A CHURCH OF THE POOR

D1560014

A CHURCH OF THE POOR

*Pope Francis and
the Transformation of Orthodoxy*

CLEMENS SEDMAK

ORBIS BOOKS
Maryknoll, New York 10545

ORBIS BOOKS
Maryknoll, New York 10545

Fathers and Brothers
MARYKNOLL™
TOGETHER IN GOD'S MISSION OF MERCY

Founded in 1970, Orbis Books endeavors to publish works that enlighten the mind, nourish the spirit, and challenge the conscience. The publishing arm of the Maryknoll Fathers and Brothers, Orbis seeks to explore the global dimensions of the Christian faith and mission, to invite dialogue with diverse cultures and religious traditions, and to serve the cause of reconciliation and peace. The books published reflect the views of their authors and do not represent the official position of the Maryknoll Society. To learn more about Maryknoll and Orbis Books, please visit our website at www.maryknollsociety.org.

Library of Congress Cataloging-in-Publication Data

Names: Sedmak, Clemens, 1971- author.
Title: A Church of the poor : Pope Francis and the transformation of
    Orthodoxy / by Clemens Sedmak.
Description: Maryknoll, New York : Orbis Books, Maryknoll, 2016. | Includes
    bibliographical references and index.
Identifiers: LCCN 2016024455 (print) | LCCN 2016026688 (ebook) | ISBN
    9781626982062 (pbk.) | ISBN 9781608336722 (ebook)
Subjects: LCSH: Catholic Church. Pope (2013- : Francis). Evangelii Gaudium. |
    Poverty—Religious aspects—Catholic Church. | Church and social
    problems—Catholic Church. | Catholic Church—Doctrines. | Evangelistic
    work—Catholic Church.
Classification: LCC BX2347.4 .S42 2016 (print) | LCC BX2347.4 (ebook) | DDC
    261.8/325—dc23
LC record available at https://lccn.loc.gov/2016024455

Contents

Introduction

"How I Would Like a Church That Is Poor" – Pope Francis's Vision of an Empty Church

When Pope Francis embraced Vincio Riva in early November 2013, the encounter was not only a moving moment of tenderness, it was also an expression of orthodoxy, an expression of living faith.

At the end of the general audience in St. Peter's Square on that day, Pope Francis went around greeting and blessing people. He saw Vincio and approached him without fear or hesitation and embraced him tightly. Vincio Riva suffers from neurofibromatosis, a non-infectious genetic disease; his body is completely covered with sores and swellings. Notwithstanding the risk of producing "moral kitsch" in describing this situation in some detail,[1] I would like to claim that this

---

1. The Israeli philosopher Avishai Margalit warns us of the attitude of being moved by the fact that we have been moved (like people who visit the Auschwitz museum who feel good about feeling bad about what they see). It is not helpful to develop seeming moral philosophy (or, for that matter, moral theology) invoking moral kitsch. A coherent argument cannot be made on the basis of one single moving incident, nor does one touching scene constitute a proper way of making people understand what is at stake; it is not advisable to base an argument on singular and emotionally loaded cases (such as the encounter of Pope Francis with Vincio Riva). See Avishai Margalit, "Human Dignity between Kitsch and Deification," in Christopher Cordner and Raimond Gaita, eds., *Philosophy, Ethics, and a Common Humanity: Essays in Honour of Raimond Gaita*

moment stands out as an act of teaching, bringing important truths, such as those of the Nicene Creed, to life.

The creed expresses our belief in God who created everything, including all of us; it expresses our belief in an invisible dimension of reality, our belief in the incarnation of God—beliefs that touch on the deepest and most defining features of our *conditio* and our personhood. How can anyone affirm the Nicene Creed without basing his or her life on the existential truths it expresses? Pope Francis's gesture is an act of teaching, a lesson given in and comprising the actual act of doing something. What is striking in this particular embrace is the perceptible lack of hesitation and reflection. One might be tempted to say, using Bernard Williams's memorable words, that a person reflecting on whether or not she should reach out to a disfigured man has "one thought too many."[2] Pope Francis's embrace was an expressive act without any intention of conveying a message. This "self-forgetfulness" encapsulates the meaning of "reaching out to the peripheries." This is the key to a "Church of the Poor."

In Cardinal Bergoglio's notes for his speech during the cardinals' meetings before the conclave where he was elected pope, notes made available through Havana's Archbishop Cardinal Jaime Lucas Ortega y Alamino,[3] we can see a plea for a church that would go to the peripheries, that would not be self-referential, that would overcome what some might call "theological narcissism." These points are pillars for Pope Francis's theology of a Church of the Poor, and they show how his embrace of Vincio Riva was both an important statement and an expressive gesture.

(London: Routledge, 2011), 106-20. In an attempt to counteract any risk, I will be using the example to illustrate rather than argue my point.

2. Bernard Williams, "Persons, Character, and Morality," in Bernard Williams, *Moral Luck* (Cambridge: Cambridge University Press, 1981), 1-19; cf. Susan Wolf, "'One Thought Too Many': Love, Morality, and the Ordering of Commitment," in Ulrike Heuer and Gerhard Lang, eds., *Luck, Value, and Commitment: Themes from the Ethics of Bernard Williams* (Oxford: Oxford University Press, 2012), ch. 3.

3. See zenit.org.

A Church of the Poor

In Pope Francis's first encounter with newspaper journalists and TV reporters on March 16, 2013, he underlined his deep desire to construct a "poor church" as envisaged by Francis of Assisi: "How I would like a church that is poor and for the poor!" In his interview with Antonio Spadaro, Francis talked about the central importance of discernment with special consideration of the poor: "Discernment is always done in the presence of the Lord, looking at the signs, listening to the things that happen, the feeling of the people, especially the poor."[4] Many people are familiar with the story that Pope Francis shared with the journalists during the March 2013 meeting about his commitment to the poor:

> During the election, I was seated next to the Archbishop Emeritus of São Paolo and Prefect Emeritus of the Congregation for the Clergy, Cardinal Claudio Hummes: a good friend, a good friend! When things were looking dangerous, he encouraged me. And when the votes reached two-thirds, there was the usual applause, because the Pope had been elected. And he gave me a hug and a kiss, and said: "Don't forget the poor!" And those words came to me: the poor, the poor.

Since then, this vision of a poor church and a Church of the Poor has been a defining factor in Pope Francis's pontificate. He pursues this commitment on various levels: on the level of written documents and verbal articulations, on the level of symbolic gestures, and on the level of institutional reforms (e.g., the financial management of the Vatican). The *cantus firmus*, the "fixed song" if you will, of these efforts are the motifs of emptiness and emptying. Francis emphasized this idea of a poor church on October 4, 2013, in the deeply symbolic *Sala della Spoliazione* (Room of Renunciation) of the archbishop's

---

4. Pope Francis and Antonio Spadaro, "The Heart of a Jesuit Pope: Interview with Pope Francis," *Studies: An Irish Quarterly Review* 102, no. 407 (2013): 255-78, at 258f.

residence in Assisi. He focused on the concept of divesting self of material goods, renunciation, and following in the footsteps of Jesus Christ; in other words, casting off the trappings of this world—the spirit of worldliness. He had mentioned this spirit of worldliness in his pre-conclave speech citing Henri de Lubac. In his *Méditation sur l'église* ("The Splendor of the Church") de Lubac had written of "the greatest temptation to the Church" ("the most subversive, the ever-recurrent, reappearing insidiously when all the rest are overcome")— namely, the temptation of a *worldliness of the mind,* which de Lubac takes to be "the practical relinquishing of other-worldliness, so that moral and even spiritual standards should be based, not on the glory of the Lord, but on what is the profit of man."[5] Hence, worldliness of the mind means an anthropocentric sense of orientation, which would be disastrous if it were to invade the church. It is a spirit of seeking privileges and power, rather than service to the kingdom. It is a spirit that allows for terms like "career," "success," "convenience," or "fame" to enter the church as legitimate points of reference. Nobody is "wholly immune from this sort of evil." In *Evangelii gaudium* 93, Francis characterizes spiritual worldliness as consisting "in seeking not the Lord's glory but human glory and personal well-being." Spiritual worldliness makes us build comfort zones.

Pope Francis connects this theological concept of spiritual worldliness with the motif of a fundamental and existential decision: it is the basic choice between an anthropocentric and a theocentric church. The gospel teaches us that we cannot serve two masters at the same time (Matt 6:24); this may be possible in the world of politics and business economics but not in the true way of the church. A Church of the Poor does not just "happen," it is the result of a choice, of a decision, a commitment. A committed attitude is incompatible with indifference, which is the attitude the world attributes to poverty and hardship. Interestingly, however, this indifference does not primarily mean that there is a lack of something, but that something is

---

5. Henri de Lubac, *The Splendor of the Church,* trans. Michael Mason (Glen Rock, NJ: Paulist Press 1963), 234. In the French original de Lubac uses the term "*mondanité spirituelle,*" a phrase borrowed from Dom Vonier (Henri de Lubac, *Méditation sur l'église* [Paris: Aubier, 1953], 283).

"too much." The spirit of worldliness is synonymous with "being too full"—too full of desires for convenience and comfort, for instance, including epistemic comforts. Consequently, in the address submitted for publication, Pope Francis asks:

> What should the Church strip herself of? She must strip away every kind of worldly spirit, which is a temptation for everyone; strip away every action that is not for God, that is not from God; strip away the fear of opening the doors and going out to encounter all, especially the poorest of the poor, the needy, the remote, without waiting.

A Church of the Poor is an emptied one. It is an empty church in which the Spirit can dwell; it is with empty hands that human beings can receive the grace of God. Francis of Assisi stripped himself of his garments, thus renouncing his citizenship in the earthly city, to use Augustinian language, and to express his willingness to strip away and "empty" himself of a spirit of worldliness and lead a life without and beyond. This was not just a matter of discarding garments; it was more a matter of renouncing a particular identity, of rejecting identity-conferring commitments. In short, it was a matter of conversion, a journey from a world-centered attitude to a God-centered attitude. Pope Francis's words in Assisi unambiguously reflect the theocentric nature of the church, which for that very reason makes it a Church of the Poor.

A theocentric church, then, is a kenotic church, a church that is stripped of the spirit of power and wealth. The church is called upon to empty itself because of the divine act of renouncing divine glory. In his 2014 Lenten Message Pope Francis recalled divine emptying: God "does not reveal himself cloaked in worldly power and wealth but rather in weakness and poverty: 'though He was rich, yet for your sake he became poor. . . . ' Christ, the eternal Son of God, one with the Father in power and glory, chose to be poor; he came amongst us and drew near to each of us; he set aside his glory and emptied himself so that he could be like us in all things (cf. *Phil* 2:7; *Heb* 4:15)." Francis sees deep theological value in these dynamics and states in the same message:

xii • Introduction →

By making himself poor, Jesus did not seek poverty for its own sake but, as Saint Paul says *"that by his poverty you might become rich."* This is no mere play on words or a catch phrase. Rather, it sums up God's logic, the logic of love, the logic of the incarnation and the cross. God did not let our salvation drop down from heaven, like someone who gives alms from their abundance out of a sense of altruism and piety.

The poverty of Christ is redeeming, enriching, and liberating. It is not destitution and despair, but an expression of a life-affirming attitude with a sense of what is essential. It is a way of loving, a way of being close to us vulnerable creatures, to us who may be victims of violence left half dead by the side of the road.

On August 14, 2014, Pope Francis explicitly mentioned a "Church for the Poor" again in his meeting with the bishops of Korea in Seoul: "Solidarity with the poor is at the heart of the Gospel; it has to be seen as an essential element of the Christian life; through preaching and catechesis grounded in the rich patrimony of the Church's social teaching, it must penetrate the hearts and minds of the faithful and be reflected in every aspect of ecclesial life." On this occasion Francis warns Christian congregations not to lose their ability to celebrate the mystery and not to become mediocre institutions void of the prophetic spirit "lacking the leaven of prophecy." This statement expresses great expectations from the theological input of the poor. He goes on to caution parishes not to slip into middle-class habits of "well-to-do" congregations, which a poor person might feel too embarrassed to enter. A poor church is one that welcomes outsiders with open arms. Again and again Pope Francis reminds the church that Christ is to be encountered in the face of the outcast.[6]

---

6. In his first Chrism Mass homily as pope in March 2013 Pope Francis underlines the command that the precious oil needs to reach the peripheries; in a beautiful morning meditation in the chapel of the Domus Sanctae Martae on November 17, 2014, he urges the addressees to be open to recognize the Lord in the outcasts and encourages a church "which is sitting by the roadside in Jericho . . . symbol of sin"; during that same week, on November 22, Pope Francis talked about building the church on the peripheries of the world and called the

The poor are the heart of the gospel, Francis emphasizes, as seen in Mark (Mark 2) and in Matthew (Matt 25); the poor are the prophetic leaven that the church needs (cf. 1 Cor 11:17 and James 2:1-7). This is not a statement about the humanitarian concerns of the church; this is not a statement about epistemological advantages for theological purposes when considering the voices of the poor. This is a statement about the theocentric character of a faithful church that will honor the central place given to the poor by God. In this sense a Church of the Poor is *not* a special way of being church or doing church, but rather obedience to the will of God.

No less unambiguous was the central significance the pope placed on the role of the poor in his homily given at the celebration of the Eucharist on January 16, 2015, in the Cathedral of Immaculate Conception in Manila, Philippines: "The poor are at the center of the Gospel, are at heart of the Gospel, if we take away the poor from the Gospel we can't understand the whole message of Jesus Christ." If the poor are the central pillar on which the church is built, the church should aim to build on the central message of the gospel, which is about and for the poor. However, the central issue of *being poor* does not stop there; the next consideration must be how such a church with such a message will impact life in general—every day: "For all of us, it means living lives that reflect the poverty of Christ, whose entire life was focused on doing the will of the Father and serving others."

The poverty of Christ, clearly, is not a poverty of judgment or a poverty of commitment; it is a poverty of the Son of God, who so emptied himself that God could dwell in him; it is the poverty of the Lord who seeks only to fulfill the will of the Father, thus emptying his own will, or, more strongly, rendering his own will void. The poverty of Christ is not to be defined in terms of items that are missing or that have to be sacrificed but rather by the liberating orientation toward what is good. It is an expression of the quest for the Ignatian *magis*, striving for love and hope and divine glory.

Theologically speaking, it seems to be the litmus test of proper church life and a morally decent life in general to look at the impact

---

poor the first ones the church meets "our evangelizers, for they point out where the Gospel still needs to be proclaimed and lived."

on and the connection with the poor. In his 2015 encyclical letter *Laudato si'* (LS), Pope Francis uses this litmus test when he calls for special attention for the poor (e.g., LS 158), for direct contact with the poor (LS 50), for giving the poor access to basic resources (LS 109). He speaks of "the tragic effects of environmental degradation on the lives of the world's poorest" (LS 13; see also LS 20, 48), "the intimate relationship between the poor and the fragility of the planet" (LS 16), the fact that "many of the poor live in areas particularly affected by phenomena related to warming" (LS 25), and the special concern about the availability of water to the poor (LS 29). The encyclical explicitly and repeatedly makes the point that one cannot have proper ecological attitudes without a proper social conscience: "A sense of deep communion with the rest of nature cannot be real if our hearts lack tenderness, compassion and concern for our fellow human beings" (LS 91).[7] Understood in this way, a Church of the Poor is also a church following integral ecology.

Perhaps Pope Francis's clearest declaration to date can be found in his programmatic text *Evangelii gaudium* (EG)[8]; here he underlines the "special place of the poor in God's people," and in paragraph 198 reminds us of the testimony of Christ, who lived his life among the poor, a sign that they would always have a special place in God's heart: "This is why I want a Church which is poor and for the poor. They have much to teach us. Not only do they share in the *sensus fidei*, but in their difficulties they know the suffering of Christ." As agents of *sensus fidelium,* the poor are the subjects of the evangelizing spirit in their bringing us all nearer to Christ in a way only they can do. They are teacher and evangelizers. "We need to let ourselves be evangelized by them."

---

7. Similarly in *Laudato si*, 117: "When we fail to acknowledge as part of reality the worth of a poor person, a human embryo, a person with disabilities—to offer just a few examples—it becomes difficult to hear the cry of nature itself."

8. Cf. Stephen B. Bevans, "The Apostolic Exhortation *Evangelii gaudium* on the Proclamation of the Gospel in Today's World," *International Review of Mission* 103, no. 2 (2014): 297-308, at 305f.; see also Ursula Notelle-Wildfeuer, "Eine Frage der Authentizität," *Arme Kirche—Kirche der Armen: Stimmen der Zeit* 232 (2014): 579-90.

A New Epistemic Praxis?

Against this background of Pope Francis's plea for a Church of the Poor we could ask a simple question: What are the epistemological consequences of a Church of the Poor? In other words, how will this commitment affect theological method and epistemic cultures of doing theology? And yet again differently, what does a Church of the Poor mean for an understanding of *orthodoxy*?

It seems obvious that a Church of the Poor would impact the world. It might affect everyday pastoral care and mission; it might impinge on church administration and the way dioceses are structured. In other words, it would be felt in the daily lives of Christians no matter where they live. While all these aspects are of equal importance, I should like to focus on one particular aspect, namely, what a Church of the Poor would mean for the epistemic praxis of the church, as grounded in mystery and expressed in orthodoxy.

Evangelii gaudium makes explicit statements about theological work, which is encouraged to engage in dialogue with nontheological sciences and other experiences (in order to broaden its horizon and go beyond limited and particular questions [EG 235]) and beyond a state of "desk-bound" (EG 133). There is no excuse for academic theologians not to be close to the poor (EG 201). The document warns of the temptation to treat normative texts by applying them to other people in mind, thereby avoiding the hard questions of consequences for one's own life (EG 153). Theology should not cloud those clear commitments (of justice and mercy to the poor) that Jesus exhorted us to hold.[9] He exhorts a way of embracing the Catholic Social Tradition as a positive force offering proposals for change (EG 183) without watering down principles so that they remain "mere generalities which challenge no one" (EG 182). Good theology, then, is challenging: "It is irksome when the question of ethics is raised" (EG 203).

Is it also irksome to do theology as if poor people mattered? Is it also irksome to have to let poor people get in the way of theology? It has

---

9. "Jesus taught us this way of looking at others by his words and his actions. So why cloud something so clear?" (EG 194). There is always the danger of key issues to be "exploited by a rhetoric which cheapens them" (EG 203).

been recognized that the option for the poor called for in this apostolic exhortation has implications for the person of the theologian as well as for theology in terms of being taught by the poor.[10] We could push this question even further. If we think of the image of a church that is stripped of power, would that also imply "epistemic power," "power of judgment"? What does it mean for the church's capacity to judge the world? A theocentric church, as I have mentioned, is a kenotic church, a church that is stripped of a spirit of power and wealth. One could be tempted to ask whether this is also an invitation to renounce particular theological language. Ludwig Wittgenstein, for example, once observed that the Gospels present us with a simple vision that has been transformed; "in the Gospels—as it seems to me—everything is less pretentious, humbler, simpler. There you find huts; with Paul a church."[11] Even if one does not agree with Wittgenstein on this point one will have to admit that there is a difference, if not a gap, between the language we find in the Gospels and the language of much academic theology or many church documents. There are huts and there are palaces of fine theological architecture—maybe a Church of the Poor would be more a church of linguistic huts?

10. Sergio Silva, "La exhortación apostólica del papa Francisco como desafío a los teólogos," *Teología y vida* 55, no. 3 (2014): 549-69, at 565. Silva recognizes the epistemological dimension of a theology following the exhortations in *Evangelii gaudium* (especially 135, 139, 198-207, 220, 268-73): "Para que sea auténtica teología, debe ser hecha en la escucha atenta del clamor de los pobres, porque Dios los escucha y porque, en su sentido de fe, tienen mucho que enseñarnos; para ello, el teólogo debe estar cerca de los pobres, sin buscar excusas de ningún tipo. Dicho de otra manera, su lugar epistemológico –el horizonte desde el cual hace su teología—debe estar lo más posible en el pueblo de los pobres" ("In order for theology to be authentic it has to listen to the cry of the poor because God hears the poor and the poor can teach us a lot about their sense of faith. For Pope Francis the theologian has to be close to the poor without looking for excuses of any kind. In other words, the theologian's epistemological place—the horizon against which theology is done—has to be as much as possible in the villages of the poor") (ibid.).

11. Ludwig Wittgenstein, *Culture and Value*, ed. G. H. v. Wright in collaboration with H. Nyman; trans. P. Winch; rev. ed. by Alois Pichler (Oxford: Blackwell, 1998), 35.

Will, and this is the guiding question of this book, a Church of the Poor change our epistemic practices in the church, in theology?

By *epistemic practice* I mean *forms of agency that lead to knowledge claims in the pursuit of orientation as the ability to administer spectrums of judgment thus leading to a change in the inner situation and the self-situatedness of the person.* Epistemic practices pursue epistemic goals such as truth, knowledge, and security of agency; they change the inner or epistemic situation of persons (their sets of beliefs, memories, desires, and emotions). Epistemic practices change and shape the way a person interacts with the world and coordinates her plans with other stakeholders. Spectrums of judgment (i.e. the spectrum between "true" and "false," "appropriate" and "inappropriate," "right" and "wrong," which allows and enables us to place entities into a system of orientation) are also shaped by epistemic practices. To break this down in plain language: epistemic practices are all we do and have to do in order to know something.

With regard to the church, we are interested in institutional epistemic practices; questions of truth are pursued as a community and within a community, and truth claims are administered within an institutional setting. Institutional epistemic practices could be framed in terms of a social epistemology, in terms of collective or social agency employed to generate knowledge claims. Institutional epistemic practices could also be framed in a manner more akin to Alisdair MacIntyre's famous definition of practice[12] as *coordinated, cooperative, coherence-inspired, institutionally and socially established and theologically grounded ways in which we express our understanding and perception of Truth, and strive to acquire and process all knowledge*

---

12. "By a practice I am going to mean any coherent and complex form of socially established cooperative human activity through which goods internal to that form of activity are realized in the course of trying to achieve those standards of excellence which are appropriate to, and partially definitive of, that form of activity, with the result that human powers to achieve excellence, and human conceptions of the ends and goods involved, are systematically extended" (Alasdair MacIntyre, *After Virtue*, 2nd ed. [Notre Dame, IN: Notre Dame University Press, 1997], 187). Institutional and social epistemic practices will generate goods such as truth, orientation, and strong beliefs honoring standards of justification.

related to it. The search for truth within the church does have a fundamental basis in divine agency; it has taken on a social face that requires
coordination and cooperation as well as a commitment to past commitment and hence a sense of the normative meaning of coherence
(generally speaking, later magisterial teachings have to be coherent
with binding previous teachings). In other words, a document can
take certain teachings from previous documents for granted (cf. EG
51); there is no need to repeat past relevant documents in a new script
(cf. EG 163).

Epistemic practices can change. Pope Francis himself has begun to
transform the epistemic culture of his office by putting new emphasis on listening. *Laudato si'*, for instance, works with research-based
claims (LS 15, 48, 132, 135, 140). Francis also expressed this new
culture of listening in the above-mentioned interview. "This means
that 'thinking with the Church' now means, as well as respect for the
hierarchical Magisterium and theologians, a close listening to what
the faithful are saying, in particular those who are poor. Hence the
frequent references in the interview to dialogue and consultation, a
consultation that is real, not simply token or ceremonial. And truth
is to be 'discerned'—Francis is here referring to a prayerful reflection
on lived experience which includes, but cannot be reduced to, rational
discussion."[13]

Listening is an epistemic practice. Listening demanding and
resulting in attention is hard work, hard work for oneself. "Listening"
is an obvious trait of presence, of being present in a situation, of being
attentive and open. This move toward presence and attentiveness is
the invitation *Evangelii gaudium* exhorts us to make "that we may be
docile and attentive to the cry of the poor" (EG 187). Missionary listening is not an oxymoron, but may be acknowledged as an expression of taking the signs of the times seriously. Rowan Williams talks
about the "authoritative urgency to communicate the good news" and
continues by saying that "the urgency must often be channelled into
listening and waiting, and into the expansion of the Christian imagination itself into something that can cope with the seriousness of the

---

13. Gerry O'Hanlon, "The Pope's Interview: A Reflection," *Studies: An Irish
Quarterly Review* 102, no. 407 (2013): 279-82, at 279.

world."[14] This mindset also requires a sense of "attention" in Simone Weil's understanding of the word; an attitude of openness to the world, an attitude that allows an object to impress itself on the person who has suspended her own self-concern.[15] A Church of the Poor will engage in singular ways of listening to the poor as evangelizers. This change in attitude, this renewal, this conversion will result in new and renewed epistemic practices leading to a new and renewed epistemic culture. But what are these new or renewed epistemic practices?

Orthodoxy and a Church of the Poor

The question of epistemic practices in more general terms can be translated into a more specific focus on "orthodoxy." Within a church context orthodoxy (*orthodoxeia*) signifies "right belief" or "purity of faith," which is not subjective but based on proper instruction and in accordance with the teaching authority of the church. Fundamentally speaking, orthodoxy on its simplest level means accepting a set of beliefs; hence, on this basic level, denying the truth of a correct statement or maintaining the truth of a misconception is a violation against orthodoxy. Orthodoxy accepts propositions as true and holds truths—maybe paradoxically about orthodoxy itself and about terms like "poverty of Jesus," "Church of the Poor," etc.

The Christian concept of orthodoxy is a colorful one; it has at least three sets of properties: It is based on epistemic and social claims (i.e., it operates with knowledge claims, truth claims, power claims, and claims about the social order); it is institution-anchored and institution-inducive (which is to say, it presupposes institutional settings and is also institution building since it needs to be administered); it is based on and expressed in existential commitments (it touches on the deepest layers of a person's identity and is linked to a personal relationship with Jesus Christ). The concept has been contrasted

---

14. Rowan Williams, "The Judgment of the World," in Rowan Williams, *On Christian Theology* (Oxford: Blackwell, 2000), 29-43, at 40.

15. Simone Weil, "Reflections on the Right Use of School Studies with a View of Loving God," in Simone Weil, *Waiting on God* (New York: Fount, 1977), 53-61.

with "heresy," even though this scheme has been denounced "as a dichotomy of Eurocentric interpretive categories that fails to grasp the pluralism and complexity characteristic" of, for example, Muslim religious life or human realities in general.[16]

The term orthodoxy is inextricably linked to truth as ideal value and epistemic goal. It would be difficult to hold on to this concept without a substantial and robust understanding of truth and with commitments regarding the possibility of truth. Questions of truth are negotiated within an institutional church setting. The concept of orthodoxy cannot be separated from the institution of the Magisterium; in fact, the Magisterium protects epistemic practices enabling and safeguarding orthodoxy. Teaching, doing theology, and evangelization are the cornerstones of epistemic practice in the church. The Magisterium is outcome and expression as well as framework and basis for church epistemic practices. In its narrower sense, the teaching function of the church can be exercised only by the pope, the college of bishops, and those who administer that function, such as the Bishops' Conference, the ecumenical council, synods, and the congregations of the Vatican Curia; in its wider sense, the ministry of teaching can be seen as an integral part of the church's mission of annunciation.[17] A "Church of the Poor" transforms the mission of annunciation and proclamation, as is made clear in *Evangelii gaudium* and forms the basis of our present enquiry.

Evangelii gaudium explicitly broaches the issue of orthodoxy when discussing the relationship between form and content and the difference between deposit of faith and its expression.[18] It also makes

---

16. This observation about the mental reservation vis-à-vis this concept has been observed (without necessarily stating the authors' opinions) by Robert Langer and Udo Simon; see R. Langer and U. Simon, "The Dynamics of Orthodoxy and Heterodoxy. Dealing with Divergence in Muslim Discourses and Islamic Studies," *Die Welt des Islams*, N.S. 48, nos. 3-4 (2008): 273-88, at 273.

17. Cf. Clemens Sedmak, *Katholisches Lehramt und Philosophie* (Freiburg/Breisgau: Herder, 2003), 43-48.

18. "There are times when the faithful, in listening to completely orthodox language, take away something alien to the authentic Gospel of Jesus Christ, because that language is alien to their own way of speaking to and understanding one another" (EG 41).

the point about insufficient orthodoxy when reflecting on the possibility of ignorance toward and acceptance of intolerable situations of injustice without falling into doctrinal error (EG 194). One could also read this passage to embrace a wider understanding of orthodoxy transcending the level of propositions.

Would a Church of the Poor change our theological understanding of orthodoxy? Would a commitment to engender a Church of the Poor cast a new light on our understanding of mystery and orthodoxy? Of course, such questions should not be allowed to shake the foundations of the ministry of teaching or the idea that the revelation is in principle concluded. Notwithstanding, the implications inherent in the question would seem to be both meaningful and significant for epistemic practice within the church. There is no suggestion that there could be an understanding of orthodoxy that would not reflect the traditional use protected by the Magisterium. There is, however, the question whether a Church of the Poor would challenge certain interpretations of orthodoxy and call for not only a new theological style in talking about orthodoxy but also for a new way of accepting elements (such as listening to the voices of the poor) as constitutive for orthodoxy. This study makes the claim that a Church of the Poor will have implications for the way we think about orthodoxy.

This Book

This book is a small and fairly simple contribution to an already extensive theological debate; it sets out to show that a Church of the Poor will also be characterized by a particular way of knowing, learning, and understanding, and these epistemic practices have consequences for the understanding of what it means to be orthodox.

This argument is developed in five chapters. The first chapter, entitled "The Joy of the Gospel," offers a reading of *Evangelii gaudium* as an invitation to a new epistemic praxis. It reconstructs the motif of "joy" as an epistemological motif and develops Pope Francis's understanding of epistemic practices in the light of divine creativity and mission, living structures of a non-self-centered church, and the recognition of the poor in a commitment to a *sensus fidelium*. The second chapter ("The Gospel of Joy") explores Jesus' efforts to build a Church of the Poor as well as epistemic practices invoked and advocated by Jesus in the Gospels, looking at the transfiguration of the Lord and the nocturnal visit of Nicodemus. There are grounds to argue that Jesus invites an understanding of orthodoxy as discipleship and also sees discipleship as a new way of getting to know and understand the world. Chapter 3 ("Poverty and the Wound of Knowledge") looks at the experience and epistemic situation of poverty and asks whether the experience of poverty leads to epistemic or moral privileges. The fourth chapter explores the notion of a Church of the Poor in Christian theology, tracing some of the pillars of a theological understanding of poverty and also asks the question whether the theory of goods that can be found in the documents of the Catholic Social Tradition can be applied to epistemic goods as well. The last chapter discusses the concept of orthodoxy; it attempts to show that a Church of the Poor will lead to an understanding of "transforming orthodoxy" that focuses on one key question: What does it mean to love God? The epilogue will address this question.

This study is meant to be a response to Pope Francis's appeal to take the "important consequences" and the "programmatic significance" (EG 25) of *Evangelii gaudium* seriously. I attempt to do this for its epistemological dimension without trying to walk alone, but rather in conversation with others and under the leadership of bishops (cf. EG 33). This book, even though a product of "desk-bound theology," may allow us to recognize some of the down-to-earth and on-the-ground consequences of reading the signs of the times (cf. EG 51) as hearers of the word and as hearers of the cry of the poor.

Chapter 1

The Joy of the Gospel: A Call to Respond to Love

Does an orientation toward an option for the poor call for a new epistemic praxis? That question is the central theme of this study, and is connected to the central theme threading its way through Pope Francis's apostolic exhortation *Evangelii gaudium*: the invitation to transformation, to "a real commitment to applying the Gospel to the transformation of society" (EG 102), and "the transforming power of the Gospel" (EG 116).[1] Transformation signifies renewal by changing the "form," which can also be understood as standing for major, fundamental, and substantial change. This transformation is nothing less than a conversion. The first disciples, "immediately after encountering the gaze of Jesus, went forth to proclaim him joyfully: 'We have found the Messiah!' (*Jn* 1:41)" (EG 120). This breakthrough realization is the beginning of a journey; transformation is an ongoing process of being transformed (cf. EG 160). Conversion is not primarily "a moment," but is setting out on a path that will allow *meta-noia*, "thinking beyond all known."

The task of evangelization "implies and demands the integral promotion of each human being" (EG 182). The desire to change the world and "leave this earth somehow better than we found it" (EG 183) are part of this deep experience. In *Laudato si'*, written in the same spirit, Pope Francis asked: "What kind of world do we want to leave to those who come after us, to children who are now growing

---

1. Cf. EG 162, referring to Romans 8:5.

up?" (LS 160; cf. LS 179, 183). This is a profound question to make people think about the "good life" and about ways of looking at life as a whole. Recognition of what is good fills a person with a desire to change the world for the better. Transformation is both commitment and the result of this commitment to goodness. One important aspect of transforming heart and mind is changing epistemic practices. A transformation of epistemic practices represents changing not only the form of knowledge but also its acquisition. Different avenues toward knowledge will lead to different types of knowledge. Scott Wright, in his biography of Oscar Romero (another person dear to the heart of Pope Francis), mentions a conversation in Rome between Cesar Jerez, the Jesuit provincial, and Archbishop Romero. Jerez had asked the bishop, "Monseñor, you've changed. Everything about you has changed. What's happened?" The reply: "'You know, Father Jerez, I ask myself that same question when I'm in prayer.' He stopped walking and was silent. . . . 'It's just that we all have our roots, you know . . . I was born into a poor family. I've suffered hunger. . . . When I went to seminary (in Rome) I started to forget about where I came from. I started creating another world. . . . Then they sent me to Santiago de Maria, and I ran into extreme poverty again. Those children were dying just because of the water they were drinking. . . . And what happened to Father Grande. . . . So yes, I changed. But I also came back home again.'"[2] Oscar Romero changed his epistemic practices by being with the poor; this changed the content and the framework of knowledge he had and would have of the poor. It is, we could assume, this kind of transformation that Pope Francis has in mind.

Pope Francis calls for a change of epistemic practices regarding poverty and the poor. We are called upon to transform such epistemic practices as blaming the poor and blaming poor countries (EG 60). It is a transformation based on the joy of the gospel. "Some people do not commit themselves to mission because they think that nothing will change and that it is useless to make the effort" (EG 275). The exhortation, for that matter, is a call to renewal and transformation. It

---

2. Scott Wright, *Oscar Romero and the Communion of Saints* (Maryknoll, NY: Orbis Books, 2009), 53.

is an invitation to see the gospel with fresh eyes and to become a witness to the gospel on the basis of this experience.

We will explore these topics by discussing the nature and epistemological relevance of *Evangelii gaudium* (1.1), the central role of joy in a Christian life (1.2), the challenge of divine creativity (1.3), and the (implicit) understanding of orthodoxy informing Pope Francis's apostolic exhortation (1.4).

1.1 An Exhortation to New Epistemic Practices?

The document *Evangelii gaudium* is an apostolic exhortation intended to encourage (hence *exhortation*) the addressees to live in a particular manner, to embrace particular forms of practice, to change patterns of being and doing. An exhortation is an exercise in *paraklesis,* in summoning help, in encouraging, in admonishing. An exhortation is an act to bridge the gap between thinking and doing, between principles and application, between epistemic universe and pragmatic horizon. An exhortation entails both a message about direction and a message about motivation to move in this direction. It confirms "courage," the virtue of holding on to the good in spite of challenges, difficulties, and adversities.[3]

An exhorter is one who encourages and strengthens others. Biblical texts referring to the act of exhorting can be found in the book of Deuteronomy (Deut 26:16—divine exhortation to keep the covenant) and in the book of Tobit (Tobit 12:6—the angel Raphael exhorts Tobiah and Tobit to give thanks to God). The book of Tobit indicates that an exhortation is based on a clear vision of a good to be aspired to and the content of the exhortation is to make people see the point of this good; Proverbs 3:11-12 is a reminder to live the discipline of the Lord, a reminder called an exhortation in Hebrews 12:5. The New Testament recalls situations of exhortation in numerous passages, for example, in Luke 12:4 (Jesus exhorts the disciples to have courage) and in Acts 13:15 (Paul and his brothers are encouraged to give an exhortation by the synagogue official in Antioch: "My brothers, if one of you has a word of exhortation for the people, please

---

3. Aquinas, *Summa Theologica* II-II, 123:2 resp.

speak"). Here "exhortation" seems to be a wisdom-based act of providing a sense of direction as well as motivation. Romans 12:8 characterizes the gift of exhortation as a charism; Philippians 4:2 ("I urge Euodia and I urge Syntyche to come to a mutual understanding in the Lord") is a passage that places the exhortation in the context of making a person pass the threshold from belief to action.

Exhortation is a particular social practice aimed at leading a person into the right moral direction. It is meant to foster moral nurturing, opening possibilities for moral growth.[4] When talking about the proper understanding of biblical texts (to get to their principal message) Pope Francis talks about a distinction between consolation, exhortation, and teaching: "If a text was written to console, it should not be used to correct errors; if it was written as an exhortation, it should not be employed to teach doctrine; if it was written to teach something about God, it should not be used to expound various theological opinions" (EG 147): Pope Francis draws that fine line distinguishing exhortation from consolation and from teaching. Exhortation is not about consoling people in a difficult situation, nor is it about, so it seems, telling them something new; it is a reminder of what they already know and the forceful encouragement to act on that basis. In this sense, it is not surprising that an exhortation may involve a moment of strictness, which Pope Francis articulates: "If anyone feels offended by my words, I would respond that I speak them with affection and with the best of intentions" (EG 208). The one exhorting may well have to pay the high price of losing the acceptance of the one exhorted, but here again the issue of the good to be held on to comes in (a good higher than the temporary emotional quality of relationships).

Obviously, an exhortation that can inflict or sustain lasting damage on relationships will not serve its purpose of motivating people to act in a particular way toward a particular goal. An exhortation is an act of encouragement, and any element of encouragement calls for a moment of persuasion in the presentation of such a text. Pope Francis masters

---

4. Abraham J. Malherbe, *Moral Exhortation: A Greco-Roman Sourcebook* (Philadelphia: Westminster Press, 1986), ch. 3; letters were a well-established means for providing exhortations in the Greco-Roman world (ibid., 79-84).

the challenge of persuading by offering a new "tone" in the document, a much more personal tone based on experience.[5] He quotes George Bernanos (EG 83 n. 64) and gives a vivid example of the acceptance of suffering by the testimony of St. Thérèse of Lisieux (EG 91 n. 69). These examples show a moment of persuasion rather than argumentative force. Such a moment of persuasion has been named a typical element of therapeutic arguments, of a way of speaking that can heal the ills of (mis)orientation.[6] It has been noted that this exhortative style is characteristic of Pope Francis's papal magisterium, focusing on persuasion to make people seek an encounter with Christ.[7]

The normative status of a papal exhortation is lower than that of an encyclical or apostolic letter, which is telling in terms of the "epistemic poverty" displayed. I hasten to add that by "epistemic poverty" I do not mean lack of coherence or lack of quality of argument, but a conscious restraint in the strength of knowledge claims; this restraint

---

5. "This Exhortation is completely different in style and language from all the previous documents of the Church. This is like a face to face and heart to heart conversation. It is easy to read and can be understood by ordinary people. *EG* is completely different from the other documents on the Church's missionary work" (Suresh Matthew, "Evangelii gaudium: Pope Francis' Magna Charta For Church Reform," *SEDOS Bulletin online* 45, nos. 11-12 [2013]: 2). Sergio Silva has also identified such a "novedad del 'tono'": "Por un lado, el papa Francisco habla de experiencias que todos hacemos (o podemos hacer), de modo que la gente lo comprende. Por otro—y este rasgo es el que me parece más desafiante—no habla desde su rol, sino desde su persona" (Sergio Silva, "La exhortación apostólica del papa Francisco como desafío a los teólogos," *Teología y vida* 55, no. 3 [2014]: 549-69, at 552).

6. Cf. Martha Nussbaum, "Non-scientific Deliberations," in Martha Nussbaum, *The Fragility of Goodness* (Cambridge: Cambridge University Press, 2001), 290-317.

7. "Es posible reconocer que el 'carácter exhortativo' no sólo es un rasgo de *Evangelii gaudium*, sino que puede ser considerado como elemento característico del estilo magisterial del papa Francisco. Un estilo exhortativo que, a partir de la propuesta del encuentro gratuito con Jesucristo, pone delante del fiel cristiano el camino que tiene ante si' para responder al don de la fe y a la dinámica de cambio—conversión, personal y comunitaria—que dicho camino implica" (Gabriel Richi Alberti, "Evangelii gaudium y la índole pastoral del magisterio," *Scripta theologica* 46 [2014]: 611-34, at 618).

can serve as an invitation to open dialogue. The document could be seen as an exercise in "weak thinking,"[8] that is, thinking with cautious knowledge claims.

Pope Francis describes the nature of the document as the presentation of "some guidelines" (EG 17; cf. EG 33). For these reasons Pope Francis's approach has been labeled "weak theology" ("Central to weak theology is the deflation of moral-theological claims. Moral statements may still be made, but they are stated without any emphasis on dogmatic certainty"[9]). Mark Cherry, who coined the term, insists on the possibilities for dialogue opened up by the pope's emphasis on pastoral concerns. The pope intends to show practical implications rather than to provide an exhaustive treatise (EG 18). He does not intend to offer a detailed and complete analysis (EG 51), but sets out to provide a programmatic document (EG 25) for the faithful.[10] He is well aware of the changing landscape of document reception. By proceeding in this way, Pope Francis generates an open-ended document that is complete only with follow-up and substantial conversation carried out in a spirit of courage and generosity (EG 33). In other words, an exhortation is an act of speech that is only successful if people act on it; this is, we could say, the proper characterization of a proper exhortation, moving people toward proper action.

As a postsynodal apostolic exhortation, the document is intended to communicate the concerns and action points gathered by the inter-

---

8. Cf. Gianni Vattimo, "Dialectics, Difference, Weak Thought," in G. Vattimo et al., eds., *Weak Thought* (Albany: State University of New York Press, 2012), 39-52.

9. Mark J. Cherry, "Pope Francis, Weak Theology, and the Subtle Transformation of Roman Catholic Bioethics," *Christian Bioethics* 21, no. 1 (2015): 84-88, at 85.

10. Even though addressed to the faithful, there is a passage in EG where the pope addresses "financial experts and political leaders," namely, "to ponder the words of one of the sages of antiquity: 'Not to share one's wealth with the poor is to steal from them'" (EG 57). This is a remarkable sidestep or even step outside of the previously defined circle of addressees and expectations. It shows that the kind of exhortation chosen by Pope Francis is understood to be convincing, at least partly, even to those who do not share the experience of the joy of the gospel.

national synod of bishops (the status of which is open to theological debate[11]). *"Evangelii gaudium* may be one of the most collegial post-synodal apostolic exhortations to emerge from the papal magisterium, Catherine Clifford has noted. "In all, it draws explicitly from the *propositiones* of the synod no less than thirty times."[12] The pope explicitly says that he is "reaping the rich fruits of the Synod's labors" (EG 16); moreover, the document contains his own concerns and advice he himself has sought. An interesting element in the document is a moment of explicit self-application when the pope talks about a conversion of the papacy ("since I am called to put into practice what I ask of others"; EG 32). Here again, a more personal tone rings through.

This element can also be seen in the reference points: *Evangelii gaudium* reflects a history of thought connected with the pope's biography. The 2007 final document from the Fifth General Conference of the Bishops of Latin America and the Caribbean in Aparecida, Brazil,[13] is the most quoted magisterial document in *Evangelii gaudium* and can serve as a hermeneutic key. Cardinal Bergoglio was appointed the chairperson to draft the final text of the Aparecida document, which reminds addressees of the welcome Jesus extends: "The first invitation that Jesus makes to every person who has lived an encounter with Him, is to be His disciple, so as to follow in His footsteps and to be part of His community. Our greatest joy is that of being His disciples!" (Inaugural Session, no. 2). The joy of being a Christian is another way of talking about the joy of the gospel. Again and again this document talks about "joy" (no. 7: "hope against all hope, and the joy of living even under many difficult conditions"; no. 14: "rediscover the beauty and joy of being Christians"; no. 17: "our

---

11. Should it be an instrument of papal teaching or something like an advisory body? See Jan Grootaers, "The Collegiality of the Synod of Bishops: An Unresolved Problem," *Concilium* 4 (1990): 18-30; Ludwig Kaufmann, "Synods of Bishops: Neither Concilium nor Synodus," *Concilium* 4 (1990): 67–78.

12. Catherine Clifford, "Pope Francis' Call for the Conversion of the Church in Our Time," *Australian eJournal of Theology* 21, no. 1 (2015): 33-55, at 34.

13. Fifth General Conference of the Bishops of Latin America and the Caribbean, *Disciples and Missionaries of Jesus Christ, So That Our Peoples May Have Life in Him. Concluding Document* (Aparecida, May 13-31, 2007).

joy is based on the love of the Father in sharing the paschal mystery of Jesus Christ"; no. 18: "Knowing Jesus Christ by faith is our joy"; no. 28: "the joy of being disciples of the Lord"; no. 29: "We want the joy that we have received in the encounter with Jesus Christ, whom we recognize as Son of God incarnate and redeemer, to reach all men and women wounded by adversities"; no. 117: "Being loved by God fills us with joy"). The Aparecida document presents "the disciple's joy" as "remedy for a world fearful of the future and overwhelmed by violence and hatred" (no. 29), but also talks about "the joyful spirit of our peoples" in a more cultural sense, "the joyful spirit of our peoples who love music, dance, poetry, art, and sports, and cultivate firm hope in the midst of problems and struggles" (no. 106). Joy is presented as a basic force in spirituality as well as cultural identity.[14] Joy is even presented as an element in leadership ethics: "bishops must be close joyful witnesses of Jesus Christ (no. 187). Joy is the criterion for proper faith (no. 280d: "An authentic Christian journey fills the heart with joy and hope and moves believers to proclaim Christ continually in their life and their environment"); in other words, it will be difficult to argue a case for joyless orthodoxy in the light of this document. *Evangelii gaudium* is an exhortation to a personal and communal culture of joy.

The significance of the document lies in its defining nature, shaping the expectations and hopes of Pope Francis's pontificate. *Evangelii gaudium* lays out, so to speak, the main concerns of Pope Francis; the mission can be compared to the first encyclical published by Pope Paul VI under the title *Ecclesiam suam* in 1964. In this "simple conversational letter," as Pope Paul VI had called it himself (*Ecclesiam suam* 6), he wanted to convey three policies that shaped his thinking about the pontificate ahead of him; the first is deeper self-knowledge of the church, which is a justification for renewed efforts in the light of insights into failures and imperfection: "A vivid and lively self-awareness on the part of the Church inevitably leads to a comparison between the ideal image of the Church as Christ envisaged it, His holy and spotless bride ... and the actual image which the Church

---

14. See also *Aparecida* 259 for the joy of being part of a community and *Aparecida* 356 for other joyful moments of communion.

presents to the world today.... But the actual image of the Church will never attain to such a degree of perfection, beauty, holiness and splendor that it can be said to correspond perfectly with the original conception in the mind of Him who fashioned it" (*Ecclesiam suam* 10). Hence, "the Church's heroic and impatient struggle for renewal: the struggle to correct those flaws introduced by its members which its own self-examination, mirroring its exemplar, Christ, points out to it and condemns" (*Ecclesiam suam* 11). This struggle leads to the second policy, an exhortation, "to bring the members of the Church to a clearer realization of their duty to correct their faults, strive for perfection, and make a wise choice of the means necessary for achieving the renewal we spoke of" (*Ecclesiam suam* 11). The third policy is a call to dialogue. Self-examination, correction, and renewal and dialogue as the pillars of this pontificate are close to Pope Francis's concerns; this is even more obvious when we see Pope Paul VI's commitment to "the spirit of poverty, or rather, the zeal for preserving this spirit" (*Ecclesiam suam* 54); it has to be made "clear to pastors and people how the spirit of poverty should regulate everything they do and say" (*Ecclesiam suam* 54). Paul VI even calls for directives that are "such as will teach us and the men of this era that spiritual goods far outweigh economic goods" (*Ecclesiam suam* 55).[15] This is a clear vote against a spirit of worldliness. It is a reminder that the spirit of poverty is not a marginal aspect of the church but is at the center of the church's identity. For Pope Francis this identity is inextricably linked to mercy and joy.

1.2 Joy and the Inner Condition

Evangelii gaudium puts joy at the center of faith and mission and exhorts the faithful to be joyful—not as an imperative ("be joyful!" is not a felicitous command), but as a reminder of the "original call" and the "reasons of joy." Addressed to the faithful, this apostolic exhortation is in this sense a document *ad intra*, one that

---

15. In this context Paul VI affirms "the Church's traditional social teaching" on wealth and the common good orientation of the use of property (*Ecclesiam suam* 55).

presupposes the experience of the joy of being a Christian. It is the joy of a person who has encountered Christ, the joy of a person whose "right faith" ("orthodoxy") is based on this encounter and experience. This joy is the very foundation and core of the document. Joy changes one's sense of inner self. A famous example of this experience is C. S. Lewis's autobiography, *Surprised by Joy*. Lewis characterizes joy as the sublime experience of the transcendent and sees his journey toward the Christian faith as a quest for the joy he experienced as a boy, when he was surprised—even overwhelmed— by the joy he found in Christianity. This joy changed his whole life both in outlook and action; it led to a conversion of beliefs, ideals, and inner self. *Evangelii gaudium*, one could argue, is also about the (re)discovery of joy and a corresponding conversion. As an exhortation presenting a reminder of the original experience of joy in Christ or the authentic encounter with the joy of the gospel, this document calls for a change in epistemic practices. It does make a difference both for one's general inner condition and for one's own cognitive processes whether the basic motif for exploration, encounter, and acquaintance is joy or doubt. Joy transforms epistemic practices, it shapes and changes that inner attitude of persons in a way doubt never can.

Evangelii gaudium addresses dimensions of that inner state of the human individual; it talks about the joy that "fills the heart," thus overcoming "inner emptiness" (EG 1), the fruits of "a complacent yet covetous heart" (EG 2) or a heart "gripped by fear and desperation" (EG 52). The inner state, that is, the epistemic condition of a person with her intentions, desires, emotions, and beliefs, is a key element in epistemic practices. The inner state of a person reflects her moral and spiritual condition. It is the place where attitudes and maturity levels are taken on board or abandoned, it is the place where dispositions, decisions to act, and ways of dealing with the social world are confronted and processed. The finely tuned inner state is affected by truth: "every authentic experience of truth and goodness seeks by its very nature to grow within us" (EG 9). This is an expression of a spiritual law that talks about the fertility of goodness and truth. The good and the true are dilatory; they expand and bear fruit.

An inner life that is out of kilter will have repercussions on the social dimension of the way we lead our lives: "Whenever our interior life becomes caught up in its own interests and concerns, there is no longer room for others, no place for the poor" (EG 2). Here the document establishes an explicit link between individual interiority and the politics of poverty. Pope Francis refers to that state of "being incapable of feeling compassion at the outcry of the poor" (EG 54). There are good reasons to believe that while a particular inner inclination can petrify a poverty situation because of the inner obstacles that have been constructed, other beliefs may work against and prevent people from responding to the light of others. An example of the former would be Liane Phillips's observation about inner obstacles within people enduring a condition of long-term unemployment: "Some of the biggest issues that interfere with work are: fear, poor self-esteem, lack of self-confidence, poor work ethic, and feelings of powerlessness."[16] Such people find themselves trapped in patterns of self-sabotage and inappropriate attitudes. The experience of poverty is sometimes linked to the experience of an inner cage,[17] a lack of a sense of possibility. An example of the latter—beliefs preventing people from being sensitive to poverty—would be Daniel Dorling's study of the persistence of poverty based on central beliefs Western culture encourages such as elitism and the advantages of greed.[18] The inner state is clearly connected to the outer one.

There is a toxic "thirst for power and possessions" (EG 56) that poisons a person's common-good orientation; other "poisons" mentioned in the document are skepticism and cynicism (EG 79), defeatism (EG 85), unhealthy suspicion (EG 88), or a self-centered mentality (EG

---

16. L. Phillips and E. M. Garrett, *Why Don't They Just Get a Job?* (Highlands, TX: aha! Process, 2010), 54f.

17. Cf. Rachel Hosmer, "Poverty and Human Growth," *The American Journal of Psychoanalysis* 34 (1974): 263-69, esp. 264-65; see also for the same point Martin Kämpchen, *Leben ohne Armut. Wie Hilfe wirklich helfen kann—meine Erfahrungen in Indien* (Freiburg/Breisgau: Herder, 2011), 52-65.

18. Daniel Dorling, *Injustice: Why Social Inequality Still Persists* (Bristol: Policy Press, 2015).

208). Taking up an important concept from early Christian sources, the concept of *acedia*, Pope Francis talks about "pastoral acedia" (EG 82)—an unbearable fatigue nourished by over-ambitiousness, impatience and vanity-based attachment. It is a well-known trap that poses a risk for many: "Disillusioned with reality, with the Church and with themselves, they experience a constant temptation to cling to a faint melancholy" (EG 83). This inner state of mind prevents a person from entering social relationships. "Acedia" has well been diagnosed, especially through Evagrius Ponticus, an influential Christian monk of the fourth century.[19] One of the dangerous elements of acedia is the creeping and gradual process of its settling in a person's soul. There are many tell-tale signs of carelessness, which gradually take up more and more space; slowly, sometimes over an extended period of time, it becomes clear that acedia has kicked in. Pope Francis talks about patterns inhabiting and characterizing one's inner being changing quietly and gradually: "Almost without being aware of it, we end up being incapable of feeling compassion at the outcry of the poor, weeping for other people's pain, and feeling a need to help them, as though all this were someone else's responsibility and not our own" (EG 54). Proper social orientation, on the other hand, is an indication of a healthy inner life. Improper spiritual mindsets can emerge on the basis of just a few religious exercises that discourage engagement with others (EG 78). This is, it seems, an exhortation to a healthy and well-balanced diet of religious exercises; an indication of the appropriateness of this diet is its capacity to curb individualism, to develop a clear sense of one's identity, and to foster a strong commitment to the original fervor.

The inner self is also affected by political issues: toxic ideologies undermining the primacy of the human person (EG 55) suggesting the autonomy of the marketplace and financial speculation (EG 56) and offering false hopes (EG 60). It is a well-established idea in Catholic Social Tradition that the micro level and the macro level interact. There is permeability at work here, the dynamics of inner forces shaping external realities and vice versa.[20] This would also suggest

19. Cf. Gabriel Bunge, *Despondency: the Spiritual Teaching of Evagrius Ponticus on Acedia* (Yonkers, NY: St. Vladimir's Seminary Press, 2012).
20. Cf. Clemens Sedmak, "Utility and Identity: A Catholic Social Teaching

that political conditions shape epistemic practices and that epistemic practices shape politics. Political frameworks can enhance or hinder the nurturing of a proper inner culture. They can also hinder or foster a culture of joy. A "joyless economy" (to quote Tibor Scitovsky) presupposes structures and political conditions.

The interior state is properly and rightly governed by joy, and joy is the key to the new epistemic practices Pope Francis is calling for. In other words, the epistemic proto-situation, that is, the basic epistemic disposition leading to new practices, is not Platonic awe or Cartesian doubt but the joy of the gospel. This is significant. Doubt and awe both lead to asking questions, motivate an attitude of exploration and curiosity, a sense of not being epistemically content with the current order. But what about joy? Joy is a strong affirmation of (aspects of) reality, along with the energy to transform that same reality. The joy of the gospel as the joy about being created and being saved is the source of motivation to transform the world. In his *Ethics*, Spinoza defines "joy" as "that passion by which the mind passes to a greater perfection."[21] Hence, joy is the passion one experiences in the transition to an increased power to strive; this power is based on the experience of surpassing expectations. Here again, there is the observation that joy leads to a "more" of energy and vitality. Joy, according to Spinoza, is pleasure in the present accompanied by the idea of something past, which has to do with an issue beyond our hope.[22] There is then a propositional element in joy, according to this analysis, namely, some beliefs about the past and some future expectations that could be translated into propositions in the here and now. Furthermore, joy as an affirmative emotion is based on beliefs about the present situation and perhaps even on beliefs about the fundamental structure of reality.

Evangelii gaudium characterizes *joy* in this very way—as an overwhelming affirmation of reality, as an experience of being affirmed,

---

Perspective on the Economics of Good and Evil." *Studies in Christian Ethics* 28, no. 4 (November 2015): 461-77.

21. Spinoza, *Ethics* IIIp 11s.

22. Ibid., XVI.

of being loved: created, accompanied, and saved. Joy in the apostolic exhortation has at least the following six properties:

(1) The joy of the gospel is an invitation extended to all; no one is to be excluded from this condition or proto-situation (EG 3, referring to Paul VI's apostolic exhortation *Gaudete in Domino* 22; EG 23). It is not a privileged position to be in; it is not a theologically or spiritually elitist conception, and it is presented as the natural state of the Christian self. If there is a *conditio Christiana,* it is characterized by joy.

(2) Joy as the joy of salvation is a biblical motif (EG 4), which can also be understood to mean: there are reasons for this joy; the joy is *docta laetitia,* a kind of joy that is neither blind nor empty but well grounded and substantial in the sense that the content of the joy (what is this joy about?) can be clearly discerned. *Docta laetitia* can provide answers as to the "why" and the "aboutness" of the joy being experienced. The ultimate "aboutness" of the joy of the gospel is the experience of love: it is joy nourished by "our personal certainty that, when everything is said and done, we are infinitely loved" (EG 6; cf. EG 11). In this sense, joy is a response to this love (EG 81); it is well founded because it is responsive. That is why there are different kinds of joy in response to different kinds of experiences, such as the joy in finding the lost sheep (EG 237).

(3) Joy in the Christian tradition is not only *docta,* it is also a kind of *laetitia crucis.* When we read, "The Gospel, radiant with the glory of Christ's cross, constantly invites us to rejoice" (EG 5), we understand that the joy of the gospel is not "pure" in the sense that it is incompatible with pain; the joy of the gospel is a joy "suffered," it is a joy that can inhabit our hearts alongside the experience of pain. This pain does not go away; "faith always remains something of a cross" (EG 42); the pain of the cross is part of the joy of the gospel.

(4) Joy has to be nourished and can be restored through proper nourishment (EG 3). There are stages in the development of joy. It can start with small beginnings and develop into "quiet yet firm trust" (EG 6), even in its initial stage. In this sense, joy can be built up, can grow, if it is nourished properly. Joy can be nurtured and fostered "amid the little things of life" (EG 4). First and foremost it can be nourished by drinking "of the wellspring of his brimming heart" (EG 5); it can be nourished by being close to people (EG 268: "To be evan-

gelizers of souls, we need to develop a spiritual taste for being close to people's lives and to discover that this is itself a source of greater joy").[23] Joy can be nourished through proper preaching (EG 11) and proper teaching. The poor can teach all of us about joy (EG 7), a joy that is not based on conditions. In fact, there cannot be human-made conditions that would ever take this joy away (EG 84).

(5) Joy is an overflowing,[24] cooperative good, a good that people wish to share (cf. EG 15); it is a "missionary joy" (EG 21, 271) and a good that is multiplied and increased through sharing. By that it offers, we could say, a sense of a "more" of life. The joy of the gospel is energizing; it gives strength to embrace sacrifices joyfully (EG 76).

(6) There are also social and political conditions for joy. There can be frameworks that make it more difficult to express and live joy, especially conditions that create fear (see EG 52).

If we were to construe a theology of joy we would have to remember that joy is a fruit of the Holy Spirit according to Galatians 5:22. Joy is a sign of the fruitfulness of the gospel (EG 21). Joy has to be nurtured. An important source of joy is beauty, a category that features in *Evangelii gaudium*, which speaks of the beauty of the gospel (EG 42) and beauty in the liturgy as a fruit of joy (EG 24). Pope Francis's encyclical *Laudato si'* reminds us that "the world is a joyful mystery to be contemplated with gladness and praise" (LS 12) and that struggles and concerns must not take away the joy of our hope (LS 244). However, realism and joy are not mutually exclusive (EG 109); there is joy as a fundamental affirmation of the world that gives grounds to accept and embrace reality. This sense of the real induced by joy is further nurtured by epistemic practices, especially remembering, silence, and detachment. An important epistemic practice that nourishes joy is grateful remembering: there is a link between joy and gratitude and between gratitude and memory: "The joy of evangelizing always arises from grateful remembrance" (EG 13); the document

---

23. Cf. EG 269: being close to people as "the result of a personal decision" can bring us joy and can give meaning to our lives.

24. Cf. EG 5, where Pope Francis talks about "this great stream of joy." In EG 272 he makes it very clear: "A committed missionary knows the joy of being a spring which spills over and refreshes others."

talks about the practice of remembering as a source of joy (EG 142), which brings us to a proper "ethics of memory" in connection with joy. "Remember in a way that nourishes your joy!" could then be an imperative to be followed. It becomes apparent that not all remembering or ways of remembering nourish joy. William Blake illustrated the destructive nature of harboring resentment in his famous poem *A Poison Tree*: resentful memories will only bring death and destruction both to others and to self. Joy is also nourished by the practice of silence, listening and "abiding in God": Pope Francis talks about "the quiet joy" of God's love (EG 2). The key to nourishing our joy is the spirituality of "abiding in God"; the document (EG 5) quotes John 15:11 ("I have said these things to you, so that my joy may be in you, and that your joy may be complete"), which is embedded in the theology of abiding ("remain in me, as I remain in you" [John 15:4]; and in John 15:10 we read: "If you keep my commandments, you will remain in my love"). The document also mentions the practice of simplicity and detachment (EG 7) as a source of joy, that is, a special way of positioning oneself in the material world.

In our spiritual struggles joy can be seen as "a countervailing, centripetal force, a sign and surety of adhesion to God and neighbor."[25] Joylessness then is a sign of the absence of the Spirit. John Cassian talked about sadness as a principal fault of the soul. Jonathan Edwards had described joy as the fuel of Christian life. Robert Roberts has characterized joy as a spiritual emotion.[26] If we take those elements together, the idea of "joyless orthodoxy" crystalizes as a contradiction. In one of his last homilies (January 6, 1980), preaching on the three Magi, Archbishop Oscar Romero talked about the motif of joy: "What else do the Magi receive? The gospel states explicitly that *they were overjoyed at seeing the star....* Happiness is so lacking in our time. Why? Because there is no faith and because we are not aware of God as the source of our happiness. This is one of the signs of being with

25. Adam Potkay, "Spenser, Donne and the Theology of Joy," *SEL Studies in English Literature 1500–1900* 46, no. 1 (2006): 43-66, at 43.

26. Robert Campbell Roberts, *Spiritual Emotions: A Psychology of Christian Virtues* (Grand Rapids, MI: Erdmans, 2007), 114-29.

God, for even in the midst of the difficulties of history we are joyful because the Lord is near. The Magi experienced this joy." Proper Faith and joy are inextricably linked. The Magi experience the joy of discovery and disclosure, a joy not entirely dissimilar to the epistemological value of joy described by philosopher Moritz Schlick in his theory of knowledge in which he discusses the joy of seeing a prediction come to pass, "the joy in knowledge" as "the joy of verification," the joy of the *"heureka"* moment, the joy of finding orientation.[27] In this reading, joy presupposes a certain mode of longing and a certain type of expectation relating to reality and experience. The fulfillment of this longing or a surprising over-fulfillment of expectations will lead to joy. "Joyful orthodoxy," then, is based on the experience of being surprised by God.

1.3 Open Epistemic Practices: Divine Creativity and a Church of the Poor

The experience of being surprised by God cannot be separated from the experience of being witness to divine creativity. Pope Francis talks about a "real newness": "the newness which God himself mysteriously brings about and inspires, provokes, guides and accompanies in a thousand ways" (EG 12). But is this newness expressed only in pastoral care or in epistemic praxis, too? In EG 22, Pope Francis refers to the image of the Word of God being like a seed of corn left to grow and develop freely: "The Church has to accept this unruly freedom of the word, which accomplishes what it wills in ways that surpass our calculations and ways of thinking" (EG 22).[28] There seems to be a twofold challenge for the theologian: accepting the freedom and certain autonomy of the world yet at the same time

---

27. Schlick used the term "Erkenntnisfreude"; Moritz Schlick, "Über das Fundament der Erkenntnis," *Erkenntnis* 4 (1934): 79-99, 82f.

28. Silva, *La exhortación apostólica del papa Francisco*, 569—the main challenge for the theologian is the acceptance of the freedom of the Word: "El desafío para el teólogo es, a mi parecer, aceptar la libertad de la Palabra." Acknowledging the freedom of the Word has obvious implications for an understanding of "possessing the Word" and for a concept of "divine creativity."

accepting the freedom and creativity of God. Accepting the freedom of the world indicates a commitment to learn from the world and what it can teach. Accepting the freedom of God may, after Ockham and the suspicions he managed to stir up, be more difficult. The distinction between *potentia Dei absoluta* and *potentia Dei ordinata* may be helpful in this regard, but at the same time challenging. The former is closer to "potency"; the latter closer to will[29] and also more personalist in the sense that it expresses divine personhood. Divine freedom cannot be exhausted by human reconstructions of order and law. There is always a "more" of God's agency. There always is the inexhaustability of God, and a part of this mystery is the inexhaustibility of a person. "Pope Francis echoes the personalist understanding of divine disclosure embraced by the Second Vatican Council's Dogmatic Constitution on Divine Revelation."[30] Revelation is personal, touching upon the deepest layers of identity, *cor ad cor loquitur*. The truth of revelation, in this sense, is also social; it is truth generated within a relationship and for the sake of a relationship. God does not reveal order, but "order for us"; God does not reveal "law," but "law to us."

There is, however, a price to pay for transformative orthodoxy: creativity can undermine the need for safety. The Holy Spirit enriches the entire church with different charisms, which are gifts of renewal for the church and, to quote Pope Francis,

> not an inheritance, safely secured and entrusted to a small group for safekeeping; rather they are gifts of the Spirit integrated into the body of the Church, drawn to the center which is Christ and then channeled into an evangelizing impulse. A sure sign of the authenticity of a charism is its ecclesial character, its ability to be integrated harmoniously into the life of God's holy and faithful people for the good of all. (EG 130)

---

29. Jürgen Miethke, *Ockhams Weg zur Sozialphilosophie* (Berlin: de Gruyter, 1969), 152.

30. Clifford, *Pope Francis' Call for the Conversion of the Church*, 38—cf. *Dei verbum* 2.

The Spirit stirs things up, and may even be disruptive.[31] The flip side to epistemic reliability providing a deep sense of trust and security is self-contained predictability. Pope Francis writes: "Jesus can also break through the dull categories with which we would enclose him and he constantly amazes us by his divine creativity. Whenever we make the effort to return to the source and to recover the original freshness of the Gospel, new avenues arise, new paths of creativity open up, with different forms of expression, more eloquent signs and words with new meaning for today's world. Every form of authentic evangelization is always 'new'" (EG11).[32] There is a freshness in every genuine encounter of love; and there is freshness in any deep human experience. An example of this experience of newness can be found in the life of C. S. Lewis. On more than one occasion he spent a great deal of time in deliberating about and pondering the question of theodicy—once in 1940 in *The Problem of Pain* and then again in a private diary after the death of his wife in 1960, later published as *A Grief Observed*. The time and space between the unruffled theological theory put forward in the polished work of 1940 and the rough style and language of the 1960 book, with its emotional outbursts reflecting the bitter inner battle between belief and disbelief, could be a key indicator in highlighting the difference between epistemic praxis with the living God at its center and other practices. One of the images used by Lewis in his 1960 book is the one of an iconoclast who shatters our limited imaginations: "My idea of God is not a divine idea. It has to be shattered time after time. He shatters it Himself. He is the great iconoclast. . . . Could we not almost say that this shattering is one of the

---

31. Karl Rahner made this point as well: "Do we not all too often seek in vain the Spirit in the visible Church? Are not many true indeed to the letter without possessing the Spirit, orthodox without being moved by the Spirit of God?" (Karl Rahner, "The Church as the Subject of the Sending of the Spirit," in Karl Rahner, *Theological Investigations* VII, trans. David Bourke [London: Darton, Longman and Todd, 1971], 186-92, at 190).

32. The main thing is to express those unchanging truths "in a language which brings out their abiding newness" (EG 41) Forms of expression need to be renewed—not estranged—for people to be able to accept and understand in their *own* language.

marks of His presence?"[33] Lewis does not see divine creativity simply as a fresh breeze but as an ominous whirlwind necessitating sacrifice; he experienced firsthand a disruptive God.

A deep experience transforms the person from within. These are experiences of growth, and these experiences of growth involve risks; an "iconoclastic God," a "God of surprises," will invite the person and the church to grow. Against this background we could identify a need for a proper "theology of fallibility" as an interpretation of *"ecclesia semper reformanda."* Such a theology would have to respect and carefully consider the 1975 document *Mysterium ecclesiae,* with its teaching on the infallibility of the church and the infallibility of the Magisterium; such a theology would perhaps have to distinguish between "infallibility" and "perfection"; it would have to negotiate the fact that teachings of the church, for example, the moral teachings with regard to usury, marriage, slavery, and religious freedom,[34] have changed over the course of time, that divine creativity calls for "living structures" and the epistemic risks that learning experiences entail. "We are not asked to be flawless, but to keep growing and wanting to grow" (EG 151). "It would not be right to see this call to growth exclusively or primarily in terms of doctrinal formation. It has to do with "observing" all that the Lord has shown us as the way of responding to his love" (EG 161).

Here we enter the discourse on orthodoxy as a relationship with God that must not be reduced to propositional correctness. The concept of "orthodoxy" is anchored in the idea of a set of beliefs that can be contained or in a missionary faith that enters the risk of encounter. We constantly build epistemic comfort zones, by phrases like "We have always done it this way" (EG 33) or by living a life "which appears outwardly in order but moves through the day without confronting great difficulties" (EG 44). Pope Francis challenges the idea of closed-off epistemic security, which is incompatible with a missionary heart (cf. EG 45). This is a call to an openness toward divine creativity and toward the cry of the poor. A church of the poor

---

33. Clive S. Lewis, *A Grief Observed* (London: Faber and Faber, 1966), 55f.

34. John T. Noonan Jr., "Development in Moral Doctrine," *Theological Studies* 54 (1993): 662-77.

will respect voices of the disadvantaged as theologically relevant; this is risky since the logic could be the following: a hospital without patients would be so much easier to manage! So would a school without students; so would a supermarket without customers. Similarly, a church without the poor would be so much easier. Let us just imagine a church whose members are satiated, materially well off, socially well situated, and even spiritually well fed. Wouldn't that be easier? Could that not be a temptation to think about a church without wounds and bruises?

This temptation is precisely what Pope Francis is talking about: he compares a church of the poor to an open house, which has to be a bit dirty and a bit "bruised":[35] "The Church is called to be the house of the Father, with doors always wide open. . . . Everyone can share in some way in the life of the Church; everyone can be part of the community, nor should the doors of the sacraments be closed for simply any reason" (EG 47). As the pope had already indicated in Korea, ecclesial structures should not be allowed to create exclusion mechanisms or barriers. Quite the reverse in fact; they should undermine them. The image of a bruised church implies that this is the prize (rather than the price) of an ecclesiology of an open house. A church with open doors cannot at the same time be one that lives in fear and dread of making mistakes, since this attitude will inevitably lead to the church closing its doors on its own self, shutting itself off from its believers: "my hope is that we will be moved by the fear of remaining shut up within structures which give us a false sense of security" (EG 49). EG 33 highlights boldness as the epistemic virtue with the capacity and willingness to shoulder risks—against all odds—for the sake of good.

Preaching the gospel by way of encounter is risky, since encounter means entering the realm of messy situations. This requires patience as well as courage; the gospel, when "preached in categories proper to each culture, will create a new synthesis with that particular culture. This is always a slow process, and we can be overly fearful. But if we allow doubts and fears to dampen our courage, instead of being

---

35. "I prefer a Church which is bruised, hurting and dirty because it has been out on the streets, rather than a Church which is unhealthy from being confined and from clinging to its own security" (EG 49).

creative we will remain comfortable and make no progress whatsoever" (EG 129). The pope reminds us: "to run the risk of a face-to-face encounter with others" (EG 88) means avoiding becoming fixated on those "rules which make us harsh judges," and not falling into "habits which make us feel safe" (EG 49). One might at this point think that things that "rightly disturb us and trouble our consciences" (EG 49) are those disruptive forces that enable us to see people in need, and we may then ask ourselves whether the "habits" mentioned might not be epistemic habits and the "rules" relevant to dogmatic formulas.[36]

An encounter with disadvantaged people has its own singular dynamic; we may find ourselves "at the margins," and this deep and powerful experience leaves "tattoos on the Heart."[37] Gregory Boyle, who coined this phrase after working for years with former gang members in Los Angeles, tells the story of a phone call at three o'clock in the morning when Cesar, one of the tough guys of the streets, asked him: "Have I been your son?" Boyle was deeply moved; this man discovered that he was a son worth having. This insight was transformative both for Cesar and Boyle.[38] Any genuine encounter transforms the persons involved; it will change the epistemic situation of a person, her beliefs and emotions, her knowledge and her way of knowing and thinking. This idea of knowledge as encounter was expressed

---

36. In a beautiful passage Karl Rahner pointed out the necessity and the risk of asking questions: "It is preferable simply to look at the facts, that is to say at Christology itself—always providing that one has the courage to ask questions, to be dissatisfied, to think with the mind and heart one actually has, and not with the mind and heart one is supposed to have. One can then be confident that after all something will perhaps emerge which we ought to be thinking today. . . . The only thing one can do in this situation is not to suppose that it is necessary to deny who one is (out of anxiety or distrust or falsely understood orthodoxy), but rather allow oneself honestly to have one's say, and really build on the fact that God" can give his grace to this age of ours, too, as he once gave it to sinners" (Karl Rahner, "Current Problems in Christology," in Karl Rahner, *Theological Investigations* I, trans. Cornelius Ernst [London: Darton, Longman and Todd, 1961], 149-214, at 153-54).

37. Gregory Boyle, *Tattoos on the Heart: The Power of Boundless Compassion* (New York: Free Press, 2010).

38. Ibid., 31.

by Cardinal Bertone in his address at a philosophical symposium for "Friendship among People," held in Rimini in 2009.[39] Knowledge is generated in encounters, the process of obtaining knowledge can be described in the language of encounter. It is in encounter that a poor church has a duty to invite those people outlined in Matthew 25, who recognize Christ in their own singular way and who need to be given space and possibilities to receive the gospel God has sent them. People who depend on God without the illusion of self-sufficiency have, generally, "a special openness to the faith; they need God" (EG 200). The poor as teachers will challenge closed spaces.

Pope Francis also underlines the importance of encounter and friendship by warning against self-centeredness and developing a mindset that leaves no space for the poor and where "God's voice is no longer heard" (EG 2). He even mentions the "self-absorbed promethean neo-pelagianism of those who ultimately trust only in their own powers . . . instead of opening the door to grace" (EG 94). The encounter and friendship ensuing from open dialogue require boldness because they abandon the familiar ground of "we have always done it this way" (EG 33) and break through the surrounding fence of habit. The epistemic praxis of new encounter depends for its very

39. "Contemporary epistemological reflection has brought to light the crucial role of the subject of knowledge of the actual act of knowing. . . . The most important consequence of this situation is that knowledge cannot be described as the registration of a detached spectator. On the contrary, involvement with the known object by the knowing subject is a *conditio sine qua non* of knowledge itself. Therefore, it is not detachment and the absence of involvement that are the ideal to seek in vain in the search for "objective" knowledge, but rather an appropriate involvement with the object, an involvement likely to impart its specific message to the person who is questioning knowledge. This is why knowledge can be an 'event.' It 'happens' like a real encounter between a subject and an object. That this encounter is necessary in order to speak of knowledge does not make us look at subject and object as two important things that can be kept at an ascetic distance from each other to preserve their purity; on the contrary, they are two living realities that influence each other when they come into contact" ("Message of His Eminence Cardinal Tarcisio Bertone on Behalf of His Holiness Benedict XVI on the Occasion of the 30th Meeting for Friendship among Peoples Held in Rimini on 17 August 2009").

existence on the virtues of bravery and boldness. It requires boldness to revise the church's "rules or precepts which may have been quite effective in their time, but no longer have the same usefulness for directing and shaping people's lives" (EG 43). It may leave bruises to the perfect architecture of the doctrinal building; it may be incompatible with epistemic purism.

This is precisely what Pope Francis is exhorting us to embrace—the image of a bruised church. A bruised church is a church that has gone out bearing the risk of those who leave safe havens. There are different ways of leaving safe places: it may be the exodus of Abraham, who was called to leave his home; it may be the exodus from safe bondage into unsafe freedom; it may be the exodus of the shepherd looking for the lost sheep; or it may be the exodus of a younger son leaving the family home. Exodus involves risks; a church that "goes out" and leaves the safe places of structures and habits takes risks. Would there also be space to accommodate a concept like "bruised orthodoxy"?

It might be fascinating to pursue the thought that Jesus used in Luke 15 in the parables of the lost sheep, the lost coin, and the lost son to describe the dynamics of joy. We can pose some deeper questions: What is the importance of the lost sheep for the flock? What happens within the flock once the lost sheep has been returned? The parable of the prodigal son focuses on the image of the home, a place that is safe and secure, a place well able to host celebrations. If we accept the idea that orthodoxy is about the right relationship with God we could compare these two types of orthodoxy: the orthodoxy of the older son, who has never left home, and the orthodoxy of the younger son, who has returned from the land of the lost. The first orthodoxy is "safe"; the second is "bruised." A theology of proper fallibility will reflect on the possibility of bruised orthodoxy that has mastered a learning curve, an experience of growth, appropriated through exodus and error. Is there such as thing as "*felix error*"?

1.4 The Idea of Orthodoxy

Orthodoxy connotes having the proper relationship with God; it is about having the right faith, since faith is primarily about the quality of a relationship and not about the quality of a person's epistemic situation. The relationship shapes the epistemic situation with beliefs and convictions: "Faith also means believing in God, believing that he truly loves us, that he is alive, that he is mysteriously capable of intervening, that he does not abandon us and that he brings good out of evil by his power and his infinite creativity" (EG 278). A person enters a relationship with God; this relationship is based on beliefs, of course, but if there is a living relationship the experience of the relationship cannot be reduced to beliefs. A "second-person perspective" cannot be exhausted by beliefs. The belief that God truly loves us is not a belief that could be properly expressed or understood without an experiential element; without appropriate experience we cannot understand the meaning of the words "to be loved." "Belief in" with its moment of trust cannot be reduced to "belief that." Moreover, one cannot claim to have understood the belief "God truly loves us" without encountering reality in the light of this belief; in other words, this belief will change the kinds of experiences that we will have. The experience will fill us with joy (a thought that is like the *cantus firmus* of *Evangelii gaudium*), will change the way we see the world, the way we see ourselves, the way we enter commitments.

Orthodox faith, proper faith, is the result of a "fundamental option," or, more specifically, the experience of falling in love "in a quite absolute, final way," as a quote attributed to Pedro Arrupe puts it. This commitment will be such that all other commitments will appear in a new light, which may be the deeper meaning of the warning: "No one can serve two masters. . . . You cannot serve God and Mammon" (Matt 6:24). The commitment that corresponds to the experience of being loved by God is final: "If we wish to commit ourselves fully and perseveringly, we need to leave behind every other motivation. This is our definitive, deepest and greatest motivation, the ultimate reason and meaning behind all we do: the glory of the Father which Jesus sought at every moment of his life" (EG 267). The motif of doing everything and living life *ad majorem Dei gloriam* expresses the nature of orthodoxy.

Let me now reconstruct the main insights into the nature of orthodoxy in *Evangelii gaudium* in seven points: (1) orthodoxy has as its center a loving relationship with God; (2) orthodoxy is healing; (3) orthodoxy is dynamic; (4) orthodoxy is humble; (5) orthodoxy is missionary; (6) orthodoxy is compatible with healthy pluralism; and (7) orthodoxy is costly.

(1) "The primary reason for evangelizing is the love of Jesus which we have received" (EG 264); orthodoxy is responsive to the experience of divine love: "Before all else, the Gospel invites us to respond to the God of love who saves us, to see God in others and to go forth from ourselves to seek the good of others" (EG 39). Love defines the concept of doctrine and not the other way round; "relational orthodoxy" defines "positional and propositional orthodoxy" and not the other way round. Without the central meaning of love there is the risk "that it is not the Gospel which is being preached, but certain doctrinal or moral points based on specific ideological options" (EG 39). The criterion for orthodoxy is not primarily the correspondence to positions within a coherence theory of orthodoxy, but primarily the correspondence to the spirit of the gospel in the light of a relationship with God whereby truth is personal ("I am the Truth" [John 14:6]). It is not so much "truth as coherence" as "truth as encounter."[40] It is truth as an expression of love and not as the result of conclusions. It is in the light of this love that all aspects of life will be "personalized," appropriated in the light of the experience of personal love. In this sense, orthodoxy has to be "ratified" or "authenticated" as a living relationship with the living God: "We need to remember that all religious teaching ultimately has to be reflected in the teacher's way of life, which awakens the assent of the heart by its nearness, love and witness" (EG 42).

(2) Orthodoxy is healing; a proper relationship with God will heal wounds and brokenness. Orthodoxy has to be approached in this light of love; the confessional should be regarded not as "a torture chamber but rather an encounter with the Lord's mercy which spurs us to do our best" (EG 44). The pope reflects on misleading attitudes: "Frequently, we act as arbiters of grace rather than its facilitators" (EG 47); "we need to approach it [this reality] with the gaze of the Good Shepherd, who seeks not to judge, but to love" (EG 125); the "preparation for preaching requires love" (EG 146). Orthodoxy is a response

---

40. See *Deus caritas est*, 1, on Christianity as based on encounter.

to the experience of being truly loved by God. This experience will address personal and social ills in the spirit of the gospel: "The unified and complete sense of human life that the Gospel proposes is the best remedy for the ills of our cities" (EG 75). The healing nature of orthodoxy comes through in the fact that orthodoxy provides a "haven"; a relationship with God provides a sense of home that cannot be taken away. It is also part of the dynamics of providing a haven that there is epistemic security, as the pope reminds his audience: The church cannot change things; there is no space for a superficial understanding of "progress" in certain issues (EG 214); there are "objective moral norms" (EG 64) that are binding. It is healing to be in a safe place without confusion and with clear points of reference. It is also part of the healing nature of orthodoxy that a proper relationship with God opens doors to the experience of mercy. It is healing to offer mercy— works of mercy are central to the Christian message; this point "is so clear and direct, so simple and eloquent, that no ecclesial interpretation has a right to relativize it" (EG 194); there can then be no such thing as "merciless orthodoxy." Orthodoxy is healing because it builds bridges; it is healing to overcome differences: People wounded by historical divisions will find "the witness of authentically fraternal and reconciled communities . . . luminous and attractive" (EG 100).

(3) Orthodoxy is dynamic, "living." The church "needs to grow in her interpretation of the revealed word and in her understanding of truth" (EG 40). There is an idea of magisterial and ecclesial growth expressed in this seemingly simple statement. The acknowledgment of growth goes hand in hand with the acknowledgment of an *esprit de finesse* in connection to doctrine. "For those who long for a monolithic body of doctrine guarded by all and leaving no room for nuance, this might appear as undesirable and leading to confusion" (EG 40). As a culture of living encounter, orthodoxy is also discerning, a process: "We need to distinguish clearly what might be a fruit of the kingdom from what runs counter to God's plan. This involves not only recognizing and discerning spirits, but also—and this is decisive—choosing movements of the spirit of good and rejecting those of the spirit of evil." (EG 51). There is a need for constant discernment in order to preserve the vitality of orthodoxy; there is a "demand that we constantly seek ways of expressing unchanging truths in a language which brings out

their abiding newness" (EG 41). Discernment processes are spiritual processes, expressions of a rich inner life. Orthodoxy as dynamic and living is a spiritual process rather than a mental state; it is definitely not a mechanical application but rather the "enactment" of doctrine. Ministry is not about imposing a multitude of doctrines (EG 35); it is not about making use of "fixed formulations learned by heart" (EG 129). It is about enacting the spirit of doctrine and allowing the Holy Spirit to touch people's minds and hearts with divine creativity.

(4) Orthodoxy is humble: reading a biblical text is listening to the Word of God, which requires "the humility of the heart which recognizes that the word is always beyond us" (EG 146). This demands patience and attention, a spirit of waiting but also openness, an emptying of oneself in order to allow Christ's message to "penetrate and possess the preacher, not just intellectually but in his entire being" (EG 151). This is the humility of being willing to be guided. Another aspect of humility is realism and a commitment to keeping one's feet on the ground (EG 234: "We also need to look to the local, which keeps our feet on the ground"), which is incompatible with being "stuck in the realm of pure ideas" (EG 232). As an expression of this honesty to reality Pope Francis formulates the principle "Realities are greater than ideas" (EG 233) based on the incarnation of the Word. Orthodoxy as humble recognition of created and cultivated reality is honest to the real, open to be guided by truth, eternal truths but also truths about the changing faces of reality.

(5) Orthodoxy is missionary. Orthodoxy is not "closed" and "safe"—a missionary heart "never closes itself off, never retreats into its own security, never opts for rigidity and defensiveness" (EG 45). "Let us not stifle or presume to control this missionary power!" (EG 124). An authentic faith "is never comfortable or completely personal—[it] always involves a deep desire to change the world" (EG 183). There is a social dimension of orthodoxy, a deep sense of having to engage with the world. We are committed to building a new world "not as a burdensome duty but as the result of a personal decision which brings us joy and gives meaning to our lives" (EG 269).[41]

---

41. *Evangelii gaudium* has clearly a social dimension and a commitment to the poor; see Ginés García Beltrán, "La dimensión social de la evangelizacion en

Orthodoxy as proper relationship with God is "overflowing," eager to share in the sense of Acts 4:20 ("It is impossible for us not to speak about what we have seen and heard").

(6) Orthodoxy is compatible with healthy pluralism[42] in terms of content as well as in terms of form. There is propositional orthodoxy and there is nonpropositional orthodoxy. Popular spirituality, or "the people's mysticism," a spirituality incarnated in the culture of the lowly, as the Aparecida document states (*Aparecida*, 263), is not "devoid of content; rather it discovers and expresses that content more by way of symbols than by discursive reasoning, and in the act of faith greater accent is placed on *credere in Deum* than on *credere Deum*" (EG 124). Here Pope Francis is referring to STh II-II,2,2. There is not only epistemic value in nonpropositional orthodoxy, there is also a sense of the irreducibility of orthodoxy to propositional aspects: "Faith always … retains a certain obscurity which does not detract from the firmness of its assent. Some things are understood and appreciated only from the standpoint of this assent, which is a sister to love, beyond the range of clear reasons and arguments" (EG 42). Beyond this fundamental distinction of two types of orthodoxy there is space for pluralism in terms of cultural diversity, which properly understood "is not a threat to Church unity" (EG 117). In fact, attitudes of cultural ethnocentrism can be dangerous and damaging (EG 117). Orthodoxy is compatible with the recognition that "each people is the creator of their own culture and the protagonist of their own history" (EG 122). This gives grounds to argue for a contextual theology of orthodoxy. Gerard Whelan suggests reading *Evangelii gaudium* as "an exercise in contextual theology,"[43] using an inductive method that has been more

la exhortación apostólica *Evangelii gaudium*," *Scripta theologica* 46 (2014): 461-80; Joseph Loic Mben, "The concept of 'poor' in Evangelii gaudium," *Zeitschrift für Missionswissenschaft und Religionswissenschaft* 98, no. 1 (2014): 133-38.

42. EG 255.

43. Gerard Whelan, "Evangelii gaudium as 'Contextual Theology': Helping the Church 'Mount to the Level of its Times,'" *Australian eJournal of Theology* 22, no. 1 (2015): 1-10, at 1. This view has been shared by Stephen Bevans, "The Apostolic Exhortation *Evangelii gaudium* on the Proclamation of the Gospel in Today's World," *International Review of Mission* 103, no. 2 (2014): 297-308, at 302f.

consistently applied than the claim to this method in the 2007 *Aparecida* document.[44]

(7) Finally, orthodoxy is painful and costly: "Faith always remains something of a cross" (EG 42). The Christian idea of a proper relationship implies aspects of self-denial in discipleship and the recognition of the foolishness of the cross. There may be "epistemic costs" involved, explicitly mentioned by Saint Paul (1 Cor 1:21-25). It may also be painful to recognize the pluralism of charisms in communion (EG 130). Orthodoxy is costly because a person cannot claim to be orthodox without feeling concern for the poor in her life: "None of us can think we are exempt from concern for the poor" (EG 201); concern for the poor is costly since it asks for commitments that come with opportunity costs, especially the opportunity costs of a spirit of worldliness with its categories of efficiency and success.

Ultimately, *Evangelii gaudium* also invites us to ponder the possibility of a paradox, the paradox that a cost of orthodoxy could also be (a certain notion of) orthodoxy itself. A proper relationship with God will make us engage in an exodus from safe places, including epistemically safe places. Let us not forget that the spirit of worldliness as the most direct threat to orthodoxy can also manifest itself in "an ostentatious preoccupation ... for doctrine" (EG 95). It is safer to work with "the given" rather than "the found"; it is safer to use the same phrases; it is safer to hold on to the same habits; it is safer not to ask certain questions; it is safer not to enter the messiness of local realities. Orthodoxy cannot be kept in sterile containers. Persons who take the world and this life and the incarnation seriously will have to accept "the prophecy of their brothers and sisters" (EG 97). Orthodoxy is about not indulging in fantasies and not losing contact with the real lives and difficulties of our people (EG 96). Is this a case of "bruised orthodoxy"?

---

44. Jose Marins, "Base Communities, a Return to Inductive Methodology," in R. Pelton, ed., *Aparecida: Quo Vadis?* (Scranton, PA: University of Scranton Press, 2008), 93-99.

Chapter 2

The Gospel of Joy: Orthodoxy as Discipleship

"This is the time of fulfillment. The kingdom of God is at hand. Repent, believe in the gospel." More than one theologian has identified these sentences in Mark 1:15 as Jesus' message in a nutshell.[1] They encapsulate the good news. This news is good because it comes from the fountain of all goodness; it is news about the good life to come and about the good life to be lived in the here and now, since the kingdom of God is "at hand" (Mark 1:15). It is good news since it comes about in the time of fulfillment; it is news inviting a new beginning in all kinds of ways (*metanoia* and repentance, but also newness in the spirit of new wine in new wineskins, as mentioned in Matt 9:17; Mark 2:22; Luke 5:38). This good news is the source of joy, the "joy of the gospel." Pope Francis cites a number of examples about the Gospels' invitations to rejoice: "'Rejoice!' is the angel's greeting to Mary (*Lk* 1:28). Mary's visit to Elizabeth makes John leap for joy in his mother's womb (cf. *Lk* 1:41). In her song of praise, Mary proclaims: 'My spirit rejoices in God my Savior' (*Lk* 1:47). When Jesus begins his ministry, John cries out: 'For this reason, my joy has been fulfilled' (*Jn* 3:29). Jesus himself 'rejoiced in the Holy Spirit' (*Lk* 10:21). His message brings us joy: 'I have said these things to you, so that my joy may be in you, and that your joy may be complete' (*Jn* 15:11). Our Christian joy drinks of the wellspring of his brimming heart. He promises his disciples:

---

1. Thomas Söding, *Die Verkündigung Jesu: Ereignis und Erinnerung,* 2d ed. (Freiburg/Breisgau: Herder, 2012), 140.

'You will be sorrowful, but your sorrow will turn into joy' (*Jn* 16:20). He then goes on to say: 'But I will see you again and your hearts will rejoice, and no one will take your joy from you' (*Jn* 16:22). The disciples 'rejoiced' (*Jn* 20:20) at the sight of the risen Christ. In the Acts of the Apostles we read that the first Christians 'ate their food with glad and generous hearts' (2:46). Wherever the disciples went, 'there was great joy' (8:8); even amid persecution they continued to be 'filled with joy' (13:52). The newly baptized eunuch 'went on his way rejoicing' (8:39), while Paul's jailer 'and his entire household rejoiced that he had become a believer in God' (16:34)."[2] We see joy in the Magi, who were overjoyed when they found the Messiah (Matt 2:10); we see abundance in the sign at the wedding of Cana and in the feeding of the five thousand. Jesus' disciples do not fast because they cannot mourn, they are like wedding guests with the bridegroom in their midst (Matt 9:15); we see the seventy-two return "rejoicing" (Luke 10:17); we see people glorify God after a healing (Mark 2:12); the transfiguration brings the joyful "It is good that we are here" to Peter's lips (Matt 17:4). Sensing an initial understanding of the empty tomb, the women "went away quickly from the tomb, fearful yet overjoyed" (Matt 28:8).

Pope Francis expresses a commitment to a Church of the Poor and the belief that the gospel fills us with joy. What is the link between a Church of the Poor and its epistemological implications for understanding "orthodoxy" on the one hand and the gospel on the other? I want to explore this question by looking into Jesus' way of building a Church of the Poor (2.1), and Jesus' risky encounters and interactions with sinners (2.2), by reconstructing Jesus' way of challenging and changing epistemic practices (2.3), and, against the background of this enquiry, discuss the concept of "orthodoxy" ("healing faith") in the light of the gospel of joy (2.4).

2.1 Jesus Builds a Church of the Poor

Jesus left a community—before he died on the cross and after his resurrection. Was this community a "community of the poor"? There is a temptation to present "firm theology" with regard to the

---

2. EG 5.

biblical "option for the poor." It cannot be denied that there is strong theological evidence that the Hebrew Bible expresses a special commitment to attend to the poor of YHWH, that is, those who are in pain and depend on divine mercy and human support.[3] Distinctive and prescriptive measures (gleaning harvest leftovers, Sabbath year, jubilee year: Exod 23:10; Deut 24; Lev 19, 23, 25) show that concern for the poor is "tangible" in that it transforms the material and social situation. Hebrew servants were to be freed in the seventh year (Exod 21:2); foreigners were not to be mistreated (Exod 22:21; Lev 19:33), widows not be exploited (Exod 22:22); lending money to a needy person from the people of Israel was not to be treated like a business deal, which meant that no interest could be levied (Exod 22:25; Lev 25:35-37); poor people must not be denied justice in their lawsuits (Exod 23:6); a hired worker must receive his wage on the same day and not be held back over night (Lev 19:13b).[4] These measures can also be seen to point to a biblical understanding of economics, which the Czech economist Tomas Sedláček has characterized by the imperative "Do not always optimize,"[5] since there are clearly more productive ways of spending the seventh day of creation. Leviticus 19 ("the Holiness Code") expresses this limit to optimization and maximization by asking people not to reap "to the very edges of your field" and not to "gather the gleanings of your harvest" (Lev 19:9); similarly, it is prescribed, "Do not go over your vineyard a second time or pick up the grapes that have fallen, leave them for the poor and the foreigner" (Lev 19:10). This model of a Sabbath economy with built-in mechanisms of limits to growth express a preferential option for the poor, and is also common-good oriented, since it provides for membership and ownership for the entire community. The "Sabbath culture" and the idea of a sphere protected from economization seems counter-

---

3. Julio de Santa Ana, *Good News to the Poor: The Challenge of the Poor in the History of the Church* (Maryknoll, NY: Orbis Books, 1979), 1-11.

4. The *Sefer Habrit*, the Book of the Covenant (Exodus 21–24), contains the "pro poor laws" in a nutshell.

5. Tomas Sedláček, *Economics of Good and Evil: The Quest for Economic Meaning from Gilgamesh to Wall Street* (Oxford: Oxford University Press, 2011), 245.

economic. "Saturday was not established to increase efficiency. It was a real ontological break that followed the example of the Lord's seventh day of creation.... The seventh day of creation is enjoyment.... The observance of the Sabbath bears the message that the *purpose of creation was not just creating* but that it had an *end*, a *goal*. The process was just a process, not a purpose. The whole of Being was created so that we may find in it rest, accomplishment, joy."[6] The Jewish creation story with the establishment of a Sabbath culture communicates that people were not primarily created for labor or material wealth. The Sabbath year prescribed in Leviticus 25 is an expression of this Sabbath culture: "The land itself must observe a Sabbath to the Lord" (Lev 25:2). The Jubilee year is the consecrated fiftieth year during where all the inhabitants of the land were to be liberated (Lev 25:10) and property returned (Lev 25:25-28).

The loss of this "Sabbath economy" has been criticized in prophetic literature (esp. Amos and Micah), where concern for the poor is connected with the articulation of social pathologies. A healthy community, characterized by loyalty, justice, and compassion, does not exclude those with fragile membership status such as the widow, the orphan, the sojourner.[7] Social justice in Judaism "is realized in a society where the elders are honored and the physical sustenance of unfortunate members is a response to a divine commandment."[8] Even though there may be different Hebrew Bible traditions with regard to poverty (in broad strokes: poverty as a result of laziness, as described in the Wisdom Books; poverty as a result of injustice, as described in prophetic literature; poverty as a result of calamity, as described in "history" books), there is a clear sense of an obligation to help and support the poor not only for individual members of a society but for whole communities as

6. Ibid., 89.

7. Donald E. Gowan, "Wealth and Poverty in the Old Testament. The Case of the Widow, the Orphan, and the Sojourner," *Interpretation* 41, no. 4 (1987): 341-53.

8. Michael A. Signer, "Social Justice in Judaism," in Daniel Groody, ed., *The Option for the Poor in Christian Theology* (Notre Dame, IN: University of Notre Dame Press, 2007), 290-301, at 294. This also means that social justice in this tradition is based on prayer and study.

well.[9] An "option for the poor" in the Old Testament can be seen in different ways: as the liberation by God of a suppressed people in the book of Exodus; in the self-understanding of the Davidic monarchy, which proclaims itself God's instrument for the defense of the poor; as the language game of prophets speaking out against injustice; in the petitions of the psalms where the poor turn prayerfully to God.[10]

The Gospels discuss aspects of a Church of the Poor with regard to people of higher social status, in prominent places, such as the parable of the Good Samaritan (Luke 10:29-37), the parable of Lazarus and the rich man (Luke 16:19-31), Jesus' encounter with the rich young man (Mark 10:17-31; Matt 19:16-30; Luke 18:18-30), and the words on the final judgment (Matt 25:31-46). These passages, as we will see further in Chapter 4, have been extensively discussed in early Christian writings. Since Jesus is the messenger with the message in the spirit of "*Ego-eimi*-statements," Jesus' words in the Gospels cannot be separated from Jesus' life as described by the Gospels. What then, we might ask, is Jesus' attitude to poverty?

Even though one could read the manger in the stable as a symbol of poverty[11] or the sacrifice of a pair of turtle doves given at the presentation in the temple as a sign of lower socio-economic status (Luke 2:22-24), Jesus himself was probably not poor as the son of a carpenter with his own carpentry trade, which would put him into the lower middle-class. However, Jesus chose to be poor and reached out to social outcasts who at that time would have included tax collectors, robbers, herdsmen, prostitutes, and those forced to beg because of their severe disability or handicap (being blind, deaf, lame, crippled, or leprous). Jesus became a social outsider by choice.[12] He made a

---

9. Christopher J. H. Wright, *Old Testament Ethics for the People of God* (Downers Grove, IL: Intervarsity Press, 2004), 169-71.

10. George Pixley and Clodovis Boff, *The Bible, the Church and the Poor* (Maryknoll, NY: Orbis Books, 1989), ch. 1, esp. 21-48.

11. Elsa Tamez, "Poverty, the Poor, and the Option for the Poor. A Biblical Perspective," in Daniel Groody, ed., *The Option for the Poor in Christian Theology* (Notre Dame, IN: University of Notre Dame Press, 2007), 41-54, at 45.

12. Albert Nolan, *Jesus before Christianity* (Maryknoll, NY: Orbis Books, 1978), 23-26. Leslie Hoppe makes the same point referring to Jesus' decision to leave his socio-economic context: Jesus "belonged to a family that was not poor.

commitment, and in the Gospel we can read many passages where Jesus is prompting and provoking people to make choices and enter commitments. Again and again, he sides with the poor and challenges the privileged. In the Mediterranean context, the poor were those who were scarcely able to maintain their honor and sense of dignity, those struggling on a day-to-day basis to maintain some sort of social status; whereas "the rich" were characterized as those driven by avarice but nevertheless dissatisfied with their "lot," and here is the theological-ethical challenge: they freely choose to serve greed rather than serve God.[13] Jesus becomes an outcast in a world that is "dark and fearful," in a world, as Nolan describes it, that attributes misfortunes to moral failure. However, in choosing to be poor, Jesus did not choose a life without a proper material basis. This aspect touches on the interesting question of the infrastructure Jesus disposed of and used, or even possessed and owned. The latter was the point of heated debate about poverty in the thirteenth and fourteenth centuries, a point to which we will return in Chapter 4. In the Gospels, we find contradictory textual evidence. There is an indication of Jesus' infrastructure when he is asked by the disciples where he lives in John 1:39 ("Come and you will see!"); Matthew 8:20 talks about the lack of place and infrastructure ("nowhere" to lay his head; cf. Luke 9:58); the disciples are commissioned without infrastructural support (Matt 10:5-15; Luke 9:3; 10:4). The experience of homelessness endured in Bethlehem ("there was no room for them in the inn" [Luke 2:7]) is repeated only once during Jesus' ministry as itinerant preacher—when we learn about the lack of Samaritan hospitality (Luke 9:53). At the same time, there are no scenes of infrastructural exclusion, let alone severe experiences of destitution such as homelessness. Jesus is able to pay the temple tax and is not openly opposed to paying taxes; he is even depicted as one

---

His legal father, Joseph, was a *tektôn*—a builder, a contractor, a skilled laborer. But Jesus left his family and occupation" (Leslie Hoppe, *There Shall Be No Poor among You: Poverty in the Bible* [Nashville: Abingdon Press, 2004], 144).

13. Bruce J. Malina, "Wealth and Poverty in the New Testament and Its World," *Interpretation* 41, no. 4 (1987): 354-67; Sondra Ely Wheeler, *Wealth as Peril and Obligation: The New Testament on Possessions* (Grand Rapids, MI: Eerdmans, 1995).

who can provide material structures by feeding many through an act of multiplying bread, a temptation he resisted in the desert. All in all, Jesus was not without means; he had infrastructural possibilities at his disposal. He stayed in Bethany; he was able to organize Passover with his disciples using the resources of an unnamed citizen (Matt 26:18; Mark 14:13-15; Luke 22:10-12). Mark tells us that the disciples are commanded to follow a man with a jar of water into a house and ask the master of the house: "The Teacher says, 'Where is my guest room where I may eat the Passover with my disciples?' Then he will show you a large supper room furnished and ready." This is an expression of the power to move goods; the room is "large," and it is "furnished" and "ready." Jesus chooses social exclusion but builds circles and networks of social inclusion; he does not forgo material infrastructure for its own sake; he does not rebuff it in a harsh or severe manner.

Jesus proclaims good news to the poor in this dark world (Luke 4:17-19); the connection between Jesus and poverty can be summarized in seven key points: (1) Jesus chose to be poor and rejected the temptations of materialism, power, wealth, and idolatry (Luke 4:1-13); (2) Jesus preached the kingdom of God as good news to the poor as his first addressees to be offered a gospel of joy; (3) Jesus associated with the poor, including close contacts in healing situations, and shared table fellowship; (4) Jesus challenged the intellectual elites (e.g., Matt 23) and the rich (as in the encounter with the rich young man in Mark 10:17-22, or in his stern warnings in Luke 6:24-25 and Luke 12:15, or in the parable of the rich fool in Luke 11:16-21); (5) Jesus did not systematically challenge social conditions and structural issues[14]; the image of the weeds among wheat (Matt 13:24-30) may even point to a "transitory ethics of endurance with an eschato-

---

14. This laid the foundation for a type of teaching on wealth that would see wealth as morally and spiritually risky and in need of pro-poor activities as a remedy, but not as principally faulty—a position clearly expressed in 1 Timothy 6:17-19: "Tell the rich in the present age not to be proud and not to rely on so uncertain a thing as wealth but rather on God, who richly provides us with all things for our enjoyment. Tell them to do good, to be rich in good works, to be generous, ready to share, thus accumulating as treasure a good foundation for the future, so as to win the life that is true life."

logical justice perspective"; (6) Jesus lived a life of limited austerity
(Matt 9:14-17; 11:19)[15] and did not give up a culture of "wasteful celebrations" (John 2, wedding of Cana; John 11, anointing scene). There
may even be grounds to see a link between an option for the poor and
celebrations, as in the anointing scenes (Matt 26:6-16; Mark 14:3-10;
Luke 7:36-50; John 12:1-8) because it is the socially excluded woman
who plays the key part in these scenes and is the "enabler" of wasteful-
ness. (7) Theologically speaking, Jesus' identity can be described as
kenotic (Isa 53; Phil 2:7; 2 Cor 8:9).

Jesus builds a Church of the Poor, we could say, by choosing social
exclusion in siding with the poor, sometimes against the establishment, without social upheaval or a loss of a culture of celebration.
Honesty to the text, however, requires a deeper reading.

Waiting for the Text: Embracing Spiritual Unclarity

A deeper reading may prove to be painful because it challenges the
epistemic integrity of coherent vision and consistent judgment.
There is a temptation to project onto the text one's vision of the poor
Jesus of Nazareth founding the Church of the Poor. A deeper reading of the Gospels does not make for innocent reading; it is painful,
opening up wounds and plunging the reader into darkness. It is a
theological-intellectual and a spiritual-existential challenge to allow
a text to be a "thorn," to be an "axe for the frozen sea within us" (Franz
Kafka) rather than a source of comfort and consolation. Reading the
gospel in Simone Weil's spirit of *attente* is a "waiting" for the meaning
to emerge, even against our predictions and predilections, which in
turn will challenge our need for moral and spiritual clarity.[16]

If we allow ourselves to be led purely by the text rather than by our
belief in Jesus' mission to bring about a Church of the Poor, we will
find reasons to be irritated. The statement "The poor you will always

---

15. Aquinas comments on the limited austerity of Jesus' life in that Jesus
associated with people and because of that conformed to their manner of living
(STh III,40,2,resp.).

16. See Mary Gordon, *Reading Jesus: A Writer's Encounter with the Gospels*
(New York: Pantheon Books, 2009), xxii-xxiii.

have with you" (Matt 26:11) is a particularly painful eradication in the sense that it limits the imagination and makes it difficult for us to embrace the vision of a world without poverty. It seems to challenge efforts to combat poverty.[17] Moreover, there could be grounds for theological or philosophical frustration with regard to the status of the poor: the concept of "fairness," dear to liberal philosophical discourses, seems oddly out of place and inapplicable. The parable of the workers in the vineyard (Matt 20:1-16) indicates limits to fairness as much as the parable of the prodigal son (Luke 15). The term "fairness" does not work in a feudal context; it works best among peers in an egalitarian framework. A similar key challenge to the Church of the Poor is the parable of the talents in Matthew 25 with the message: "To everyone who has, more will be given and he will grow rich; but from the one who has not, even what he has will be taken away" (Matt 25:29). For good reason, Robert Merton called this dynamic the "Matthew effect" and applied it to the sociology of science with the message that well-established scientists and well-established academic institutions (as "those who have") will always and invariably receive more and more (recognition and resources), whereas unknown writers and researchers and lesser known institutions have a much harder time obtaining recognition. It is also for good reason that Merton's Matthew effect has become an established term in poverty research.[18]

An option for the poor implies judgments. It is impossible to talk about issues of social ethics, including injustice, exploitation, and structural sin without using normative judgments. There are gospel

---

17. See *Christian Aid, Report on Poverty* (London: Christian Aid, 2009), 11.

18. Robert Merton, "The Matthew Effect in Science," *Science* 159, no. 3810 (1968): 56-63; Robert Merton, "The Matthew Effect in Science, II: Cumulative Advantage and the Symbolism of Intellectual Property," *Isis* 79, no. 4 (1988): 606-23; Keith E. Stanovich, "Matthew Effects in Reading: Some Consequences of Individual Differences in the Acquisition of Literacy," *Reading Research Quarterly* 21, no. 4 (1986): 360-407; Robert H. Wade, "On the Causes of Increasing World Poverty and Inequality, or Why the Matthew Effect Prevails," *New Political Economy* 9, no. 2 (2004) 163-88; Daniel Rigney, *The Matthew Effect: How Advantage Begets Further Advantage* (New York: Columbia University Press, 2010).

passages that do not encourage the formation of judgments: "Stop judging that you may not be judged" (Matt 7:1; Luke 6:37); the same passages prompt the art of "self-accusation" with the splinter/beam metaphor ("Remove the wooden beam from your eye first; then you will see clearly to remove the splinter in your brother's eye" [Luke 6:42]). But what does this mean if it is addressed to the poor and their ability to make judgments about social situations they find themselves in? This challenge of proper judgments is deepened in Jesus' reaction to the adulterous woman where we find: "Let the one among you who is without sin be the first to throw a stone at her" (John 8:7). There are two issues here: how can a sinner (and be it a poor person) ever make a substantial judgment without violating the spirit of this passage? And, if this statement were to be applied to the criticism of inequality or the accumulation of wealth, how would social critique and moral clarity with regard to structures and individual behavior still be possible? Can you build a Church of the Poor without judging the establishment?

There are further challenges and complications. There is the issue of the heterogeneity of "the poor"; it is a challenge to reconcile the array of persons and categories grouped together in the concept "the poor."[19] Even within a group of poor people there will be a hierarchy, an insight famously established in poverty research by Charles Booth in the nineteenth century. Even within a poor household there will be a hierarchy, and inner-household patterns of resource distribution are not always transparent to the outside. This heterogeneity of the poor is also a factor in the Gospels: There are outcasts such as soldiers (the centurion in Matt 8 and Luke 7 is an outside who needs an explicit recommendation: "he deserves to have you do this for him" [Luke 7:4]) and tax collectors (Matthew in Matt 9:9 or Levi in Luke 5:27) who are different from other outsiders, including lepers, the mentally unstable and insane, and encapsulated in Matthew 15:30: "the lame, the blind, the deformed, the mute." The beatitudes, on the other hand, praise different kinds of persons, including the addressees of the beatitudes:

---

19. Bryant Myers sees at least five different groups of "poor" in the Scriptures (Bryant L. Myers, *Walking with the Poor* [Maryknoll, NY: Orbis Books, 2011], 109).

"Blessed are the eyes that see what you see" (Luke 10:23), or "Blessed are those who hear the word of God and observe it" (Luke 11:28). A difference becomes apparent that may otherwise be overlooked between those who thirst for justice and those who are excluded. Or can it be argued that exclusion is a consequence of commitment to justice? There is then also the issue of the desirability of social exclusion. "Blessed are you . . . when people exclude you," we read in the New American Bible (revised edition) translation of Luke's version of the beatitudes in the Sermon on the Plain (Luke 6:22). Is social exclusion then a desirable state if sought and practiced through the right motives? Jesus is more than clear in declaring that the price paid for discipleship is high, and an attendant knock-on effect is self-exclusion, lambs among wolves (Matt 10:16-25). Jesus is portrayed as the key cause of division in the Gospel (Matt 10:34-35). Jesus' "option for the poor" is depicted as an option against his family (Matt 12:46-50, where Jesus rejects primary affiliations with the statement: "For whoever does the will of my heavenly Father is my brother, and sister, and mother"). This tension is heightened in Jesus' being rejected in Nazareth by the people he has known all his life (Matt 13:54-58; Mark 6:1-6; Luke 4:16-29) and is not an unknown phenomenon experienced by those who side with the poor. Jesus builds and is committed to building the Church of the Poor at a personal cost; it will have affected family bonds and even family responsibilities. Undeniably, there is a moment of rejection in those passages (Matt 12:46-50; Mark 3:31-35; Luke 8:19-21). Jesus underpins the imperative of priority in passages such as Luke 14:26: "If anyone comes to me without hating his father and mother, wife and children, brothers and sisters, and even his own life, he cannot be my disciple" or Mark 10:29-30: "There is no one who has given up house or brothers or sisters or mother or father or children or lands for my sake and for the sake of the gospel who will not receive a hundred times more now in this present age." A bitter pill to swallow? The message is hard to accept; giving up children can be seen as the giving up of primary responsibility for dependents. Mary Gordon is quite harsh in her comment on Jesus' way of dealing with his family: "Jesus sounds like a teenage brat when people try to tell him to acknowledge those he was born of."[20] The text asks us to "wait for meaning." There is here the textual challenge to reconcile discipleship with well-founded moral obligations. It cannot be denied that accompanying a parent or child into death and burial of the dead are sacred duties in many cultures, including the culture Jesus was born into. Yet, Matthew 8:19-22 and Luke 9:57-60 seem to undermine this duty; "let the dead bury their dead" (Matt 8:22) is a harsh statement. What would it say to Philip Roth, who took care of his dying father and was prepared to make sacrifices for this commitment?[21] The good news constitutes an entry point for new types of exclusion (Matt 12:30: "Whoever is not with me is against me"; "whoever rejects you rejects me" [Luke 10:16; 12:49-53]); people take offense at him in Nazareth (Matt 13:57). Does Jesus build a Church of the Poor based on an expectation of self-exclusion?

There are also issues connected with the moral costs of the mission of Jesus, the massacre of the infants in Matthew 2:16, a high price for the good news that gives a central role to children,[22] or the death of John the Baptist, who prepared the way for the Lord (Matt 14:10). Moral costs can also be attached to the cynicism that people could sense if the words "Do not worry about your life and what you will eat, or about your body and what you will wear" (Luke 12:22) were addressed to the poor themselves. Too many people suffer from a lack of food and basic security and run a daily risk of being physically abused, attacked, or threatened in some way or another. What do these words say to those who are unable to feed their children? The word "X is in God's hands" can also sound cynical. Suffering in grief on the death of his beloved wife, C. S. Lewis was offered these words as consolation: "'Because she is in God's hands.' But if so, she was in God's hands all the time, and I have seen what they did to her

---

20. Gordon, *Reading Jesus*, 123, even though Jesus enforces the fourth commandment in a debate with the Pharisees (Matt 15:4).

21. Philip Roth, *Patrimony: A True Story* (New York: Simon & Schuster, 1991).

22. Rodney Stark, *The Rise of Christianity* (Princeton, NJ: Princeton University Press, 1996).

here."[23] This then is the challenge: allowing faith to change physical and material conditions; for example, in the story of the healing of a boy with a demon in Matthew 17:14-21, the disciples are surprised at their own failure to heal the boy; Jesus' rejoinder is that they lacked the necessary faith. Why then can poverty not be driven out in a similar manner?

John the Baptist's disciples are given "a list" of the fruits of Jesus' ministry: different kinds of healings, that is, changes on the material, physical level of the sufferer, but the poor are not "materially healed"; "the poor have the good news proclaimed to them" (Matt 11:5-6; Luke 7:22); the poor experience no tangible change on a material and physical level. Nor does Jesus mention the poor in describing his ministry to some Pharisees ("I cast out demons and I perform healings" [Luke 13:32]). We might be tempted to assume that healing someone from blindness or paralysis would open new possibilities for social as well as material inclusion, but this "option" is not specifically stated in the Gospels. The Gospels seem to assert the status quo of the law, a situation that has not led to liberation of the poor (Matt 5:17-18; Luke 16:17).[24] The instruction to turn the other cheek if one is struck, and to freely give one's cloak if pressed for the tunic (Matt 5:39-41) may be morally clear in the framework and context of the wealthy, but could be potentially cynical and even offensive if expected of the poor (the *skandalon* lies in the fact that the poor, who are already exploited by others, seem to be invited to add to the burden of exploitation voluntarily).[25] Some of us may also feel uneasy, even embarrassed, at the way poor people are described in the Gospels, for example, in the parable of the persistent widow in Luke 18:1-8. There may also be a sense of insinuation that the gospel appeals to an entrepreneurial mindset in the parable of the talents and in the invitation to make

23. Clive S. Lewis, *A Grief Observed* (London: Faber & Faber, 1966), 24.

24. Elsewhere the law is challenged—see Matt 15:2 and Luke 16:16 where we read: "The law and the prophets lasted until John, but from then on the kingdom of God is proclaimed."

25. On the other hand, it may be precisely an expression of respect for the poor to communicate moral expectations. The "fellowship of the least coin" worked with the idea of inviting all people to give.

friends with children of the world (Luke 16:8-9). It may also be disconcerting that the gospel extends capitalism to an eschatological dimension in the reward structure it propounds (Matt 10:40-42 for capital in heaven). John of the Cross has discussed the phenomenon of spiritual avarice in the third chapter of the first book of his *Dark Night of the Soul*. The vices of materialism can also be extended to a certain kind of "spiritual materialism."

Jesus does build a Church of the Poor, but the effort in doing is as a thorn in the flesh; it is costly and leaves room for controversy. Perhaps the "option for the poor" is more of an "option for sinners"? Jesus calls outcasts into his discipleship (Mark 2:15-17; Luke 5:30-32): "Many tax collectors and sinners sat with Jesus and his disciples; for there were many who followed him. Some scribes who were Pharisees saw that he was eating with sinners and tax collectors and said to his disciples, 'Why does he eat with tax collectors and sinners?' Jesus heard this and said to them, 'Those who are well do not need a physician, but the sick do. I did not come to call the righteous but sinners.'" In Luke 7:36-50 Jesus has been invited to the house of a Pharisee (a member of a group that Jesus criticized extensively for their sinfulness), and "a sinful woman," on hearing where he is, appears (we may assume uninvited) to anoint Jesus' feet. Here we find amazing dynamics: Jesus pursues a preferential option for the lost sheep and accepts the invitation to dine with a Pharisee (whom Jesus explicitly considers to be sinful by spiritual standards); Jesus responds to this Pharisee's reaching out to him by willingly entering under his roof. In this context a "notable sinner" approaches Jesus, sinful by the social (moral) standards of the time. The woman ("who was a sinner") shows her profound love for Jesus and a singular discernment of his social and spiritual status in the way she anoints his feet. Here again, Jesus responds immediately, both to the host who wonders at the actions of the woman and to the woman herself who is offering her heart. Interestingly, a shift takes place in focus and perspective: the sinful woman becomes the host in the house of the sinful Pharisee even though she herself is a "gate-crasher," so to speak; she performs the rites and rituals expected of a good host, such as providing water for the guest to wash his feet and a welcome kiss, acts the host himself failed to perform, thus increasing the impression of his sinfulness. The sinner teaches the sinner, and Jesus teaches about this teaching.

2.2 The Danger of Impurity

In Chapter 1 we explored Pope Francis's perception of the temptation to embrace epistemic purism and a church not willing to run the risk of getting bruised. Building a Church of the Poor that calls to sinners involves considerable risks. Notwithstanding the above-mentioned challenges, Jesus was engaged in building a community of followers significantly shaped by the concerns of a Church of the Poor. The beginning of his life was shaped by experiences of exclusion. In the version of Jesus' genealogy according to Matthew we find mention of the name of Judah as well as of Tamar (Matt 1:3); this is a story of exclusion as told in Genesis 38: Judah had forced his daughter-in-law to remain a widow in her father's house (Gen 38:11), and then—without knowing who she was—slept with her when she was disguised as a prostitute (Gen 38:14-18). This is a morally difficult story to accept as the genealogy of the savior. Joseph's intention to quietly terminate his engagement to Mary, his pregnant wife-to-be, is also morally fragile (Matt 1:19); the circumstances of Jesus' birth (born in a town away from home, in a place outside the inn) are burdensome; the flight to Egypt followed by an extended exile experience (Matt 2:14) could have easily been traumatizing. We see brokenness in the framework and foundation of Jesus' life. Jesus and his family were controlled (and, at least in some instances, humiliated) by authorities from the beginning (his birth circumstances shaped by the occupational power's imposition of taxes) to the end (suppression by Jewish authorities, interrogation and torture by the representative of the emperor). We see authorities terrorize the country (the massacre of the infants [Matt 2:16]); we see corrupt representatives of authorities (Matt 28:11-15); Jesus' first visitors and the first witnesses were shepherds (Luke 2:16-17). We see not only humble, but also fraught and burdened beginnings. From a therapeutic perspective, the first two years of Jesus' life and also the nine months in his mother's womb with its dramatic unexpectedness for the mother and the fragile marital situation were trauma inducive. Jesus built his ministry on and out of brokenness, and we see no hint of the kind of "glory" the Magi initially sought when approaching the palace of the king. These wounds are the building blocks of a Church of the Poor.

Jesus pursued close relationships and companionship with outsiders; women who were not members of high social hierarchies journeyed with him (Luke 8:1-3); he extended friendship and closeness to social and moral outsiders, including table fellowship with Judas Iscariot, who finally excluded himself from the circle of trusted friends. Judas Iscariot was clearly part of the most inner circle (Matt 10:4). He was sitting, as the Gospel account goes, at Jesus' table with Jesus knowing about his betrayal (Matt 26:21). Jesus did wonderful things for the poor, such as healing and forgiving. In a moving scene in Luke 17 we see him raise a widow's only son from the dead, a son who would have been her only source of social and economic security. By embracing the poor, Jesus built a Church of the Poor.

Jesus also built a Church of the Poor by exhorting his disciples to engage in a different business model—"lend expecting nothing back" (Luke 6:35), which blurs the lines between "lending" and "giving" and can give rise to ideas about specifically Christian ways of doing business, as outlined by Martin Luther in his treatise *On Trading and Usury*. In any case, in building a Church of the Poor Jesus can be said to be taking substantial risks. He builds the Church of the Poor by allowing the life-situation of outcasts to shape his ministry. We see overt encounters of Jesus with the epistemic situation of outcasts (the man with an unclean spirit in Mark 1:23—the unclean spirit with special knowledge of Jesus: "I know who you are—the Holy One of God" [cf. Mark 5:7; Luke 4:34]); he drove out many demons, "not permitting them to speak because they knew him" (Mark 1:34; cf. Mark 1:11). Unclean spirits or demons "knew that he was the Messiah" (Luke 4:41). Jesus accepts the risk involved in such acts, namely, that he too is perceived as someone who must be possessed by an unclean spirit: "He is out of his mind" (Mark 3:21).

Jesus builds a Church of the Poor by resisting the temptation to side with power. The three temptations mentioned in Luke 4 and Matthew 4 are temptations to improper material transformation (stones into bread), an improper reduction of the vulnerability of the human condition (angels to prevent him falling to his death), and improper worship (idolatry in exchange for power). These temptations are relevant for a Church of the Poor because the first one undermines the scarcity aspect of materially grounded human life; the second one, the fragility aspect of the human condition with its fragile bodily integrity; and the third one underpins the surrender of power to the all-powerful God. Jesus resists the temptation to build a "fed," "secure," and "powerful" community. The consequences of resisting the temptation to make the struggle for our daily bread "disappear" are acknowledgment and acceptance of responsibility: "Give them some food yourselves" (Matt 14:16; Luke 9:13) is an imperative that characterizes the duties of a church working with people who have not only spiritual but also material needs. We find the same commitment to the material reality of the human condition in Jesus' command to give Jairus's daughter something to eat after her reawakening (Luke 9:55). A Church of the Poor cannot afford to be oblivious to the body and its needs. The body is the temple of the Holy Spirit (1 Cor 6:19).[26] Lack of thirst (see Matt 5:6), lack of vulnerability, and lack of dependence are obstacles to building a Church of the Poor. Contentment, security, and power are dangerous and are indicators of entry points for the erosion of concern for a Church of the Poor. Jesus resists the temptation to "betray vulnerability" in the garden of Gethsemane: "Do you think that I cannot call upon my Father and he will not provide me at this moment with more than twelve legions of angels?" (Matt 26:53). Jesus renounces power; he is concerned, the gospels tell us, with different power structures within his community (Matt 20:26: "It shall not be so among you").

Jesus thus builds his community in a mode of contrast to existing social settings. He challenges existing hierarchies (e.g. Matt 11:11; 18:1-5; 19:14; 19:30; 20:16), outlines the transformation of criteria for status and the risks that the privileged run (expressed in the Canticle of Mary [Luke 1:52-53]). Jesus cares about "the little ones" (see Matt 11:25; 18:6; Luke 10:21) and praises the mustard seed, perhaps the underestimated and smallest of all seeds (Matt 13:31-32). Jesus also makes judgments—judgments about sinful cities (Matt 11:20-

---

26. See Tamez, *Poverty, the Poor, and the Option for the Poor*, 49.

24; Luke 10:13), judgments about human behavior (the cleansing of the temple [Matt 21:12]) and social groups (Matt 23 and Luke 11:37-54: words against the intellectual elites at the time), statements about final judgments (Matt 25:31-46).

An important element of the way Jesus builds a Church of the Poor is in his respecting outsiders' input. This is a change of epistemic practices and a change in the culture of encounter. He expects an answer to the question "What do you want me to do for you?" (e.g. Matt 20:32); throughout the Gospels there are dialogues between Jesus and the persons in need of healing. He does listen to outsiders; on a number of occasions he puts them in the middle of a situation, be it a person to be healed or a child. Outsiders have a voice, and their judgment is valued. There are a few instances where we see that Jesus taps epistemic resources from outsiders and the poor. The fact that he honors the poor widow with an exercise in situational theology by making use of the incident for instructive purposes shows the epistemic relevance of this poor widow (Luke 21:1-4); similarly, we see him use the poor in parables, most prominently, the parable of the Good Samaritan in Luke 10 and the parable of Lazarus and the rich man in Luke 16.

There are even situations where Jesus learns from the poor. If we were to accept soldiers (an occupying army) as socially excluded, we would see a learning curve in Jesus' encounter with the centurion (Matt 8:5-13: the text mentions that the centurion needed a recommendation, suggesting that he was clearly not part of the primary target group of Jesus' ministry), and in the powerful passage in Mark 7:24-30 in which Jesus encounters the Syrophoenician woman.[27] Jesus works, so the story goes, with a clear and coherent position that is expressed in mutually exclusive categories ("children," "dogs") and

---

27. See the thorough analysis by David Rhoads, "Jesus and the Syrophoenician Woman in Mark: A Narrative-Critical Study," *Journal of the American Academy of Religion* 62, no. 2 (1994): 343-75. Jane Hicks places "moral agency" in the center of her analysis: Jane E. Hicks, "Moral Agency at the Borders: Rereading the Story of the Syrophoenician Woman," *Word and World* 23, no. 1 (2003): 76-84.

in clear statements ("Let the children be fed first"; "it is not right to take the food of the children and throw it to the dogs"). This nameless woman resists this position with a twofold experience—her experience of marginalization as a pagan and her experience as a worried mother of a possessed child, of a daughter with an unclean spirit. She knows all too well what marginalization is and feels like; she is a "gentile" of "Syrophoenician origin" (Mark 7:26), and she knows what it is to be a mother—a mother of a child who is possessed by "an unclean spirit" (Mark 7:25). These two experiences empower this woman, mother, outsider to approach Jesus and "bow down at his feet"; these two experiences also enable her to counter Jesus' curt answer with an immediate and convincing line of argument (Mark 7:27). This woman knows exactly what Jesus is referring to and understands the basis of his argument; she is acquainted with these stereotypical pictures, having had to live with them all her life. Her life experience gives her the strength to approach Jesus, fall at his feet, and address him pleadingly; this experience also gives her the skill to forge a counterargument and the authority to deliver it. She must have appropriated the discriminatory category in a way that she has internalized it and made it her own: "Even the dogs under the table eat the children's scraps" (Mark 7:28). She is not questioning the authority of Jesus, calling him "Lord"; she is not calling into question the categories and distinctions he uses. She is not entering a sophisticated conceptual discussion, nuanced theological debate, or socio-political discourse. She is interested in the "cash value" of a position, which she measures in the currency of experiential value. She does not question Jesus' position, but she reminds him of the practical realities of this position which work to her favor. This woman speaks about what she knows and represents that point of view—that difference between theory and practice as epistemic resource. She offers, we could say, "raw experience." It is a type of experience that has not been "intellectually cooked" with subtle terminology that allows for a distancing from everyday life.

Jesus' rejection of an outcast is even more strongly depicted in Matthew's version of the episode, where a Canaanite woman approaches Jesus with the words: "Have pity on me, Lord, Son of David! My daughter is tormented by a demon" (Matt 15:22). Jesus rejects the woman in the most severe way a person can be humiliated—by silence: "He did not say a word in answer to her" (Matt 15:23). This is an expression of "blindness to the human aspect," which can be seen as an erosion of the recognition of dignity.[28] Ignoring a person in a way that the person knows that she is being deliberately ignored is an expression of agency; the ignored person knows that the ignoring agent could act differently if he or she wanted; in other words, the subject on the receiving end of "ignorance" knows that the subject realizes she is being ignored. The woman is a nuisance in the eyes and sensibilities of Jesus' disciples, who want him to "get rid of her." Her insistence is impressive; she cannot afford not to insist; she cannot afford to give up or to consider etiquette and rules of politeness. Jesus makes his point twice, once indirectly in talking to the disciples ("I was sent only to the lost sheep of the house of Israel") and once directly to the nameless woman herself ("It is not right to take the food of the children and throw it to the dogs" [Matt 15:24, 26]). The first statement carries the credibility of a first-person statement; the second, the authority of an objective claim. The first seems to be less rude since it contextualizes Jesus' mission into a context beyond Jesus' mandate, for Jesus was sent by the Father.[29] The woman is not the least bit impressed by the limits of the mission, believing in Jesus exercising power that transcends this limited mandate. She performs yet again an act of homage (paired with the kind of impertinence that insistence implies). She kneels before him and makes a second plea ("Lord, help me!") before countering Jesus' second statement. Her counterclaim against his position is even more self-effacing than the version in the Gospel of Mark: "Even the dogs eat the scraps that fall from the table of their masters" (Matt 15:27). Jesus replies a second time—compelled to change both his act of ignoring and his seeming ignorance: "O woman, great is your faith! Let it be done to you as you wish!"—and the daughter is healed by the

---

28. Avishai Margalit, *The Decent Society* (Cambridge, MA: Harvard University Press, 1996), 96-103.

29. The statement could be seen as more rude if compared to John 10:26, where Jesus seems to give "faith" as the criterion for belonging to his flock, being among his sheep.

active agency of a mother who breaks through rigid social boundaries for the daughter she loves.

What we are confronted with here is a nameless, unknown woman revealing and offering up epistemic "knowledge" specific to her own plight, and in doing so she is contesting the validity of healing, saving resources; in other words, she is contesting the tight restrictions to access. The particular plight of this particular woman is an epistemic resource that is relevant for a poor church; it is a plight that questions the sense and meaning of propositions in the bitter realities of everyday experience. Our understanding of *orthodoxy* is modified in the light of the above, and focus invariably shifts toward living faith and faith lived in considering those epistemic resources that only the poor have entry to. This shift in understanding could at the same time also mean that our understanding of epistemic vulnerability, particularly as manifest by the church, also takes on a new meaning when we realize that existing coherent categories of propositions are vulnerable to change and will be deeply impacted by the "new" epistemic resources the poor bring with them when they risk trust in the church.

Jesus' building a Church of the Poor is a high-risk venture. A risk is a step into the unknown that cannot be fully controlled. One of the risks he takes is the transformation of epistemic practices.

2.3 Jesus Transforms Epistemic Practices

Jesus' mission was one of transformation, but transformation that astonishes and surprises. Jesus brought good news to the poor (cf Luke 4:18), news that transformed their lives. The Gospels describe how Jesus astounds and amazes people—as an expression of the Father's love for the Son ("For the Father loves his Son and shows him everything that he himself does, and he will show him greater works than these, so that you may be amazed" [John 5:20]). People were astonished at his teaching (Matt 22:33; Luke 4:32; Mark 1:22), asking, "What kind of wisdom has been given him?" (Mark 5:6:2); they were amazed on witnessing a healing and ask one another, "What is this?" (Mark 1:27); they were "filled with great awe" when he calmed the storm (Mark 4:41) and "astounded" them when he walked on the water (Mark 6:51); the crowds were astounded (Matt 12:33; Luke 2:47) and amazed at his words (Matt 15:31; Luke 4:22) and at his healing (Luke 4:36) and amazed at works performed (Luke 9:43; John 7:21). But they were also irritated, perhaps even "shocked" (John 6:61), "enraged" (Luke 6:11) and fearful (Luke 7:16); they also "ridiculed him" when he challenged the pronouncement that the synagogue official's daughter was dead (Mark 5:40). Jesus was more than aware of the fact that he symbolized dissent for many, provoking dissension and disagreement among all; he said according to Luke, "Blessed is the one who takes no offense at me" (Luke 7:23).

Jesus provokes astonishment, and in doing so opens up people's imagination. People are astonished when they see the impossible happening before their very eyes; people are astonished when they are confronted with something beyond their wildest dreams and imagination; people are astonished when suddenly they no longer understand and cannot find an obvious answer. Being astonished is being open, being able to see; it is a mark of wisdom to be truly astonished and at the same time suggests being dumbfounded to the extent that one can only gasp, as though robbed of one's cognitive faculties. Being astonished, amazed, or able to marvel is the first step toward philosophizing.[30] Being amazed is a liminal or threshold state.[31] There is an openness, a need for "continuation" or "closure," since an epistemic divide has opened up. Jesus challenges the limits of established imagination and sense of possibilities. The "sense of possibilities" is to sense what could be rather than what is. The term was coined (as "Möglichkeitssinn") by Austrian writer Robert Musil, who described the task of the poet as working with a sense of possibility. Jesus does just that: he pushes the boundaries of the imagination. William Abraham observes that Jesus, at least in the Gospel of Mark, has an epistemic

---

30. Plato, *Theaetetus* 155d; Aristotle, *Metaphysics* I 2, 982b12f.

31. Being amazed is comparable to that state of liminality as described by Victor Turner from a socio-anthropological perspective (Victor Turner, *The Forest of Symbols* [Ithaca, NY: Cornell University Press, 1967], 93-111). Being amazed is that state between what no longer is and what has yet to come: one's established system of orientation is insufficient and as yet no new system has been developed.

focus, "not on deducing conclusions from premises but on the proper renovation and use of our cognitive faculties."[32] Jesus transforms the epistemic situation of his audience by expanding epistemic horizons:

> First, Jesus expands our vision of human capacities to include the capacity to hear the Word of God and see the activity of God in creation, in our own lives, and in his life and ministry.... Second, Jesus expands our account of the sources of malfunction to include not just ordinary vice like the lust for power but also spiritual rebellion against God.... Third, Jesus expands our account of the background conditions affecting the use of our cognitive capacities to include demonic agency and action.... Fourth, Jesus teaches that the use of our cognitive capacities involves a divine–human synergism that highlights both divine assistance and human responsibility.[33]

Jesus transformed the epistemic situation of his followers and also of his opponents, thus inviting a singular way of learning.[34] Think of the simple way he called the first disciples. In the version of Mark he invites two fishermen: "Come after me, and I will make you fishers of men" (Mark 1:17). What effect did this invitation have on the two men? It provided them, we could say, with new social roles, new experiences, and new encounters they would have never had. The boundaries of their imagination were extended, horizons broadened, and they began to see the world in new ways. The Gospels give us the good news that the savior is transforming the face of the earth and the inner landscape of our soul. Jesus is transforming situations, materially (there is bread, there is healing), socially (there are new hierarchies, there are new roles for foreigners and outcasts!), and epistemically

32. William J. Abraham, "The Epistemology of Jesus: An Initial Investigation," in Paul K. Moser, ed., *Jesus and Philosophy* (Cambridge: Cambridge University Press, 2008), 149-68, at 158.

33. Ibid., 166.

34. Mark A. Noll, *Jesus Christ and the Life of the Mind* (Grand Rapids, MI: Eerdmans, 2011).

(there are new epistemic practices, there are new epistemic situations!). Jesus is depicted again and again as challenging established categories. He challenges the category "asleep" versus "dead" in Mark 5; in John 9:1-12 Jesus challenges the imagination of all those who can only see blindness as a result of sinfulness rather than an invitation to reveal the glory of God. People have a hard time accommodating personal experience into their epistemic horizons (John 9:8). Jesus communicates the need to reorder epistemic habits in the light of the gospel.[35]

Jesus communicates the good news in a way that is subject to debate in the Gospels. The disciples ask him about the parables (Mark 4:10), and he explains that the epistemic practice of telling parables is a way to communicate to outsiders the mystery of the kingdom of God. There is an inner link between medium and message; the parable is not only a teaching tool but also a way of seeing reality in a parabolic way. Thus, Jesus challenges established ways of finding orientation. One way is his invitation to "turn to the inner." This turn is most powerfully expressed in the Sermon on the Mount, when Jesus says, "You have heard that it was said, 'You shall not commit adultery.' But I say to you, everyone who looks at a woman with lust has already committed adultery with her in his heart" (Matt 5:27-28). Jesus does not "replace" external, "objectifiable" criteria that can be administered in the social sphere (see Matt 5:17: "Do not think that I have come to abolish the law or the prophets. I have not come to abolish but to fulfill"), but adds a layer of depth to them, thus opening a door to an inner space that reminds the person of her interiority as well as of her relationship with God in the sanctuary of her soul. A turn to the inner is also expressed in Matthew 19:8: "Because of the hardness of your hearts Moses allowed you to divorce your wives"; in Luke 16:15 ("You justify yourselves in the sight of others, but God knows your hearts; for what is of human esteem is an abomination in the sight of God"); in John 2:19 ("Destroy this temple and in three days I will build it up"); and in the reminder that evil comes from within (Mark 7:21-23: "From within people, from their hearts, come evil thoughts,

---

35. Bruce D. Marshall, *Trinity and Truth* (Cambridge: Cambridge University Press, 2000), 124.

unchastity, theft, murder, adultery, greed, malice, deceit, licentious-
ness, envy, blasphemy, arrogance, folly. All these evils come from
within and they defile"). This turn to the inner is significant for an
understanding of poverty (even material poverty) since it allows us to
see poverty more in terms of an inner situation that includes issues of
identity rather than primarily looking at the external material aspects
of poverty.

The Transfiguration Account

Jesus not only transforms epistemic practices, he "transfigures" them
by "showing" rather than "teaching." This is powerfully told in the
account of the transfiguration.

Jesus changed epistemic situations and human lives by "being"
and not only "doing." In Matthew's account of the transfiguration
story (Matt 17:1-9) Jesus carefully selects three disciples and calls
them to witness and even share an experience of transfiguration. He
leads them to a high mountain. Furthermore, Matthew notes that
this happens "after six days," which may indicate a moment of new
creation and new divine action here. Maximus the Confessor, in his
interpretation of this passage, emphasizes the idea of a new creation
and points out that the three disciples symbolize the key virtues of
faith (Peter), love (John), and hope (James).[36] On top of the mountain Jesus is transfigured before the three disciples, "his face shone
like the sun, and his clothes became (as white as the light) dazzling
white" (Matt 17:2b). The disciples are witnesses of a scene that can be
described only in metaphorical and comparative language ("like the
sun," "as white as light"). They are exposed to a powerful and extraordinary event that by its very nature tells them something. They are
taught a lesson without words. Jesus does not talk to them; he is
transfigured. Jesus does not provide them with knowledge based
on propositions; the three disciples are exposed to something that
is "shown" to them. In other words, the scene described in Matthew

---

36. Maximus Confessor, *Answers and Doubts*, questions 191-92; see also
Andrew Louth, *Maximus Confessor* (London: Routledge, 1996), 67-69, 92ff.,
105f.

56 • *A Church of the Poor*

17:2 is not about "saying" but about "showing."[37] Ephrem the Syrian, in his "Sermon on the Transfiguration of Our Lord and God and Savior, Jesus Christ," points out that Jesus wanted to show his disciples his glory; he wanted to show them his true identity. Ephrem interprets the transfiguration story as a story about identity and the challenge of accepting the transformation of identities. By entering "into" an experience the disciples obtain access to a kind of non-propositional knowledge based on "showing" and "being shown."

The transfiguration changes the epistemic situation of the disciples, especially the situation of Peter. During the transfiguration Peter expresses a sense of well-being and his desire to stay by saying, "Lord, it is good for us to be here. If you wish, I will put up three shelters/dwellings/tents—one for you, one for Moses, and one for Elijah" (Matt 17:4). Peter is still speaking when he is interrupted by a loud voice and a bright cloud, which seems to descend and cover them; thus the disciples initially experience only darkness since the cloud has engulfed them. Here we have an experience of an abrogated knowledge claim. Peter's desire to stay is frustrated; his speech is not only interrupted but even disrupted; he is moved into darkness by a bright cloud. The claim of knowing the dynamics of the situation, "we are here and we could stay here together with Jesus and the two prophets," is overwrit-

---

37. The distinction between "saying" and "showing" is, of course, famously associated with Ludwig Wittgenstein's *Tractatus Logico-Philosophicus*. In the famous passage 6.54 Wittgenstein writes, "My propositions are elucidatory in this way: he who understands me finally recognizes them as senseless, when he has climbed out through them, on them, over them. (He must so to speak throw away the ladder, after he has climbed up on it.) He must surmount these propositions; then he sees the world rightly." This is the penultimate proposition in Wittgenstein's text and gave rise to a particular ("therapeutic") reading of the *Tractatus*. According to a therapeutic reading Wittgenstein does not intend to present a "view" or "theory," but rather a way of speaking and looking. Cf. James Conant and Cora Diamond, "On Reading the Tractatus Resolutely," in M. Kölbel and B. Weiss, eds., *The Lasting Significance of Wittgenstein's Philosophy* (London: Routledge, 2004), 46-99; James Conant, "The Method of the Tractatus," in E. Reck, ed., *From Frege to Wittgenstein: Perspectives in Early Analytic Philosophy* (Oxford: Oxford University Press, 2002), 374-462; Cora Diamond, "Throwing Away the Ladder," *Philosophy* 63, no. 243 (1988): 5-27.

ten. Peter's epistemic situation is changed; his claim to understanding what is happening in the situation is abrogated. He obtains new knowledge that revalidates the map of knowledge claims and renders certain claims invalid. John Chrysostom, in his commentary on Matthew's Gospel, highlights Peter's frustration: He has understood so little. Peter has not understood—he wants Jesus to be safe and secure and invites Jesus to stay so as not to suffer in Jerusalem. He is clearly moved by his love for the Lord, but fails to understand some key points. He suggests building three dwellings, as if Jesus was on the same level with Moses and Elijah. Peter suffers the fate of "abrogated knowledge," knowledge painfully replacing other knowledge, establishing itself as an alternative to a well-received and well-accepted, even much-loved knowledge claim. Abrogated knowledge is at the same time "about something" and "about the frustrated knowledge of something." This kind of knowledge is not only "knowledge that p" but also "knowledge that the knowledge claim that q is wrong." This is not the first time that this has happened to Peter. It happened to him in the memorable rebuke in Matthew 16:18 just before the transfiguration account.[38]

The abrogation of knowledge can be the expression of a living relationship with God; it may change doctrinal perspectives: "in some cases, an existential faith discovers and develops goods that are outside what orthodoxy has proposed, but then these goods change official orthodoxy. The primary example of this change in orthodoxy, of course, occurred with Jesus. First, the disciples fell in love with Jesus. But the then-current understanding of the messiah, so well represented in Peter's rejection of Jesus' prediction of his own death, could not admit a messiah who dies on a cross."[39] Abrogated knowledge is obtained through letting go. Abrogated knowledge tells us some-

38. Abraham comments on the background to the rebuke of Peter in Matthew 16:18: "Peter is not functioning properly as an epistemic agent. His sight is not entirely reliable; it is altered for the worse by inappropriate background beliefs, interests, desires, anxieties, and expectations" (Abraham, *The Epistemology of Jesus*, 151).

39. Edward Collins Vacek, "Orthodoxy Requires Orthopathy: Emotions in Theology," *Horizons* 40, no. 2 (2013): 218-41, at 235.

thing about the "authority of what is found," the authority of what has been encountered, the authority of an experience that tells a much more complicated story than systematic doctrinal accounts would be able to give. Orthodoxy in the face of the experience of the abrogation of knowledge is not so much "holding onto the right beliefs" but "keeping faith when one's beliefs are shattered." A Church of the Poor will accept the possibility for abrogation in the light of divine creativity; a Church of the Poor will respect faith experiences of poor people as epistemically shattering transfigurations.

The Nocturnal Encounter with Nicodemus

An exemplary scene that reveals Jesus' transforming epistemic practices is the nocturnal encounter between Jesus and Nicodemus (John 3:1-10). Let us look at this passage from an epistemological perspective: From the outset of John, chapter 3, there can be no mistaking Nicodemus's epistemic and social status.[40] At this point in the proceedings, Nicodemus's epistemic authority is high. He expresses his claim of knowing (*oidamen*) not in the first person singular but the first person plural, thus unmistakeably making a claim for self as representative of a group, in other words, a title to knowledge that is primarily based on knowledge perceived and experienced. At the same time, Nicodemus addresses Jesus commensurate with a socially recognizable "group" that Nicodemus is acquainted with and accepts as authority: "*rabbi*" (Rabbi) is a form of address reserved only for those who are highly esteemed, teachers with epistemic authority.

---

40. "What stands out in this passage is that Nicodemus is depicted as *the* teacher (ὁ διδάσκαλος) of Israel (τοῦ Ισραελ)—not just a teacher, but *the* teacher—in contemporary language, *the* teacher *par excellence*, like an academic professor in Jewish historical studies and literature. It is also depicted in John chapter three that this Nicodemus was representing the Pharisees. . . . Nicodemus was a member of the Sanhedrin. This body consisted of seventy top Jewish members that were regarded as the highest religio-political authority of the Jews. . . . Within this body, Nicodemus was regarded as one of the best, the best of the best, in other words, simply outstanding" (J. M. Johan Ras, "Jesus, Moral Recognition and Crime in the Gospel of John," *Inkanyiso. Journal for Humanities and Social Sciences* 2, no. 2 [2010]: 115-21, at 116).

The interactive dialogue logically concludes: (1) Jesus does signs. (2) "No one can do these signs that you do," which endorses the theory that God is with him. (3) If God is with X, then X has come from God. (4) Hence, "Jesus has come from God." Substantial theological propositions are being relayed here based on the supposition that there is a relation between communion with God and origins in God. Nicodemus is wielding highly charged theoretical categories, showing himself to be a teacher, someone equipped with sound theological knowledge that he is able to apply in epistemic challenges.

Jesus however seems to be questioning and rattling the cage of Nicodemus's sound beliefs and knowledge, knowledge he has acquired and molded to fit his own way of life: Jesus now poses questions that disrupt the epistemic card house of habits Nicodemus has constructed for himself, including knowledge, attitudes, and perception that have all become so matter of fact that he is no longer aware of where knowledge acquired begins and convictions end. Jesus challenges those habits with an authoritative warning: "Amen, amen, I say to you." This utterance not only disrupts Nicodemus's way of thinking and listening but also any planned, preconceived line of dialogue he may have been expecting since his counterpart in this exchange has his own perception of communication and does not as custom might demand follow on naturally in the line of argument begun. Jesus introduces a new and unexpected notion that shocks Nicodemus out of any complacent cognitive meanderings he may have envisaged: "no one can see the kingdom of God without being born from above" (John 3:3). Jesus is expressing a proposition with a claim to truth and in doing so applies an epistemic category that does not fit into Nicodemus's set of categories. He is unable to grasp the concept of being born "from above." This is new to his vocabulary of knowledge, and as such he does not know how to react, how to reply; it goes beyond the categories of his own thinking, his overriding sense of incredulity. And that he does not have the right words to cope becomes evident in his answer, which he can only formulate as: "How can a person once grown old be born again? Surely he cannot reenter his mother's womb and be born again, can he?" Nicodemus's question encompasses his sense of inadequacy. Confronted with a new concept beyond his comprehension, beyond the limits of his own knowledge, he is clearly at a disadvantage and realizes it. Lost for words (literally), he tacks on a question in a vain attempt to cover up his own lack of knowledge. The question is an attempt to regain ground lost in the discussion by referring to universal truths based on universal human experience. However, this move does more than that; it rejects the epistemic resource—knowledge—being offered to him. This is a category too far, one too many for Nicodemus who is trapped in his rigid box of categorizations.

Jesus challenges what can only be termed as Nicodemus's blinkered vision and narrow perspective. What should not be forgotten in this context is also that Nicodemus should be able to understand the core concept of the dialogue if for no other reason than Jesus is expounding upon a well-known and familiar theology from the Hebrew Scriptures. Carson goes so far as to suggest that Nicodemus ought to be able to comprehend Jesus' allusions since they are anchored in the teachings Nicodemus himself bases his own beliefs on: "nothing could make clearer the fact that Jesus' teaching on the new birth was built on the teaching of the Old Testament."[41] Jesus even makes a second attempt to break through Nicodemus's fortress of categories by introducing a new motif, "being born of water and Spirit" (John 3:5). Nicodemus is thus given categories with which he can identify and should be able to work with, namely, "water" and "Spirit" (*hydatos* and *pneumatos*), particularly if we also consider that these are standard Old Testament images with which Nicodemus would be more than well acquainted.[42] The assistance offered in these images is theologically weighted. They are "signposts," "markings" that should signal to Nicodemus the line of interpreta-

---

41. D. A. Carson, *The Gospel According to John* (Grand Rapids, MI: Eerdmans, 1991), 198.

42. R. V. McCabe, "The Meaning of 'Born of Water and the Spirit' in John 3:5," *Detroit Baptist Seminary Journal* 4 (1999): 85-107. Admittedly, the category itself is complex and poses an exegetic challenge in that this extract has always been seen to suggest a theology of baptism; William Grese's understanding of baptism in this context was more the granting of a capacity—aptitude—to see the revelation of God. (William C. Grese, "'Unless One Is Born Again': The Use of a Heavenly Journey in John 3," *Journal of Biblical Literature* 107, no. 4 [1988]: 677-93).

tion he should take and where to place this *new* knowledge within this *new* category of being born "again." From the dynamics of the discussion, it becomes immediately apparent that Jesus is preparing the ground for Nicodemus to take this new category of "born of the Spirit" on board and incorporate it into his own system of categorization. In the course of the interaction Nicodemus is increasingly lost for words; his contributions to the dialogue become fewer and lose both immediacy and significance, perhaps a sign that the influence of established doctrine is on the wane: "A certain tension is developing. It is noticeable that the contributions made by Nicodemus decrease in length, from twenty-four words (v. 2), to eighteen words (v. 4), to only four words (v. 9), and to a zero response to Jesus' question of v. 10."[43] Nicodemus is losing epistemic authority, but could perhaps be growing spiritually.[44]

---

43. P. Cotterell, "The Nicodemus Conversation: A Fresh Appraisal," *The Expository Times* 96, no. 8 (1985): 237-42, here 240. Authority is questioned in this nightly encounter ("νύκτος"); Craig Bloomberg comments: "Whatever possible historical reasons—fear, secrecy, convenience—which may have prompted this timing, John surely sees it as symbolic of Nicodemus' spiritual darkness" (Craig L. Bloomberg, "The Globalization of Biblical Interpretation: A Test Case John 3-4," *Bulletin for Biblical Research* 5 [1995]: 1-15, here 6). The nighttime hour seems to bear a certain significance, as stated again in John 19:39, when Nicodemus is mentioned a third time in the Gospel and the hour specified. Saint Augustine highlights the difference between the light of Christ and the darkness of the unredeemed in his essay on John's Gospel (*Tractatus in Iohannis Euangelium*, 11).

44. Nicodemus, mentioned a second time in John 7:50-52 and a third time in John 19:39, is portrayed as a human being making spiritual progress due to his close proximity and relationship to Christ, yet, at the same time he remains an ambivalent character: "If anything, the ambiguity grows stronger, and this ambiguity arises at least in part because Nicodemus is persistently defined from two perspectives: his point of origin (the 'Jews,' Pharisees, night) and his present location (coming to Jesus, confessing him as 'Teacher sent from God': defending him, and attending to his burial rites). Thus, when Nicodemus buries Jesus, he does so as a 'Jew'; when he defends him, he does so as a Pharisee; when he confesses him, he does so at night. The result is that Nicodemus falls between the two major anthropological categories in this Gospel: he is defined as neither fully a 'Jew' nor fully a disciple, but as somehow bearing traits of both" (J. M.

Jesus transforms and transfigures epistemic practices, establishes categories and ways of using categories in order to invite people to grow.

2.4 Jesus and Healing Faith

Jesus neither wrote nor published a theological text. His teaching was based on encounters. He built relationships and in so doing taught us a lot about orthodoxy as proper relationship with the Lord. Jesus places person over proposition, second-person perspective (relationship) over third-person perspective (position). By so doing, Jesus seems to be rejecting self-righteousness and "cold" orthodoxy. Jesus warns of underestimating the fragility of one's spiritual and moral condition, for example, in his description of the casting out of unclean spirits which may return and bring companions (Matt 12:43-45; Luke 11:24-26). *Metanoia* is an ongoing process; seen in this light, orthodoxy is more of a pilgrimage and less of a state. The question as to the right relationship with Jesus shapes the transformability of situations: in Nazareth, Jesus "was amazed at their lack of faith" (Mark 6:6) and because of that he "was not able to perform any mighty deed." This lack of faith is based on wrong beliefs about Jesus ("only the son of a carpenter"). Faith is powerful and has healing properties, encapsulated in the formula "your faith has healed you." There are some passages that point to faith as the foundation of a "good human life in the here and now." Proper faith is compatible with healing on the Sabbath and the eating of holy bread (Matt 12:1-8). Poverty imposes a heightened sense of vulnerability and instills a deep sense of a need for healing that will challenge normative boundaries. Innovation, also moral innovation, is more plausibly based on the experience of pain than on the experience of saturation.

By challenging normative boundaries, a poor person in need of healing makes a contribution to an understanding of orthodoxy. This becomes most apparent when we look at Jesus' encounter with the woman with a hemorrhage: Mark 5:24-34 describes a woman with

---

Bassler, "Mixed Signals: Nicodemus in the Fourth Gospel," *Journal of Biblical Literature* 108, no. 4 [1989]: 635-46, here 641).

an "issue of blood"—a continuous hemorrhage. We are not told her name; she remains nameless, but we are told that she has been suffering for twelve years. Her epistemic situation has been shaped over twelve years by her belief, "I am suffering." This belief was certainly identity conferring and influenced her self-perception. She finds herself in a situation where she has become an expert on her health, a dimension of her life made visible through her illness and not kept hidden as in so many cases of people without health issues where health is taken for granted.

This woman had spent all she had, all her assets. She finds herself deprived of any sense of possibility. At this point she not only suffers from her hemorrhaging; she also suffers from the consequences of her condition: deprivation of assets, deprivation of vital aspects of the everyday life, probably even deprivation of social acceptance. "She had suffered greatly at the hands of many doctors" (Mark 5:26). She is suffering from her suffering, including her frustrated efforts and desires to find healing or at least alleviation. "She had heard about Jesus," we read in Mark 5:27; she may have formed an opinion on the basis of what she has heard, and these beliefs about Jesus give rise to new hope. She is in possession of "knowledge by description" of Jesus of Nazareth. With this knowledge and against the background of her illness-related epistemic situation for some reasons beknown or unbeknown to herself she believes that she needed only to touch his clothes in order to be healed. This conviction endows her with the power and strength to act, to strive toward her goal despite the physical resistance of the large crowd. This belief could be characterized as "magic," in terms of causally transferring power through touch. We are being told in Matthew 14:36 that this belief was widespread (people "begged him that they might touch only the tassel on his cloak, and as many as touched it were healed"). The woman comes up behind Jesus; she does not even attempt to seek a face-to-face encounter. She seems to be more interested in the gifts than the giver. She is not seeking Jesus but his healing powers. She may even be seen to instrumentalize Jesus and his clothes. Her epistemic state changes on account of a physical change taking place inside: "She felt in her body that she was healed of her affliction" (Mark 5:29). This feeling indicates subjective certainty. Similarly, Jesus shows himself to be Lord over his power; he too had felt something because he was "aware that power had gone out of him" (Mark 5:30). As though out of the blue he suddenly asks the question, "Who touched me?" thus addressing this seemingly invisible, nameless, and unknown woman. The situation is explosive; it harbors the potential to turn into something uncomfortable. A line has been crossed; the boundaries of Jesus have been transgressed. He has been "used" or utilized and in a sense ("power gone out of him") "exploited." It would be difficult to argue a case that the woman's relationship with Jesus was "orthodox" in the sense that it was based on and in proper faith. Without Jesus' active action and attitude she would not have come forward; she (and the cure) would have gone unnoticed. We find her coming up to Jesus, falling down before him (again not showing her face), and confessing the truth. Jesus' response is remarkable: "Your faith has saved you. Go in peace and be cured of your affliction" (Mark 5:34). What was this woman's faith? We are in no position to judge, but did she believe (as Peter confessed in Matt 16:16) that Jesus was the Messiah, the Son of the living God?

In any case, her faith is accepted, it seems, in a generous way. Jesus is generous in the kinds of relationships he accepts. Jesus allows people to approach him: "he remained outside in deserted places, and people kept coming to him from everywhere" (Mark 1:45). But why? This is, of course, open to speculation, but, given the previously mentioned experience of a leper who was cleansed, a key motivation may have been utter exasperation and action of "last resort." It seems that Jesus even allows "instrumentalization" as a step on the journey. This is generous. This is very generous. Is this an invitation to think about "generous orthodoxy"?

Chapter 3

Poverty and the Wound of Knowledge

The gospel invites us to share the joy of those who are saved. Pope Francis sees a Church of the Poor as the privileged place to nurture this joy. A Church of the Poor will also drink from the wells that only the poor can give. In this chapter I want to reflect on the "epistemic situation of poverty." What does it mean to gain understanding through poverty? What does it mean for the church to gain an understanding of poverty? What does this mean for the joy of the gospel, the gospel of joy, and the Church of the Poor?

The main and spiritually most relevant characteristic of poor people is their experience of vulnerability and dependence. Poverty in its many forms is an encounter with a reality that is more powerful than the person. Vulnerability can be characterized as the condition of being "susceptible to harm, injury, failure, or misuse."[1] You can be damaged, even destroyed, or your plans obstructed. Vulnerability means that we cannot reduce life's risks to zero—risks that are understood as potential impediments to reaching important life goals. And this means that we are not in full control of our lives. Or, in Robert Goodin's words, "Vulnerability amounts to one person being able to cause consequences that matter to the other."[2] Vulnerability also

---

1. Paul Formosa, "The Role of Vulnerability in Kantian Ethics," in C. Mackenzie et al., eds., *Vulnerability* (Oxford: Oxford University Press, 2014), 88-109, 89.

2. Robert Goodin, *Protecting the Vulnerable* (Chicago: University of Chicago Press, 1985), 114.

comprises the circumstances, health issues, and environmental challenges to change a person's life situation. Poverty makes a person's vulnerability visible and tangible. Vulnerability is commonly experienced by all of us at some time or another in our lives, but wealth and material security can lead to the temptation to overlook our "nakedness." Thus seen, poverty forces persons to eat from the tree of knowledge and recognize their human nakedness and need for protection.[3] Well-to-do people can live their lives for years and years without any profound sense of vulnerability. They may feel they are "self-made," "makers of their world," "creators of their destiny," "autonomous agents." But under the surface of these illusions is the reality of vulnerability and human interconnectedness. Poverty is a thorn in the flesh of complacent societies trying to live in a paradise without a tree of knowledge (such as Huxley's *Brave New World*).

In the following I want to explore the wound of knowledge (3.1), the experience of poverty (3.2), the epistemic situation of poverty (3.3), and the idea of an option for the poor (3.4).

3.1 The Wound of Knowledge

John Rawls famously created a foundation to develop a theory of justice in the hypothetical scenario of a veil of ignorance. If all members of a society were to come together without any knowledge of their personal and specific situation, which principles would they agree on for just community living?[4] The point of Rawls's thought experiment is that there needs to be a commitment to impartiality and a way of making moral judgments from an impersonal or super-personal standpoint. The price to be paid for this scenario is the loss of personal agency; the different discussants are interchangeable. In a certain sense it would be enough to have but one person think about

---

3. I am referring to Genesis 3:7—Adam and Eve ate from the forbidden yet accessible tree of knowledge: "Then the eyes of both of them were opened, and they knew that they were naked." I would like to think of poverty as a situation that makes us eat from this tree of knowledge helping us understand vulnerability and nakedness, mortality and decay, shame and a loss of belonging.

4. John Rawls, *A Theory of Justice*, rev. ed. (Cambridge, MA: Harvard University Press, 1999), 10-14.

society under a veil of ignorance since the cognitive faculties in this scenario are presented as "colorless" and "odorless," an epistemic skill that shows no features of personal appropriation and that could be taken off and thrown into a corner like a pair of shoes or a backpack.[5]

Let me suggest a different state of affairs, another starting point, not as a criticism of Rawls's theory but because this current project has more to do with humaneness than with justice. If I had a real sense of who I am and if I were to come together with the other members of my society who would also have a deep sense of who they are, which principles would we embrace? That is to say, if we had a deep understanding of our embeddedness in materially and socially limiting contexts as well as of our interior depth, what sort of society would we want to build? The kind of understanding I have in mind follows a spiritual principle that could be said to be Augustinian in spirit; it states a correlation between a sense of depth and a sense of vulnerability, and can be expressed as follows: "The deeper a person's self-knowledge is, the deeper a person's insight into her fragility, brokenness and need for healing will be." Augustine's *Confessions* reflects this idea very well; deep reflection leads to a sense of the need for healing. Paul Farmer aptly observed: "In my experience, people who work for social justice, regardless of their own station in life, tend to see the world as deeply flawed."[6] An understanding of the world as having a built-in self-destruction mechanism, an understanding of the human person in her weakness, an understanding of each person's fragile story with the experience of failure will lead to a deep insight into the need for healing, a longing for wholeness. And this is the realism humility would give us, and humility is a remedy of pride, which is an entry point for self-deception.

---

5. Michael Sandel's criticism (*Liberalism and the Limits of Justice* 8th ed. [Cambridge: Cambridge University Press, 2008], 62): "The Rawlsian self is . . . an antecedently individuated subject, standing always at a certain distance from the interests it has."

6. Paul Farmer, "Health, Healing, and Social Justice. Insights from Liberation Theology," in Dan Groody and G. Gutiérrez, eds., *The Option for the Poor beyond Theology* (Notre Dame, IN: University of Notre Dame Press, 2013), 199-228, at 214.

If spiritually mature persons with a deep understanding of their personhood gathered together to decide on the structures that would most likely engender the possibility of genuine human community, what would they decide? I am not suggesting a community of impartial observers under a veil of ignorance, and I am not suggesting a community of purely rational agents following the communication rules of discourse ethics. I am not suggesting a process of rational deliberation based on arguments, but rather a process of communal conscience formation, a discernment process based on depth of judgment rather than sharpness of analysis. If we were to have the sometimes painful knowledge of a personal standpoint, would we be equipped to make first-person statements with a deeper knowledge of what it means when we say "I"? In other words, if all members of a society had eaten from the tree of knowledge, what theory and practice of coexistence would emerge?

I propose that the sheer act of individuals gathering together with deep first-person knowledge will lead to a wound of knowledge. It is the wound of knowledge that senses and understands a person's own vulnerability (and on that basis the vulnerability of others). Vulnerability, one could suggest, has four dimensions: (1) the capacity to be wounded, (2) the contingency of the world, (3) the fragility of our existence, and (4) our human fallibility. There is the dimension of potential direct damage; there is the dimension of the unpredictability of the world, which is characterized by a horizon of possibilities; and there is the dimension of the unprotectedness of our finite existences together with the dimension of moral fragility in the sense that we make mistakes, err, and become guilty. One could also say that there is a pragmatic, an ontological, an existential, and a moral dimension to vulnerability. It affects aspects if our lives, but also our life as a whole. An understanding of vulnerability includes an understanding of moral fallibility as well as of moral failure. It includes an understanding of threatened and broken integrity. If a person understands her vulnerability, she will carry a wound of understanding, a wound of knowledge, a wound that comes with knowledge of one's wounds.

A wound of knowledge is the result of painful knowledge. Painful knowledge is knowledge that comes either as a result of experiencing adversity or is the cause of an experience of adversity. An example of the former is traumatic knowledge, knowledge based on an experience of destruction, such as the rape victim's knowledge. An example of the latter is tragic knowledge, the kind of knowledge where you know too much and too little at the same. You know too much to return to a state of childlike innocence and a naïve peace of mind, yet you know too little to know how to "fix" it. Such was the knowledge of Oedipus, who knew what he had done but not how to cope with it.[7] Knowledge can create wounds; the idea of a wound of knowledge challenges *prima facie* the well-known claim that knowledge is power; in fact, Oedipus's knowledge rendered him powerless. He had to continue his life journey with a wound of knowledge. A wound of knowledge is not to be understood in negative terms only: Augustine describes how he was blessed with a wound of knowledge, a knowledge of failure and lack; conversion quite often is an experience that give you a sense of what you lacked as something that you missed.

A wound of knowledge is a characteristic of Christian spirituality and the kind of knowledge the good news will leave in the hearers of the word. The gospel exhorts us to interrogate ourselves rather than to explore external data. The "greatness of the great Christian saints lies in their readiness to be questioned, judged, stripped naked and left speechless by that which lies at the center of their faith."[8] The saintliness of Peter was revealed in his tears after his repeated denials and betrayal: "He went out and began to weep bitterly" (Matt 26:75).

The "gift of tears" is a noble motif in the Christian tradition. Evagrius the Solitary, in his Treatise *On Prayer*, collected in the *Philokalia*, exhorts the reader: "First pray for the gift of tears, so that through sorrowing you may tame what is savage in your soul."[9] The gift of tears is given to the person who has received the gift of knowledge of vulnerability. Tears constitute a spiritual path, a mode of

---

7. Christoph Menke, *Die Gegenwart der Tragödie* (Frankfurt/Main: Suhrkamp, 2005), 18.

8. Rowan Williams, *The Wound of Knowledge*, 2d ed. (London: Darton, Longman & Todd, 1990), 11.

9. Evagrius the Solitary, *On Prayer: One Hundred and Fifty-Three Texts*, text 5; Jeremy Driscoll, "Penthos and Tears in Evagrius Ponticus," *Studia Monastica* 36 (1994): 147-63.

prayer in the Alphabetical Sayings of the desert fathers as well as in the monastic tradition.[10] Jesus "offered prayers and supplications with loud cries and tears" (Heb 5:7). Pope Francis has repeatedly reminded Christians of the preciousness of tears. In his Morning Meditation in the Chapel of the Domus Sanctae Marthae on September 14, 2013 (feast of the exaltation of the cross), he reflected:

> We can grasp "something" of the mystery of the Cross "on our knees in prayer," and in "tears" as well. Indeed, tears actually "bring us close" to this mystery. "Without shedding tears," and especially without "heartfelt tears, we shall never understand this mystery." It is the "weeping of the penitent, the weeping of our brother and sister who see so many human miseries and likewise see them in Jesus, on his knees weeping."

Similarly, at the end of his homily during his visit to Lampedusa on July 8, 2013, Pope Francis exhorted with a simple prayer: "Let us ask the Lord for the grace to weep over our indifference, to weep over the cruelty of our world, of our own hearts, and of all those who in anonymity make social and economic decisions which open the door to tragic situations like this." The gift of tears is the result of insight and surrender, the result of making oneself vulnerable to God, open to the transformative touch by God and the transfiguration. The gift of tears also expresses an understanding of one's moral and spiritual vulnerability (fallibility and failure) and an understanding of God's chosen vulnerability in the incarnation. Academic theology does not easily encourage kneeling theology, let alone weeping theology. A Church of the Poor will be based on a deep understanding of vulnerability.

A wound of knowledge will not increase the capacity to construe arguments, but rather the ability to narrate stories. Stories are also

---

10. Barbara Müller, *Der Weg des Weinens: Die Tradition des Penthos in den Apophthegmata Patrum*, Forschungen zur Kirchen- und Dogmengeschichte 77 (Göttingen: Vandenhoeck & Ruprecht 2000); Barbara Müller, "Das Gebet unter Tränen in der Benediktsregel und der Vita Benedicti Gregors des Grossen," *Erbe und Auftrag* 1 (2000): 47–59. See also Elizabeth Knuth, "The Gift of Tears in Teresa of Avila," *Mystics Quarterly* 20, no. 4 (1994): 131-42.

parables, accounts of deeper meaning beyond the words. A church carrying a wound of knowledge will be able to rethink orthodoxy in narrative terms, in terms of respecting the "more" of meaning in a story that is more than a set of propositions. We will return to this issue in Chapter 5. A wound of knowledge is painful. It was painful in the creation story for Adam and Eve to live with the wound of knowledge of their nakedness. I will claim that experiencing poverty leads us to a deep insight into our nakedness, human nakedness understood as vulnerability (lack of protection and safety). A Church of the Poor, I claim, is a church deeply shaped by a wound of knowledge, a bruised, even scarred church. Paradoxically, the joy of the gospel is based on painful knowledge; the joy about God's salvific offer presupposed an understanding of the need for salvation or at least a longing for salvation and healing. The gospel of joy is based on people's openness to see their need for *metanoia*, their deep need for conversion. A Church of the Poor, then, will be a church with a deep knowledge of the theological conviction "*ecclesia semper reformanda*."

I suggest that when people gather together not under a veil of ignorance but in deep personal knowledge, the experience of togetherness will lead to a recognition of a politics of the wound of knowledge. It is a politics that recognizes solidarity as a moral necessity and not as supererogatory; it is a politics that translates solidarity into structures that build a culture in which people can forgive one another on the basis of a shared and common vulnerability. Rather than "fairness," it will be values such as "attentiveness" and "care," "solidarity," and a recognition of interconnectedness and dependence that will emerge. This will have implications for levels of remuneration, privileges, taxation.

A politics of compassion can be built on deep first-person knowledge. The claim of "deep first-person knowledge" implies a deep knowledge of my life situation, which is not the same as a general knowledge of the human condition. There is what could be called "uninhabited knowledge" of the human person, a kind of knowledge that can be expressed in general statements and universal principles. This is knowledge, but knowledge not embedded in existential interests and the dynamics of personal appropriation. "Inhabited knowledge" is knowledge that has an "owner" and that cannot be separated from that owner without significant semantic losses. One could be tempted to distinguish between inhabitable and non-inhabitable knowledge. A proposition such as "When a triangle has a right angle, and squares are made on each of the three sides, then the biggest square has the exact same area as the other two squares put together" could be a candidate for uninhabitable knowledge, knowledge that may be "mastered," but not "personalized" and translated into "important sentences." Important sentences, according to nineteenth-century Austrian philosopher Bernard Bolzano, are sentences that have a direct impact on virtue and happiness.[11] It could be argued that propositions that do not express existential truths express noninhabitable knowledge. Only knowledge about existential truths, that is, knowledge about truths that touch on questions of identity and those questions that Ludwig Wittgenstein called "the problems of life" in his *Tractatus*,[12] can be inhabited. I would like to challenge this idea in the sense that for a believer there is no nonexistential truth, given the idea that everything speaks of God. It is, one could suggest, a challenge of spiritual epistemology to inhabit all kinds of knowledge as a believer, including seemingly nonexistential truths. For good reason Simone Weil took the beauty of mathematics as an illustration of spiritually relevant beauty. A believer is invited to transform uninhabited into inhabited knowledge. We can see this invitation to "transfigure" knowledge many a time in the Gospels. An undeniable feature of Jesus' way of interacting with people is the personalization of his addresses: a person cannot hide behind a position or some formula. Nicodemus, as we have seen, is pushed toward understanding that he is not a great teacher after all, which is painful. He learns something about his person. The Samaritan woman at the well in John 4 also learns something about herself, her thirst and the possibility of satiating that thirst. Jesus does not make it easy for people to hide behind "frozen statements" taken out of cold storage. We can see this in his encounter with Martha after Lazarus has

---

11. See Bernard Bolzano, *Lehrbuch der Religionswissenschaft*, Teil I (Stuttgart: Frommann-Holzboog, 1994), 49-50.

12. Ludwig Wittgenstein, *Tractatus Logico-Philosophicus* (London: Kegan Paul, 1922), 6.52.

died: "Martha said to Jesus, 'Lord, if you had been here, my brother would not have died.' ... Jesus said to her, 'Your brother will rise.' Martha said to him, 'I know he will rise, in the resurrection on the last day.' Jesus told her, 'I am the resurrection and the life; whoever believes in me, even if he dies, will live'" (John 11:21-25). Jesus challenges Martha's abstract knowledge about salvation and resurrection and makes her see the personal, existential truth. He makes it impossible for her not to inhabit this knowledge about the resurrection; the knowledge becomes personalized and embedded within encounter and relationship. Jesus does not allow Christian charity to be nonpersonal. The account of the final judgment in Matthew 25 is an expression of deeply personalized charity.[13] Christians cannot *not* inhabit the knowledge of the entrusted response to vulnerability. Again, it is knowledge based on encounter and relationship.

Deep personal knowledge will create the wound of knowing that we have failed, that we are wounded, that we live in the midst of fragility. This wound of knowledge will lead us into accepting our vulnerability as a key to the hermeneutics of the human condition. Understanding vulnerability as a defining feature of the human condition is different from understanding my own individual vulnerability. A criterion for understanding my vulnerability is the way I conduct my life. Knowing about vulnerability will make me understand the need for connectedness and the need for forgiveness. Since we are vulnerable we depend on others; we live lives full of risks. We need to trust. And trust involves dependence, a recognition of interconnectedness. Hannah Arendt has suggested that we see forgiving as a fundamental human act because of the fragility of our condition and its social nature.[14] Because of the boundlessness of the consequences of our actions, human agency falls in the category of the unpredictable. "The reason why we are never able to foretell with certainty the outcome and end of any action is simply that action has no end."[15] Our

---

13. Helen Rhee, *Loving the Poor, Saving the Rich: Wealth, Poverty and Early Christian Formation* (Grand Rapids, MI: Baker Academic, 2012), 199-210.

14. Hannah Arendt, *The Human Condition* (Chicago: University of Chicago Press, 1958), 237.

15. Ibid., 233.

actions have consequences that could become chains unless there is forgiveness. The insight into the need for forgiveness is painful; knowledge of one's moral failures constitutes a wound. And it is from this wound that we nourish a sense of life that will make us see the world and act in a particular way. Let me explain further what I mean by the implications of a wound of knowledge. We all know people who suffer from dementia or Alzheimer's disease. There are moving accounts of the social and moral costs of these conditions. Lisa Genova has written a beautiful novel about a high-achieving academic who is diagnosed with early Alzheimer's disease and has to live with the wound of the knowledge of the diagnosis.[16] Alzheimer's disease means gradually losing the sense of self and being forced to depend on others who suddenly find themselves in the role of carer with responsibilities. There is a loss of feeling at home in the world, a loss of familiarity as well as a loss of confidence in a world that is increasingly experienced as alien and adverse. If I knew now, with my full mental capacity that I will end my days with Alzheimer's disease depending on the care of others, how would I live my life now? Would I not see the need for communion and a life nurturing a culture of communality? Would I not live with and in a sense of humility, that is, a realistic understanding of the limits and the dynamics of decline?

The wound of knowledge provides us with knowledge of our "capacity to be wounded,"[17] the existential knowledge of our own fragility. As we will see in the next section, vulnerability is not something to be romanticized. It is hard and rough, painful and scary to be exposed to vulnerability. The creation story talks about the transformation of belonging into longing after the loss of paradise; it talks about the experience of nakedness, the experience of the adversity of the world that will bring pain (Gen 3:16) and "thorns and thistles" (Gen 3:18). The creation story gives an account of our human condition that does not allow us to be "at home" in this life. Albert Camus described this

---

16. Lisa Genova, *Still Alice* (New York: Simon & Schuster, 2009).

17. Hans Martin Füssel, "Vulnerability: A Generally Applicable Conceptual Framework for Climate Change Research," *Global Environmental Change* 17 (2007): 155-67, at 155.

alienation as "the absurd," the abyss between the cry of humanity and the silence of the world, the abyss between infinite longing and the finitude of life. Our material condition with its built-in structures of decline and decay, with the dynamics of aging bodies and failing health, changing circumstances and the impossibility of holding on to power creates not only a sense of vulnerability but also a sense of woundedness in the disproportion between longing and belonging.

If all members of our society were to gather together carrying the wound of knowledge in the recognition of individual and communal vulnerability we would be able to build a society based on the loving acceptance of vulnerability. There is the darkness of the wound and the light of its recognition; there is the darkness of one's pain and the light of the longing for sources of healing and consolation. This is a kind of enlightenment that appeals more to wisdom than to reason, more to the "logic of the heart" than to the common-sense thinking of the mind. The recognition of vulnerability will lead to communion. "If we deny our weakness and the reality of death, if we want to be powerful and strong always, we deny a part of who we are. . . . To be human is to accept and love others just as they are, weaknesses and strengths, because we need each other. Weakness, recognized, accepted, and offered, is at the heart of belonging, so it is at the heart of communion with another."[18] A wound of knowledge makes it easier for us to accept that "behind our roles, and the masks we often wear, we are all vulnerable and struggling human beings whose hearts are more needy than we would dare to admit at times."[19] So a first effect of recognizing vulnerability as part of the human condition is an understanding of "relational autonomy," of dependence and connectedness: of kinship.

A deep recognition of vulnerability will lead to a deep recognition of our woundedness. There is not a single person on this planet not carrying wounds—such as the wounds of a childhood with its own undeniable brokenness. You cannot mature without wounds; you

---

18. Jean Vanier, *Drawn into the Mystery of Jesus through the Gospel of John* (Mahwah, NJ: Paulist Press, 2004), 191.

19. Thomas Kearney, *A Prophetic Cry: Stories of Spirituality and Healing Inspired by L'Arche* (Dublin: Veritas, 2000), 76.

cannot become an adult without carrying wounds, and "your child-hood" wounds enter interactions with your own children.

Vulnerability threatens our integrity, and our woundedness under-mines integrity understood as "wholeness." Wounds create broken-ness and injury and constitute a state of "integrity lost." The wound of knowledge that I suggest as the framework for the discernment of life questions leads to an understanding of the loss of integrity as well as to a deep longing for healing this loss. I see how a "veil of ignorance" could lead to "fairness" as its central orientation point. I could, how-ever, also see that a wound of knowledge will lead to "integrity" as key value. Integrity has emerged as a key concept in moral philosophy.[20] I understand integrity to mean (1) wholeness, (2) sincerity, (3) epi-stemic haecceity, (4) robust concern. Wholeness means "being unbro-ken"; sincerity means honesty and an earnest desire to live a good life; epistemic haecceity suggests developing, holding, and defending a position on important questions of life (entering epistemic commit-ments); and robust concern means caring about something deeply, accepting the burden of responsibilities and commitments, having found something worth fighting for. The latter can be illustrated with an insight communicated in Alan Paton's novel *Ah but Your Land Is Beautiful*. Mr. Nene, the protagonist, understanding the brokenness of the political situation, is willing to engage in the political struggle. His family is worried about him, but he is clear about his commit-ment: "When I go up there, which is my intention, the Big Judge will say to me, Where are your wounds? And if I say I haven't any, he will say, Was there nothing to fight for?"[21]

---

20. Damian Cox, Marguerite La Caze, and Michael P. Levine, *Integrity and the Fragile Self* (Aldershot: Ashgate, 2003); Mark Halfon, *Integrity: A Philo-sophical Inquiry* (Philadelphia: Temple University Press, 1989); Lynne McFall, "Integrity," *Ethics* 98 (1987): 5-20; Carol V. A. Quinn, "On Integrity," *Interna-tional Journal of Applied Philosophy* 23 (2010): 189-97; Greg Scherkoske, *Integ-rity and the Virtues of Reason: Leading a Convincing Life* (Cambridge: Cambridge University Press, 2013); Bernard Williams, "Integrity," in J. J. C. Smart and Bernard Williams, *Utilitarianism: For and Against* (New York: Cambridge Uni-versity Press, 1973), 108-17.

21. Alan Paton, *Ah, but Your Land Is Beautiful* (New York: Scribner Paper-back, 1996), 66f.

Integrity in this sense is an expression of understanding the weight and gravity of life and life's questions, the urgency of facing the challenge to live life well. Vulnerability senses that having a full life is not a given, but constitutes a task and a challenge; an understanding of woundedness leads to the belief that a full life is not possible without scars, which in turn leads onto the idea of a permanent "thorn in the flesh." In the same way as scarcity creates value, scarcity of wholeness, that is, wounds and brokenness, creates preciousness. Life is precious. We face the challenge of "making something out of our lives," precisely because it is "open" as well as "broken."

A deep understanding of vulnerability and woundedness leaves no space for any illusion that integrity is possible, at least not in the sense of "wholeness without wounds and scars." After the fall, "first integrity" is no longer an option. We are left with the beauty and depth of "second integrity." Second integrity is integrity with wounds and scars. It is integrity with broken wholeness, healed wounds. We cannot return to "first integrity" (as we cannot return to "first naïveté," to use Paul Ricoeur's term).[22] First integrity was lost in the fall. A deep illustration of this second integrity can be found in Genesis 32, in Jacob's wrestling with God. He enters the confrontation in full strength and leaves the encounter with a new blessed identity, but limping. The new blessed identity, however, was made possible (in the sense of *felix culpa*) by the brokenness suffered in the encounter. This passage shows the transition from first integrity to second integrity. I suggest that a Church of the Poor is a church that has moved from a self-understanding of first integrity to second integrity. German poet Hilde Domin has beautifully expressed this second integrity in her poem "Please," which reminds readers that longing for a landscape this side of the border of tears doesn't work, that longing to remain unscathed doesn't work, but that out of the flood, the lion's den and the furnace, we can renew ourselves "even more wounded and even more healed."[23]

---

22. Paul Ricoeur, *The Symbolism of Evil*, trans. Emerson Buchanan (Boston: Beacon, 1969), 349-51.

23. Hilde Domin, "Please," at http://hildedomin.megtaylor.co.uk.

3.2 The Experience of Poverty

Living in poverty is harsh; Our Lady lived a simple life in Nazareth, we can assume; she may even have been a widow at some point, left to raise a son on her own. But we have no reason to assume that she was destitute. Madonna, on the other hand, is a twenty-first-century American woman. She was raised by her mother, who suffered from acute depression, dropped out of college for financial reasons after two years, entered a short-lived marriage to a man with character (honesty) issues, and found herself in the role of a single mother with a daughter to bring up. "With no college degree and a sporadic work record, the best position she could find was a daytime shift as a cashier ... which paid $9 an hour."[24] After eight years in the job her cash drawer came up $10 short. "She was summarily dismissed, given no benefit of the doubt, despite her years of service and the small amount of money involved.... That's when things really started to fall apart."[25] She fell behind on her rent payments, was evicted, could not move in with her father's new family, and had to enter a succession of homeless shelters. We can be sure that she kept all her experiences in her heart (cf. Luke 2:51), so much so that these memories built up memory banks, traces of the many experiences of rejection and humiliation, exposure to fate, frustrated hopes, and a bitter sense of vulnerability.

Vulnerability is a key, if not the most significant feature, of poverty. Poverty is a hard taskmaster and a strict teacher, teaching lessons both hard to bear and hard to understand. Poverty teaches lessons in vulnerability. We can describe the wounds of poverty and human vulnerability in the most poetic and beautiful language, but no amount of hyperbolic oxymoron can deny its ugly reality. Poverty has an insidious, repulsive face, not one in fact but many. Carolina Maria de Jesus, born in 1913 in Sacramento, Brazil, ended up raising three children in a favela of São Paulo as a single mother, trying to make ends meet as a garbage collector. She kept a diary about her life, a version of which, edited by Audalio Dantas, was published in 1960 under the title *Quarto de*

---

24. Kathryn J. Edin and H. Luke Shaefer, *$2.00 a Day: Living on Almost Nothing in America* (Boston: Houghton Mifflin Harcourt, 2015), 3-4.

25. Ibid., 4.

despejo. Through this book, a classic in poverty studies, Carolina Maria de Jesus established herself as "a kind of tour guide through the usually hidden world of poverty."[26] She made some money from the sales of the book but could not manage it and had to return to her life of collecting wastepaper and cans. She died in 1977 in poverty. Her diary provides deep insights into the ugly nature of poverty. She experiences shame, being ashamed of the clothes she has to wear: "If I walk around dirty it's because I'm trapped in the life of the favelado."[27] She talks about the absence of beauty in her life. She experiences poverty as a deprivation of beauty. She recounts the constant struggle of a life in poverty. The first entry in the published version of her diary reads: "*July 15, 1955* The birthday of my daughter Vera Eunice. I wanted to buy a pair of shoes for her, but the price of food keeps us from realizing our desires. Actually we are slaves to the cost of living. I found a pair of shoes in the garbage, washed them, and patched them for her to wear."[28] We learn from these few lines that although there are special days that merit special, well-justified, and morally relevant gestures, the situation of poverty makes it impossible to live up to these expectations. This can be the road to despair: "I heard women complaining with tears in their eyes that they couldn't bear the rising cost of living any more."[29] Again and again Carolina Maria de Jesus talks about battles and struggles in her stressful life, the lack of peace of mind, the lack of tranquillity. There is no rest and no relaxation for the poor. Life is a constant struggle, a fight: "Here in the favela almost everyone has a difficult fight to live."[30] The constant struggle makes her ponder suicide and leads to a permanent state of tiredness. "I'm tired of working so hard."[31] Life is hard: "Hard is the bread that we eat. Hard is the bed on which we sleep. Hard

---

26. Robert Levine, Afterword to Carolina Maria de Jesus, *Child of the Dark: Quarto de Despejo* (London: Penguin, 2003), 184. "Her descriptions of favela life do not romanticize its poverty, but hack away at it with a machete" (ibid., 186); cf. Robert Levine, "The Cautionary Tale of Carolina Maria de Jesus. Working Paper 178," Kellogg Institute for International Studies (Notre Dame, 1992).

27. De Jesus, *Child of the Dark*, 35.

28. Ibid, 3.

29. Ibid., 86.

30. Ibid., 28.

31. Ibid., 169.

is the life of the favelado."[32] She describes how she forgets how to smile; she witnesses violence, hatred, and loss of compassion and tenderness in her neighborhood. A major stress factor is the lack of food security. Hunger is Carolina's constant companion; "my problem is always food."[33] May 27, 1958, was one of the even more difficult days: "I didn't have any breakfast and walked around half dizzy."[34] On August 7 in the same year we read: "I got out of bed at 4 a.m. I didn't sleep because I went to bed hungry. And he who lies down with hunger doesn't sleep."[35] She sees how children prematurely die of hunger; she suffers from the fact that she cannot properly provide for her children. There are days without lunch; there are days without dinner; there are days without food; there are Sundays with only hard bread and beans. This is one of the ugliest sides of poverty: You have well-justifiable and well-justified moral standards—such as providing proper food for the children—and you cannot fulfill those standards. "A mother is always worried that her children are hungry."[36] In other words, "The worst thing that a mother can hear is the symphony: 'Mama, I want some bread! Mama, I am hungry!'"[37] Despair and frustration are the siblings of the struggle for survival and the lack of basic securities: "I was furious with life and with a desire to cry because I didn't have money to buy bread."[38]

Let us be very clear here: This not a desirable life situation. Carolina Maria de Jesus describes a situation of extreme vulnerability: she has to be afraid of health issues, violence issues, lack of food security, moral failures. She lives with the wound of knowledge that her children have to grow up under adverse circumstances and that there are children who have so much more than she can ever dream of providing. The experience of poverty gives Carolina Maria de Jesus a deep understanding of vulnerability and woundedness. Her material poverty reminds us in a painful way of resources that are missing,

32. Ibid., 33.
33. Ibid., 43.
34. Ibid., 37.
35. Ibid., 98.
36. Ibid., 108.
37. Ibid., 55.
38. Ibid., 173.

because the loss or lack of these resources makes it more difficult, if not impossible, to live a justifiably desirable life, a life that satisfies well-justifiable desires. It is not desirable not to be able to fulfill well-justifiable moral expectations and the expectations of a good life; it is not desirable not to be able to nourish the soul with beauty and tranquillity. It is not desirable to live in a polluted area, in a town that hosts an incinerator. Wealthy neighborhoods have resources to prevent such health threats. Social injustice leads to environmental injustice.[39]

It is not desirable to live in moral vulnerability. It is not desirable to be exposed to "moral poverty," "growing up surrounded by deviant, delinquent and criminal adults."[40] Joseph Wresinski talks about his childhood growing up poor; he talks about his father, who would shout all the time, who would beat his older son, who would curse his wife, who would create a climate of fear. "It was only much later, when I was a grown man sharing the life of other men like my father and of other families like our own, that I understood my father was a humiliated man. He suffered because he felt he had failed in life; he was ashamed not to be able to give his family security and happiness." He goes on to comment: "This is the true consequence of extreme poverty. A person cannot live such a humiliating life without reacting."[41] This is not desirable. It is not desirable to be pushed into situations that make you act against your own deeply rooted personal beliefs; it is not desirable to be forced to sell children, as happened during the early period of Christianity.[42] Poverty is humiliating and poverty is stressful; Wresinski recalls how his parents talked only about money. This is not desirable. It may remind us of a concern expressed in *Rerum novarum* that the soul of the working

---

39. Kristin Shrader-Frechette, "Liberation Science and the Option for the Poor. Protecting Victims of Environmental Injustice," in Dan Groody, ed., *The Preferential Option for the Poor beyond Theology* (Notre Dame, IN: Notre Dame University Press, 2013), 120-48.

40. Bryant L. Myers, *Walking with the Poor* (Maryknoll, NY: Orbis Books, 1983), 130.

41. Joseph Wresinski, "A Young Boy Caught in the Vicious Circle of Violence," in Gilles Anovil, *The Poor Are the Church: A Conversation with Father Joseph Wresinski* (Mystic, CT: Twenty-Third Publications, 2002), 3.

42. Susan Holman, *God Knows There's Need: Christian Responses to Poverty* (Oxford: Oxford University Press, 2009), 59.

man must not be neglected and that it needs proper rest.[43] It is not desirable to be under constant pressure. It is not desirable to be so restricted in your choices that you are forced to make "stupid decisions," as Linda Tirado describes from a twenty-first-century experience of poverty in the United States.[44] In her book, Linda Tirado also talks about the pitiful lack of rest, the fact that with two part-time jobs and a family she would not get more than a few hours of sleep. She describes in some detail her lack of hope, the lack of well-justified prospects to change her situation because she would not even be able to afford the kinds of clothes necessary for a job interview. She feels trapped. It is not desirable to be "trapped in poverty," a trap Robert Chambers described as an interconnected system of material poverty, physical weakness, isolation, vulnerability, and powerlessness.[45] It is not desirable *not* to be able to build assets;[46] it is not desirable to be in a situation where you cannot make plans and where it is difficult to make promises. The experience of involuntary poverty is rarely pleasant.

To experience poverty is to experience vulnerability, the vulnerability of identity. Poverty is a situation of "lack," "exclusion," and "deprivation": lack of assets and lack of access to assets, lack of life-world spaces (spaces of learning, spaces of recreation, spaces of encounter), exclusion from standardized cultural activities ("social exclusion"), exclusion from access to institutions and systems (educational system, labor market, health institutions, economic markets), deprivation of capabilities, or deprivation of identity resources.[47] The latter is the understanding of poverty that I would like to pursue here in this enquiry. Poverty as deprivation of identity resources is a personal situation characterized by identity malnourishment. Identity

43. *Rerum novarum* 20, 40, 42.

44. Linda Tirado, *Hand to Mouth: Living in Bootstrap America* (New York: Penguin, 2014).

45. Robert Chambers, *Rural Development: Putting the Last First* (Harlow: Longman, 1983), 103-39.

46. James Bailey, *Rethinking Poverty: Income, Assets, and the Catholic Social Justice Tradition* (Notre Dame, IN: University of Notre Dame Press, 2010), esp. ch. 4.

47. For capability deprivation, see Amartya Sen, *Development as Freedom* (New York: Basic Books, 1999), ch. 4.

needs resources to grow, to flourish. Resources can include a real sense of belonging or recognition, coherent narration or structures of care and concern. A *sense of belonging* means being part of an identifiable group that provides group and individual identity. *Recognition* happens when self and things of self are acknowledged and identified by third-party "others" as stemming from this self. *Coherent narration* is the ability to tell one's—my—own unique and singlular life story with all it implies with none of the bits being left out or needing to be left out. *Structures of care and concern* result from the interested involvement of B or C in the life of A, with their serious appreciation and acceptance of the things that matter, really, really matter to A. People in poverty have a hard time with all of the above. In being socially excluded by whatever mechanisms dictate, people lose all sense of belonging; they receive no recognition, and gaining access to a group that provides identity is well-nigh impossible.

Ultimately, poverty is linked to identity questions. Social exclusion makes it difficult for a person, in Adam Smith's classic words, "to go about without shame." The dynamic of social exclusion means that basic social affiliations and attachments are withheld and vital social connections are missing. Material poverty points to identity poverty as well as to the fact that material goods have an identity dimension. Lack of assets and lack of access to assets affect identity issues. British anthropologist Daniel Miller looked at the subjective "worth" of "things" in people's homes in one road in south London.[48] The things a home "has" are rarely there by chance and often have a "story" attached to them; they mean something to the owner, are there for a reason, and as such are alive in a certain sense of the word for the owner. Their impact has affected the life and soul of one or more persons in one particular household. Things are not mere things; they are perceived as part of a person's life, contributing to a person's identity. Postcards are kept for years—a lifetime—as are love letters, souvenirs of holidays, mementoes, and photographs of special occasions. Some people collect football trophies; others are mad about stamp collecting. A home is a portrait of its owners. Trinkets and ornaments

---

48. Daniel Miller, *The Comfort of Things* (Cambridge: Polity, 2008).

may be "externalized memories" that strengthen the recollection of having had *this* or *that* experience—the experience the object stands for and embodies. Things *carry* weight; they *attach* value to things for someone; they may serve as a "prop" to trigger habits, actions, memories. Russell Belk has shown that belongings also have the power to express the self they are part of; in other words, they constitute an "extended self."[49] Material goods carry immaterial meaning because they express immaterial values. The things we buy and own carve out a part of our identity; material goods have "meaning."

People hit by poverty have a restricted scope of possibilities and rarely have options to choose from. Thus, self-expression and self-awareness as agent are severely limited. Poverty stunts the growth of agency—a vital source of identity. The fact that poverty is linked to identity puts people affected by poverty in a specific epistemic situation. Poverty is being deprived of identity-giving resources. In his research into poverty, William Vollmann pinpointed its main characteristics, namely, feelings of "invisibility," "deformity," "unwantedness," "dependence," "accident-proneness," "pain," "numbness," and "estrangement."[50] These qualifiers all suggest stumbling blocks in finding and anchoring identity. The South African literary Nobel Prize winner J. M. Coetzee gives a splendid description of the dynamics at work in the erosion process of identity resources. In his autobiographical novel *Boyhood: Scenes from Provincial Life*, J. M. Coetzee (re)traces the life of his father after he is forced to shut his law firm. He continues to leave the house at 7 a.m. on the dot as he has always done and heads off to town. The difference now is that he returns home two hours later; and that is the big secret, knowing that everyone will

49. Russell W. Belk, "Possessions and the Extended Self," *Journal of Consumer Research* 15, no. 2 (1988): 139-68; cf. Daniel Ladik, François Carrillat, and Mark Tadajewski, "Belk's (1988) 'Possessions and the Extended Self' Revisited," *Journal of Historical Research in Marketing* 7, no. 2 (2015): 184-207.

50. William Vollman, *Poor People* (New York: Harper Perennial, 2007). Joseph Wresinski makes the same point describing his mother as having a passivity caused by fatigue and fear (Anovil, *The Poor Are the Church*, 6); living in a state of increased vulnerability is tiresome and creates fear and the stress of fear and anxieties.

have left the house and it will be empty till late afternoon. He puts his pajamas back on and crawls into bed with a hip flask of brandy and the *Cape Times* newspaper crossword puzzle. Several hours later, at two in the afternoon, he gets back up again, puts his clothes back on, and leaves the house for his club before anyone else comes home and finds out that he has been there. The son discovers the father's secret by chance when, feeling unwell, he comes home early from school one day. Not only does the father no longer leave the house but he becomes an alcoholic; he hides any bills that arrive by mail, and the whole situation spirals out of control, with the family losing just about all they have. If we look at the situation being described here, we see a father who withdraws from public and even from private life. His life revolves around guarding this secret; he no longer has the resources at his disposal that would allow him to come to terms in some realistic way with this drastic change in circumstances. The father forfeits all family affiliation, and his son denies him all the benefits reserved for family members. He is bogged down in his own apathy and languid indifference to self; he lacks the capabilities and tools he once had to narrate his own life simply because he has had to flee into a world founded on and constructed out of lies. All his resources of identity have been eroded away, and he is no longer capable of developing, or even living in and with, his own real identity. His abstract world of lies brings only shame and humiliation.

There may seemingly be many forms of poverty, but, ultimately, there are only two kinds: voluntary poverty and forced poverty.[51] Voluntary poverty can be identity fostering and integrity enhancing; forced poverty will seldom have this effect. It is not desirable to build a Church of the Poor on the basis of involuntary poverty.

3.3 Poverty and the Epistemic Situation

Experiencing poverty changes the epistemic situation of a person. It cannot be denied that exposure to vulnerability is both taxing and traumatic; it influences individual beliefs about social structure, social

---

51. Aloysius Pieris, "To Be Poor as Jesus Was Poor?" *The Way* 24 (1984): 186-97, at 192.

justice, and the self. Experiencing poverty gives us a deep insight into our nakedness with its vast pillars of vulnerability, absence of protection and safety as well as nonexistent moral and social shelter. Linda Tirado, as we have seen, discusses the reduced planning possibilities in poverty and the challenges to realize prudence and take a long-term perspective. When thinking about the connectedness of personal beliefs and poverty, we are confronted with epistemic situations that disempower people to free themselves of the shackles of their poverty and the epistemic situations that provide power for poverty to persist within a society. The fact that poverty persists is not a given, but based on societal and widespread beliefs—the universally held beliefs that there will be winners and losers, for instance, the belief that social exclusion is unavoidable. People create narratives, belief systems, and structures that justify their privileged positions. "The non-poor understand themselves as superior."[52]

Poverty leads to an erosion of the sense of autonomy understood as autarchy. In the discourse on autonomy we find a sense of the autonomous subject as capable of making her own choices; involuntary poverty is a life situation that takes people on journeys and paths they would not otherwise choose; it is an experience of dependence and restriction. Experiencing involuntary poverty can be likened to experiencing pain; suffering physical or mental pain can be characterized as experiencing an adverse, pervasive condition. The same categories can be applied to poverty. Poverty and pain are epistemically relevant in the sense that they change the epistemic situation of a person. A person will obtain knowledge "in pain" that would not otherwise be available. Simone Weil, who suffered from constant migraines, was dogged by ill health during her short lifetime, and who died from exhaustion in 1943, at age thirty-four, talks about "affliction" as a source of knowledge that teaches us about the laws of the world. Simone Weil sees affliction as a primary route to truth. Suffering robs us of any vestiges of independence we might have and forces us into a state of absolute dependence on third parties and a dependence on God's grace, which only extremes of suffering can

---

52. Myers, *Walking with the Poor*, 124.

bring about and which Paul, with first-hand experience, refers to as "the thorn in his flesh" in 2 Corinthians (12:7). Affliction affects us in the same way, perhaps even more so, but is different from mere suffering. In her text *L'amour de Dieu et le malheur*, written in 1942, one year before her death, Simone Weil characterizes *malheur* ("affliction") as something overwhelming: "It takes possession of the soul and marks it through and through with its own particular mark, the mark of slavery. . . . There is not real affliction unless the event that has gripped and uprooted a life attacks it, directly or indirectly, in all its parts, social, psychological, and physical."[53] Affliction directs individual personal experience to exposure to the world the person would otherwise not have had. It is an "uprooting of life"; it brings about a particular state of mind that is unknown to those who have not experienced it. Affliction deprives a person of certain sources of identity; it transforms the relationship between person and world. It is in the state of affliction that revelation takes place, as we see in the book of Job. Job is being taught a lesson about the mystery of God that he would not have learned otherwise.[54] Affliction opens doors to the soul, allows experience to touch the very quick of that soul, to penetrate its depths. The same applies to joy and beauty: through joy, the beauty of the world penetrates the human soul, and imprints itself on the soul. Beauty is also a primary route to truth. Suffering and beauty share the power to change the epistemic situation of a person. For Simone Weil, one striking example of beauty is mathematics. It is a manifest appearance of reality: "what is beautiful in mathematics is that which makes it abundantly clear to us that it is not something which we have manufactured ourselves."[55] There is knowledge that is "imposed" rather than "chosen."

We could call knowledge that is "suffered through" rather than "construed" "directed knowledge." Directed knowledge is knowledge

53. Simone Weil, "The Love of God and Affliction," in George A. Panichas, ed., *The Simone Weil Reader* (New York: David McKay, 1977), 439-43, 439f.

54. Gustavo Gutiérrez, *On Job: God-Talk and the Suffering of the Innocent*, 12th ed. (Maryknoll, NY: Orbis Books, 1999), 82-92.

55. Simone Weil, *Notebooks*, trans. Arthur Wills; 2 vols., London: Routledge & Kegan Paul, 1956), 2:386.

based on and generated via experience, the experience of being guided; the epistemic subject is drawn to or into an experience. Directed knowledge partly "overwhelms" a subject. Directed knowledge implies an experience of something that pushes us to the edge of our limits and sets up boundaries. This experience evokes a sense of humility. For Simone Weil, both affliction and mathematics (or beauty in general) generate directed knowledge that leads a person away from herself. There is a sense of self-forgetfulness that we have observed in Pope Francis's encounter with Vincio Riva.

Poverty, we could say, imparts directed knowledge. Directed knowledge is the result of people who cannot chose the situations they find themselves in. A Church of the Poor will be shaped by directed knowledge. It is the kind of knowledge Peter was promised in John 21:18 as being led to places he would not have chosen. It is the kind of knowledge Havi Carel had to obtain. She did not choose the journey she had to undertake. Carel is a British philosopher who, diagnosed with a rare form of lung cancer, sees the epistemic possibilities for patients in a new light after she was told she too was a "patient" who was "terminally ill."[56] Just as disease changes epistemic status, so too does poverty. Overnight sometimes things—like disease—take on new meaning or lose their significance completely in the new spectrum of things; questions suddenly rear their ugly heads about which neighbors have no idea or experience. If you do not live in poverty, you cannot even begin to guess what it must be like. Certain circumstances and experience, dire though they may be, contribute toward the evangelization spirit that works within "limits" and sparks growth in understanding the gospel "and in discerning the paths of the Spirit" (*Evangelii gaudium* [EG] 45). Individuals and groups of individuals can grow spiritually in their understanding of God's will exactly because of the dire things they have to live through; and it is this experience of the lowliest, weakest, marginalized, and excluded of society that means more than anything else in contributing to the growth of a universal evangelizing spirit. We could say that the "very seeds of the kingdom are found in the fragile lives of the poor and the

---

56. Havi Carel, *Illness: The Cry of the Flesh* (Durham, NC: Acumen, 2013).

ordinary as they seek the face of God."[57] They have been led to understand something crucial about our human vulnerability and about our dependence on God and about our non–self-sufficiency.

Poverty underpins particular propositions in their first-person narration account, narrations that without that first-hand experience could not be told. Access to such accounts is barred from those who are not poor. A "poor church" will know such accounts are relevant and incorporate them as a priceless resource into the structure and connectedness of the church. Poverty imposes a particular kind of first-person knowledge that will be defining in our relationship with God.

3.4 An "Option for the Poor": Overcoming Indifference

The epistemic situation of poor people is theologically relevant: Pope Francis suggests we all learn from the sources of this epistemic situation: "This is why I want a Church which is poor and for the poor. They have much to teach us. Not only do they share in the *sensus fidei*, we need to let ourselves be evangelized by them" because "in their difficulties they know the suffering Christ" (EG 198); it is up to us: "We are called to . . . embrace the mysterious wisdom which God wishes to share with us through them" (EG 198). What is the knowledge the experience of poverty conveys? It is, as we have seen, the knowledge of vulnerability, the wisdom of a deep understanding of dependence, a deep understanding of a difficult life that cries out for transformation. It is much more difficult to develop a deep understanding of human dependence and vulnerability and need for transformation within a context of saturation and economic self-sufficiency. That is why an "option for the poor," which is an example of a "standpoint epistemology" that privileges a particular position, serves as an epistemic "corrective force" not only to correct biases but also to identify hitherto overlooked questions and unfelt epistemic needs.

The concern with an option for the poor, understood as "giving special attention to the poor," is deeply rooted in the Magisterium.

---

57. Catherine Clifford, "Pope Francis' Call for the Conversion of the Church in Our Time," *Australian eJournal of Theology* 21, no. 1 (2015): 33-55, at 44.

The first social encyclical *Rerum novarum* expresses this preferential option for the poor by making the statement that "the poor and badly off have a claim to especial consideration" (*Rerum novarum* 37). This has been echoed in *Quadragesimo anno* 18. *Octogesima adveniens* 23 talks about "the preferential respect due to the poor" and even calls the more fortunate to "renounce some of their rights so as to place their goods more generously at the service of others." These words are provocative in an entitlements-centered society. *Gaudium et spes* (GS) 69 affirms that "if one is in extreme necessity, he has the right to procure for himself what he needs out of the riches of others" (GS 69). This preferential concern for the disadvantaged is again articulated in chapter 2 of the document, which reminds us of the importance of "the desire to make the conditions of life more favorable for all, especially for those who are poor in culture or who are deprived of the opportunity to exercise responsibility" (*Gaudium et spes* 57). This preferential concern is also transferred to an international level and used to talk about interstate relations in *Gaudium et spes* 86b. *Populorum progressio* 23 quotes Saint Ambrose: "You are not making a gift of your possessions to the poor person. You are handing over to him what is his. For what has been given in common for the use of all, you have arrogated to yourself. The world is given to all, and not only to the rich." The American bishops in their influential 1986 document *Economic Justice for All* reminded the American public that "all members of society have a special obligation to the poor and vulnerable" (No. 16); they describe the poor as "agents of God's transforming power" and express the belief that embracing an option for the poor means to strengthen the whole community. The same document, within the context of talking about a preferential option for the poor, calls for "a compassionate vision that enables the Church to see things from the side of the poor and powerless" (No. 52). Is this a vision of a Church of the Poor? If so, it was forcefully brought forward on November 16, 1965, the day on which the Catacomb Pact was endorsed by a number of bishops who pledged to live as most human beings live, without extra benefits and without the luxury of privileges. Again, dealing with privileges emerges as a key question. A standpoint epistemology addresses privileges. We have to remember that there are also epistemic privileges. In a hospital environment,

Havi Carel and Ian Kidd saw the authority of the nursing staff—especially of doctors—as an *epistemic privilege* greater than that sensed and experienced by the patients themselves on the receiving end, so to speak.[58] We find such epistemic praxis in the church too, where all too frequently there is a gaping chasm between *epistemic* authority and *deontic* authority, which is equally as harmful as those in a theological elitist class who deems themselves to have the sole and "rightful" authority (and expertise) to read (in its widest context) and interpret the Holy Scriptures, to the exclusion of professional exegetes. It is not without good reason that the Congregation of the Faith sees itself as the legal guardian of those who are theologically weak. A Church of the Poor is a church that listens to those who have been epistemically excluded from society and takes them seriously.

An option for the poor will have implications for the redistribution of privileges and for any kind of choice and decision-making process. In the Third General Conference of the Latin American Episcopate, on January 28, 1979, Pope John Paul II pinpoints this option within the universal tradition of the church:

> The option or love of preference for the poor [is . . .] a special form of primacy in the exercise of Christian charity, to which the whole tradition of the Church bears witness. It affects the life of each Christian inasmuch as he or she seeks to imitate the life of Christ, but it applies equally to our social responsibilities and hence to our manner of living, and to the logical decisions to be made concerning the ownership and use of goods. (*Sollicitudo rei socialis* 42)

Centesimus annus 57 indicates the "immaterial" implications of such an "option." *Evangelium vitae* 32, *Tertio millennio adveniente* 51, *Centesimus annus* 11, and *Redemptoris mater* 37 specify similar signals and stimuli. *Sollicitudo rei socialis* characterizes the option of preference for the poor as "a special form of primacy in the exercise of Christian

---

58. Havi Carel and Ian James Kidd, "Epistemic Injustice in Healthcare: A Philosophical Analysis," *Medicine, Health Care and Philosophy* 17, no. 4 (2014): 529-40.

charity" (No. 42) and couches the language of an option for the poor in a language of subsidiarity.[59] *Centesimus annus* 11 reiterates that point and challenges the perception of the poor as "a burden, as irksome intruders trying to consume what others have produced" (No. 28). In fact, the poor, Pope Benedict XVI states, should be seen as "a resource, even from a purely economic point of view" (*Caritas in veritate* 36). This echoes the idea that a social and economic integration of the poor will benefit the community as well as the idea of community as a whole. This is an important point. An "option for the poor" is not primarily motivated by the hope of alleviating the plight of a particular "segment" of society; no, an option for the poor is grounded in a common-good orientation. It is good for the whole community if an option for the poor is pursued. It is good for the quality of discipleship and faith, and also for the quality of understanding and knowledge of the church if the church becomes a Church of the Poor.

Pope Francis, following Galatians 2:2 and 2:10, suggests the question "have you forgotten the poor?" as a key criterion to assess the moral and spiritual quality of a community (EG 195). Orthodoxy, then, is linked to authenticity, and authenticity is linked to engagement for the marginalized. The main challenge in most cases, when confronted with poverty, is not so much hostility but indifference. An option is primarily a commitment to overcome indifference; it structures one's areas of concern. An option is an expression of a choice based on robust concern.

Harry Frankfurt characterizes love as "robust concern," as that volitional aspect that has to be willingly and freely chosen.[60] An

---

59. "The exercise of solidarity within each society is valid when its members recognize one another as persons. Those who are more influential, because they have a greater share of goods and common services, should feel responsible for the weaker and be ready to share with them all they possess. Those who are weaker, for their part, in the same spirit of solidarity, should not adopt a purely passive attitude or one that is destructive of the social fabric, but, while claiming their legitimate rights, should do what they can for the good of all" (*Sollicitudo rei socialis*, 39).

60. Harry Frankfurt, *The Importance of What We Care About* (Cambridge: Cambridge University Press, 1998), 159-76; Harry Frankfurt, *The Reasons of Love* (Princeton, NJ: Princeton University Press, 2004), 10-17.

option for the poor in this sense is the acceptance of responsibility. This will be transformative. It is fundamentally transformative with regard to the relationship with God. Church documents have repeatedly outlined elements of such an option, which is primarily a theological option (EG 198) amounting to a particular "attentiveness." It is an option that has been characterized as not limited to material poverty and as not exclusive or discriminatory (*Centesimus annus* 57); however, it has to be conceded that material poverty because of its rawness teaches much about vulnerability, dependence, and interconnectedness. One could use the analogy of the relationship between "ordinary language" and "ideal language." The former provides "friction" and contact with the ground; the latter suggests refinement of the everyday way of speaking.[61] Material poverty provides friction; spiritual poverty offers refinement. Arguments for the primacy of ordinary language could be used to defend the indispensable importance of material poverty. The challenge will be to materialize spiritual poverty and to spiritualize material poverty, that is, to bring the two notions of poverty closer together, because, indeed, these are two different conceptions. "It seems that the 'poverty' that affluent Christians are obliged to live is not the same as the 'poverty' from which they are to liberate the poor."[62] The culture of encounter and sharing of life will lead to a broader learning process and the establishment of an ever-widening common ground of the experience of poverty.

An "option for the poor" is not *eo ipso* the same as "learning from the poor" or "being with the poor." It is a decision to be confronted with the life realities of poverty. It is a fact that many of us can go through our entire lives never coming into contact with—not even being aware of the existence of—certain sectors or groups of the society in which we live. An option for the poor is about showing attention and attentiveness, expecting something from the poor. In his interview with Antonio Spadaro, Pope Francis mentions Pedro Arrupe, who talked about the importance of having some time of real

61. Ludwig Wittgenstein, *Philosophical Investigations* (Oxford: Blackwell, 1967), 107.

62. John R. Schneider, *The Good of Affluence: Seeking God in a Culture of Wealth* (Grand Rapids, MI: Eerdman, 2002), 202.

contact with the poor. "This is really very important to me: the need to become acquainted with reality by experience, to spend time walking on the periphery in order really to become acquainted with the reality and life experiences of people. If this does not happen we then run the risk of being abstract ideologists or fundamentalists, which is not healthy."[63] Being in the company of poor people should not be a "project" or a "burden"; instrumentalizing the poor for the purposes of one's spiritual well-being is one important side of the "blindness to the human aspect," of treating human beings as if they were objects.

Susan Holman calls for "sensing need" as an entry into a credible option for the poor; "by 'sensing' I mean the individual's literal experience of the 'other' through the physical senses."[64] One needs to smell poverty, a smell that may be more of a stench in certain circumstances—Jesus encountering death and poverty ordered the tomb of Lazarus to be opened and Martha replied, "Lord, by now there will be a stench; he has been dead for four days" (John 11:39). This is the price of a direct encounter.

In the direct encounter we learn something we cannot learn otherwise. We enter a second-person perspective. A second-person perspective differs from *both* a first-person-singular and third-person-singular perspective.[65] A second-person perspective reveals new obligations to act upon and new ways of pursuing knowledge. Eleonore Stump develops Frank Cameron Jackson's well-known story about Mary and turns it into an experiment, "what Mary didn't know,"[66] to investigate and ponder this notion of second-person

---

63. A. Spadaro, "Wake up the World!" Conversation with Pope Francis about the Religious Life, in *La Civiltà Cattolica* 165 (2014/1), 4 (English translation by Fr. Donald Maldari, S.J.).

64. Holman, *God Knows There's Need*, 15.

65. Stephen Darwall, *The Second-Person Standpoint: Morality, Respect and Accountability* (Cambridge, MA: Harvard University Press, 2006). "Call the second-person standpoint the perspective you and I take up when we make and acknowledge claims on one another's conduct and will" (ibid., 3).

66. Frank C. Jackson, "Epiphenomenal Qualia," *Philosophical Quarterly* 32 (1982): 127-36; Frank C. Jackson, "What Mary Didn't Know," *Journal of Philosophy* 83 (1986): 291-95.

perspective and how it is impacted by narrations. [67] A girl by the name of Mary knows everything there is to know about people, even though she has never met her own mother. When she does finally meet her mother the encounter teaches her something she didn't know before: "Mary will know things she did not know before even if she knew everything about her mother that could be made available to her in expository prose, including her mother's psychological states."[68] The second-person perspective is one embedded within the framework of interaction; it is an engaged perspective, which provides a certain kind of knowledge that cannot be reduced to any other form of knowledge. Eleonore Stump thus attempts to show that this type of knowledge cannot be termed propositional knowledge ("knowledge that") and can only be expressed in and via narration; or, put another way, stories represent at least in part the distinct character of the second person in his or her account. The perspective made tangible in the account generates new aspects or shapes of reasoning, which Stephen Darwall refers to as "second-personal reasons," that is, reasons that become valid via structural relations based on acknowledging authority and accountability. An encounter will produce second-person knowledge, a kind of knowledge that can only be generated in an encounter with Other. It will be difficult to provide a precise definition of "the poor" because of "challenges raised by the encounter with the poor, who are encountered precisely as people, with all the complexities, contradictions and possibilities inherent in human existence."[69] Within a Church of the Poor there can be no claim to genuine knowledge of poverty without the expe-

---

67. Eleonore Stump, "Second-Person Accounts and the Problem of Evil," in K. E. Yandell, ed., *Faith and Narrative* (Oxford: Oxford University Press, 2001), 86-103; Eleonore Stump, "Narrative and the Problem of Evil: Suffering and Redemption," in Stephen T. Davis, Daniel Kendall, SJ, and Gerald O'Collins, SJ, eds., *The Redemption* (Oxford: Oxford University Press, 2004), 207-34; Eleonore Stump, "The Problem of Evil: Analytic Philosophy and Narrative," in Oliver Crisp and Michael C. Rea, eds., *Analytic Theology: New Essays in the Philosophy of Theology* (New York: Oxford University Press, 2009), 251-64.

68. Stump, "Second-Person Accounts," 88.

69. Tim Noble, *The Poor in Liberation Theology: Pathway to God or Ideological Construct?* (Sheffield: Equinox, 2013), 23.

rience of poverty; there can be no deep understanding without the deep encounter with poor people.

A commitment to a Church of the Poor must be to develop a real first-hand awareness of the reality of those living in poverty and not focus (and rely) on third-hand reports. *Evangelii gaudium* 46 exhorts us to go out to the fringes of humanity, to social fringes, moral fringes, epistemic fringes—to encounter those who "do not fit in." This important insight is expressed by Pedro Arrupe in his letter on poverty ("Carta sobre la pobreza," January 8, 1973), written as superior general of the Society of Jesus and addressed to Vicente D'Souza, the Jesuit provincial in India.[70] In this text, Pater Arrupe looks at our view of poverty within the context of Christian community of Christ. He considers the following points to be of central importance. (1) Evangelical poverty is a mystery that cannot be justified rationally ("*La razón, por sí sola, es incapaz de explicarla y de justificarla*"). (2) Poverty has to be felt to be understood; the longing to be poor is not enough; privation—as only the poor can know—has to be experienced first hand ("*sería ridículo decir que somos pobres si no tenemos ninguna experiencia de las privaciones que tienen los pobres*"). Privation should be experienced at some point in life even if only temporarily. (3) Those who are truly poor harvest the fruits of joy and inner freedom; experiences in poverty as witnessed in Arrupe's own country prove just how little we need to lead a happy and fulfilled life. (4) Being poor is having only that which is necessary for life and doing without what we do not need, including those little everyday things. (5) Need can only be understood by working and living with the poor; "need" experienced by individuals can be transferred to the wider, institutional context of a Jesuit community, where special attention has to be paid to benefits and privileges. These points are paramount when considering an "option for the poor" within a Church of the Poor.

French philosopher Luc Ferry suggested an interesting insight into an "option for the poor" without actually using the term itself; he talked about "the formula of a new imperative" that "could be more or less the following: "Act in such a way that the maxim of your action

---

70. http://www.sjmex.org/.

could be applied to those whom you love most. If I think about this more deeply, it strikes me that, if we conformed to such a maxim, we would treat foreigners or the unemployed differently from the way we do."[71] Indeed, we would have a thick concept of "neighbor," "sister," "brother." And indeed, we might have to think about the following question: Can there be "orthodoxy" without a proper relationship with sister and brother, neighbor and stranger? (Matt 5:23-24).

---

71. Luc Ferry, *On Love: A Philosophy for the Twenty-First Century,* trans. Andrew Brown (Cambridge: Polity, 2013), 171.

Chapter 4

A Church of the Poor

The poverty of Christ is the root of the gospel of joy, just as much as poverty of spirit is the root of the joy of the gospel. A Church of the Poor is nourished by these fountains of joy together. The joy of the gospel stands in stark contrast to the sadness of the rich young man (Mark 10:22) or the anger of the Pharisees when they feel provoked by Jesus (Luke 11:53); both reactions say something about a Church of the Poor. The poor are those who can rejoice about the gospel. The poor are those for whom the Gospels are truly "good news." Let us take a closer look at this as the criterion for a Church of the Poor; a Church of the Poor is a church that rejoices in the Gospels and is not afraid of Jesus' words directed at the intellectual and religious elites of his time. A Church of the Poor is not afraid of the Beatitudes, which express unusual sources of joy. Poverty of spirit (as expressed in the first beatitude) is costly, with its implication of renouncing everything that obstructs a nondivided heart. A Church of the Poor is nourished by these sources of "costly joy," of joy that cannot be separated from kenosis and suffering. Jesus' self-emptying is a source of joy for us, but I would also like to add that Jesus himself experienced joy, the joy of loving and the joy of being loved; he experienced the joy of hospitality, fellowship, and celebration. The first public miracle at the wedding of Cana described in the Gospel of John may be read as a symbolic expression of this joy.

Pope Francis's call for a Church of the Poor cannot be separated from an invitation to a renewal of Christian joy. It is the joy of being called by God, and it is the joy of being with brothers and sisters, especially with the poor. Being with the poor, as already stated in Chapter

98

3, is primarily a source of costly joy and not a "service" or a "work of mercy." The dynamics at work in being with the poor are similar to the dynamics of reconciliation: neither can be "sold" as a solution strategy or a strategy to offset costs; costly joy can be neither if it is genuine. A Church of the Poor is not a formal organization of poverty, but is a form of spirituality, a way of following Jesus.

In this chapter I will explore the concept "Church of the Poor" (4.1), reconstruct poverty in conversation with early Christian writers as a thorn in the flesh of the church (4.2), point out the risks and costs of a Church of the Poor exemplified in the medieval debates on poverty after St. Francis of Assisi (4.3), and offer some thoughts on the epistemological implications of a Church of the Poor (4.4).

4.1 A Call to Conversion

The exhortation to build a Church of the Poor expresses a radical vision that calls for conversion. The notion of a Church of the Poor is not new; in his radio address on September 11, 1962, Pope John XXIII emphasized the need for a global church for "all and especially the Church of the poor." Pope John is not talking about any one particular church, but the idea of a real world church rooted in poverty, with the vast majority of its believers being poor.[1] The subsequent discussion on the church and the poor during the Second Vatican Council was poignant. During the council a group known as "Church of the Poor" formed around Paul Gauthier, who was inspired by the spirituality of Charles de Foucauld.[2] The group met for the first time

1. John XXIII, Radio Message, September 11, 1962: *AAS* 54 (1962): 682. For Joseph Wresinski this message set the tone for the council: "Pope John XXIII's announcement at the beginning of Vatican Council II: 'The Church is the Church of the poor,' was a reminder of the proclamation 'The Good News is proclaimed to the poor.' This seems to me to be the essential message of Vatican II" (Gilles Anovil, *The Poor Are the Church: A Conversation with Father Joseph Wresinski* [Mystic, CT: Twenty-Third Publications, 2002], 24).

2. Desmond O'Grady, *Eat from God's Hands: Paul Gauthier and the Church of the Poor* (London: Chapman, 1965); see Gauthier's book *Consolez mon people*, which received the final editing in fall 1964 and was published in early 1965 (Paul Gauthier, *Consolez mon people* [Paris: Cerf, 1965]).

in October 1962 in the Belgian College with about a dozen bishops present. Cardinal Gerlier outlined a key concern that in the midst of human suffering the church should not be rich, but must be "mother of the Poor."[3] More than fifty bishops subsequently joined the second meeting in November of the same year, but in the months and years that followed the group dissolved because of the perceived narrowing of ideological judgment. Both Yves Congar and Henri de Lubac expressed their concern to this effect, together with the worry that a reductionist theology of the church was being brought about.[4] The group was unable to identify a proper theological basis broad enough to consider the diversity of the group. "The group's fundamental problem throughout the Council," Ian Linden concludes, "was the lack of theology that could incorporate the range of issues, doctrinal and developmental. . . . It was difficult to bring experiences as diverse as the Muslim world, the European worker milieu and missionary Sisters among black Americans, the plight of Latin American peasantry and the developing world, into a coherent story."[5] A Church of the Poor will be challenged with developing a theological vision consistent with tradition yet broad enough to incorporate the diversity of the experiences of poverty.

The motif of a Church of the Poor did not feature prominently in the council texts. We have seen in the first chapter that Pope Paul VI's first encyclical, written during the council and leaving the development of new insights explicitly to the ecumenical council, underlines the central importance of a lived spirit of poverty (*Ecclesiam suam* 54-55); these are reminders of key aspects of a Church of the Poor. The council itself did express, at least in a few passages, aspects of an "option for the poor." In the Dogmatic Constitution on the Church the self-emptying of Christ is presented with normative implications for the church, which "is not set up to seek earthly glory, but to

---

3. Joan Planellas I Barnosell, *La iglesia de los pobres en el Concilio Vaticano II* (Barcelona: Herder Editorial, 2014), 48-49.

4. Yves Congar, *Mon journal du Concile II* (Paris: Cerf, 2002), 264; Henri de Lubac, *Carnets du Concile I* (Paris: Cerf, 2007), 126.

5. Ian Linden, *Global Catholicism: Diversity and Change since Vatican II* (London: Hurst, 2009), 96.

proclaim, even by its own example, humility and self-sacrifice"; the church "encompasses with love all who are afflicted with human suffering and in the poor and afflicted sees the image of its poor and suffering Founder" (*Lumen gentium* 8). A Church of the Poor sees Christ in the moral and spiritual mirror of the poor and the afflicted.[6] The same document expresses a preferential concern for the church's "poor and sorrowing members and for those who are suffering persecution for justice's sake" (*Lumen gentium* 23). Christ is present in small and poor communities (*Lumen gentium* 26); holiness is a call to "follow the poor Christ, the humble and cross-bearing Christ" (*Lumen gentium* 41), and every Christian and every community is invited to "diffuse in the world that spirit which animates the poor, the meek, the peacemakers" (*Lumen gentium* 38). Mary, the mother of God, "stands out among the poor and humble of the Lord, who confidently hope for and receive salvation from Him" (*Lumen gentium* 55).

The commitment to a Church of the Poor is articulated in the famous opening lines of the Pastoral Constitution on the Church in the Modern World: "The joys and the hopes, the griefs and the anxieties of the men of this age, especially those who are poor or in any way afflicted, these are the joys and hopes, the griefs and anxieties of the followers of Christ" (*Gaudium et spes* 1). What does that mean? The followers of Christ must appropriate the joys and griefs of their fellow human beings. They have to share in it and make it their own. This is a leap of empathy. In *Laudato si'* Pope Francis finds words for the challenge leading to ecological conversion: "Our goal is not to amass information or to satisfy curiosity, but rather to become painfully aware, to dare to turn what is happening to the world into our own personal suffering and thus to discover what each of us can do about it" (*Laudato si'* 19); this is one way of approaching an exegesis of the opening words of *Gaudium et spes*. How can we turn what is

---

6. This mirror motif is also used in *Gaudium et spes* 88: "Christians should cooperate willingly and wholeheartedly in establishing an international order that includes a genuine respect for all freedoms and amicable brotherhood between all. This is all the more pressing since the greater part of the world is still suffering from so much poverty that it is as if Christ Himself were crying out in these poor to beg the charity of the disciples."

happening to our fellow sisters and brothers into our own joy and into our own grief? There is no other way than building common ground, entering the experiential horizon of another. Encounter presupposes and constitutes common ground.

Gaudium et spes 27 invokes the passage about Lazarus (Luke 16:18-31), one of the key passages used in the early church to describe its relationship with the poor. In language that reminds us of early Christian writers,[7] the council document identifies social injustice:

> At the very time when the development of economic life could mitigate social inequalities (provided that it be guided and coordinated in a reasonable and human way), it is often made to embitter them; or, in some places, it even results in a decline of the social status of the underprivileged and in contempt for the poor. While an immense number of people still lack the absolute necessities of life, some, even in less advanced areas, live in luxury or squander wealth. Extravagance and wretchedness exist side by side. While a few enjoy very great power of choice, the majority are deprived of almost all possibility of acting on their own initiative and responsibility, and often subsist in living and working conditions unworthy of the human person. (*Gaudium et spes* 63)

These lines express the distribution of privileges as a main challenge to society, but also to a Church of the Poor since the point about the uneven distribution of "power of choice" can also be applied to the institutional mechanisms of decision-making processes in the church, for example, in the case of the appointment of local bishops. The careful discussion of privileges, so it seems, emerges as a key tool in taking a Church of the Poor seriously. Questions like the following emerge as guiding questions: Who are the underprivileged? What kinds of privileges can be created and distributed? Who has access to and control over which privileges?

---

7. Cf. *Gaudium et spes* 69: "The Fathers and Doctors of the Church held this opinion, teaching that men are obliged to come to the relief of the poor and to do so not merely out of their superfluous goods."

This focus on a Church of the Poor comes to the fore again seven years later in the opening address of Pope Paul VI to the Latin American episcopate in 1968 in Bogotá and echoes points of the council, which closed in 1965: 14.2: hierarchy is closely affiliated with the rich; 14.3: the clergy live in safety, the poor live in fear and uncertainty; 14.18: the church should be free of all worldly ties, of dubious systems of prestige, free in spirit and thereby free of the restraints of wealth.[8] John Paul II mentions the notion of a Church of the Poor in an address to the residents of a favela in Rio de Janeiro in 1980[9] and again in *Laborem exercens*.[10] The International Theological Commission uses the term of Church of the Poor in its 1982 document *Penance and Reconciliation*, which describes the ecclesial foundations of reconciliation with an understanding of the church as the sacramental sign of forgiveness and reconciliation in a threefold way (as a church of the poor and suffering and those deprived of their rights; as a church of sinners, and as the persecuted church).[11] Here Church of the Poor is embedded in a context of spiritual and social reconciliation. It emphasizes an "option for the sinners," as we have seen in

---

8. Cf. Jon Sobrino, "La iglesia de los pobres desde el recuerdo de Monseñor Romero," *Revista lationoamericana de teología* 86 (2012): 135-55. Sobrino is here addressing the Catacomb Pact of 16 November 1965.

9. Quoted in *Redemptoris missio* 60: "As I said during my pastoral visit to Brazil: 'The Church all over the world wishes to be the Church of the poor ... she wishes to draw out all the truth contained in the Beatitudes of Christ, and especially in the first one: 'Blessed are the poor in spirit.' ... She wishes to teach this truth and she wishes to put it into practice, just as Jesus came to do and to teach" (*Address* to the residents of "Favela Vidigal" in Rio de Janeiro, July 2, 1980, *AAS* 72 [1980]: 854).

10. "For this reason, *there must be continued study of the subject of work* and of the subject's living conditions. In order to achieve social justice in the various parts of the world, in the various countries, and in the relationships between them, there is a need for ever new *movements of solidarity of* the workers and *with* the workers. This solidarity must be present whenever it is called for by the social degrading of the subject of work, by exploitation of the workers, and by the growing areas of poverty and even hunger. The Church is firmly committed to this cause, for she considers it her mission, her service, a proof of her fidelity to Christ, so that she can truly be the 'Church of the poor'" (*Laborem exercens* 8).

11. International Theological Commission, *Penance and Reconciliation* III,1.

some Gospel texts as well; it also reminds us of the spiritual dimension of poverty and thus the importance of the spiritual dimension in efforts to alleviate poverty[12] and of the realness of spiritual poverty. Because of the theological relevance of poverty it makes sense to conceive of a Church of the Poor theologically; it also makes sense to be clear about a connection between a "poor church" and a "Church of the Poor." These concerns have been outlined in an influential vision by Ignacio Ellacuría.[13] A poor church is not one living outside of the world of the poor but is one standing firmly in their midst and one providing help and assistance ungrudgingly; it is not limited by regional boundaries. The foundations of this church are theologal—that is based on the union of God with his people through Jesus Christ, who divested himself of all worldly ways. The poor enable and empower the salutary nature of the church, which in turn is incarnate in the poor; and only by devoting itself to them utterly, by literally dying for them, can it become a truly Christian tool of salvation for all humanity. The poor are the mainstay of the church (they are the core principle on which the church is structured). A poor church is one that is persecuted by the rich, an appalling reality attested on November 16, 1989, with the murder of those speaking up for a Church of the Poor. This is a church structured and constructed from within by the poor, a church that recognizes the poor as having and being the healing and salutary properties for its own existence and meaning in the world. In being incarnate in the poor, the church can become an effective sign of salvation for the whole of humankind. The church can become this sign if the church points to the kingdom, if the church "embodies" or "enacts" the kingdom of God, if the church is empty enough to be open to the kingdom. In other words, the main point of a Church of the Poor, with its calling into question of privileges, is the overcoming of a spirit of worldliness.

---

12. Cf. J. Beyers, "The Effect of Religion on Poverty," *HTS Teologiese Studies/ Theological Studies* 70, no. 1 (2014): Art. #2614.
13. Ignacio Ellacuria, "La iglesia de los pobres. Sacramento histórico de la liberación," *Estudios centroamericanos* 32 (1977): 707-22.

4.2 Poverty as a Thorn in the Flesh

The question of a spirit of worldliness is a permanent challenge for the church in the world. The reality of poverty keeps the question of the relationship of church and world, church and power, church and wealth alive. There is always the temptation "not to see" and "not to hear" (Matt 11:15). There is always the temptation to think of the church as a rose without thorns. A church without the "have-nots" may be attractive to the "haves" because poverty is a constant thorn in the flesh of those who "have," and not only in the softer sense of spiritual reminders of the value of almsgiving or the appropriateness of gratitude but in the harsher and stricter sense of the church's theory of property. The first social encyclical, *Rerum novarum*, summarized what the church's teaching had been on this point. While there is a right to private property, this right is not an absolute right: "Man should not consider his material possessions as his own, but as common to all, so as to share them without hesitation when others are in need."[14] According to Aquinas, natural law prescribes that the possession of all things should be in common, although this does not mean that natural law dictates that all things should be common possessions. There can be private property but, as property established by positive law, the ownership of possessions is not contrary to natural law but a super-addition.[15] Thus, the natural-law-based universal destination of goods supersedes private-property claims in cases of dire need. Any accumulation of wealth is morally inacceptable from a Christian point of view as long as there are people whose basic needs have not been met. This statement encapsulates the deep commitment of the Christian Social Tradition, both biblically grounded and founded in early Christian writings.

Helen Rhee summarizes the challenge in a principle "that the concern to meet others' needs takes priority over accumulation of

---

14. *Rerum novarum* 22; the significance of private property is stated in *Rerum novarum* 6–9.

15. STh II-II, 66,2, ad 1; cf. Anton Hermann Chroust and Robert J. Affeldt, "The Problem of Private Property according to St. Thomas Aquinas," *Marquette Law Review* 34, no. 3 (1950–1951): 151-82.

my surplus assets. . . . Beyond sufficiency and common enjoyment, we do not have a 'natural right' to accumulation of wealth."[16] It is difficult to argue away this challenge since the claim is strong and has many implications. It implies that possessions beyond a sufficiency (or "decency") threshold fall under the jurisdiction of a different pattern of justification. The first challenge is to identify and define this threshold: just how much is "enough"? There is a beautiful word in Swedish to express exactly this sense of *enoughness*—the concept of *lagom*. *Lagom* means "exactly enough," "just the right amount," "north of sufficiency, but still south of excess."[17] Where is the *"lagom* line" for the different types of possessions we have—shoes, for instance? Obviously, this is an ongoing challenge, a thorn in the flesh that asks for regular monitoring. This question will apply to Christian households as well as to Christian institutions within the context of a commitment to a Church of the Poor.

The second challenge is the carving out of our obligations. In an influential paper Peter Singer had argued in the early 1970s that we have a moral obligation to forgo whatever is not strictly necessary, given the plight and destitution of so many people. If you can save a life, his argument goes, without forgoing a moral good of comparable significance, you will have a duty to save this life.[18] If one agrees with this principle, the implications are deep and would not allow for unnecessary expenses.

This issue of a threshold of sufficiency and decency will be a defining feature in the way individuals but also institutional components within the church deal with property and assets. One element of the message is that poverty is a thorn in the flesh that serves as a moral mirror of society, since concern for the poor limits legitimate growth.

---

16. Helen Rhee, *Loving the Poor, Saving the Rich: Wealth, Poverty and Early Christian Formation* (Grand Rapids, MI: Baker Academic, 2012), 193-94.

17. Alan Atkisson, "The lagom Solution," in Cecile Andrews and Wanda Urbanska, eds., *Less Is More: Embracing Simplicity for a Healthy Planet, a Caring Economy and Lasting Happiness* (Gabriola Island, BC: New Society Publishers, 2010), 101-6.

18. Peter Singer, "Famine, Affluence and Morality," *Philosophy and Public Affairs* 1, no. 3 (1972): 229-43, at 231.

The Scriptures express this thorn in the flesh of a self-righteous person or in the flesh of a careless society differently—by way of theological justification for a moral life; as a repository of commands and principles; as a source of examples of moral behavior; as offering an eschatological vision of the future good.[19]

Poverty is a fourfold provocation: moral, spiritual, social, and material. Poverty pricks and provocatively wounds moral standards both in terms of judgments about the moral state of a society (i.e., what is wrong with a social system if there is persistent poverty?) and in terms of the moral challenges of a person's form of life (how can we lead a moral life in the midst of poverty?). Poverty is a spiritual provocation since it forces people to take sides and come down on one clear side of the fence. A provocation is a phenomenon that elicits a reaction, that forces people into a responsive mode. This is what poverty does; it does not acknowledge neutral moral spaces, nor does it allow or tolerate so-called innocent times. An ivory-tower notion of intellectual and moral integrity is not compatible with an attitude of indifference to poverty in the midst of affluence.

The provocative power of poverty is intensified in the Gospels with Jesus' foundational praxis of siding with the poor. "Foundational praxis" means that there is an exemplary form of life that opens up new possibilities for the social and spiritual imagination. Jesus' foundational praxis leaves us with a sense of the finality of nonresolution.[20] Early Christian writings wrestled with the implications of the foundational praxis of Jesus from the very beginning. The three main Gospel passages that were most frequently used in early Christian writings to develop teachings on poverty are the above-mentioned

19. Warner M. Bailey, "'I was hungry...'—The Bible and Poverty," *Journal of Presbyterian History* 59, no. 2 (1981) 181-96, at 182-83.

20. Oliver Davies, *Theology of Transformation* (Oxford: Oxford University Press, 2013), 205. Mary Gordon develops open questions that will not go away and ends her book on grappling with the Gospels with three questions: "Why do you weep?"; "Whom do you seek?"; "Who do you say I am?" and introduces them with the simple sentence: "I am committed to the questions, unsusceptible to final answers" (Mary Gordon, *Reading Jesus: A Writer's Encounter with the Gospels* [New York: Pantheon Books, 2009], 205).

encounter with the rich young man, the final judgment in Matthew 25:31-46 (with its clear message, "Whatever you did for one of these least brothers of mine, you did for me"), and the parable of the rich man and Lazarus in Luke 16:19-31. These passages speak not about poverty as an ascetic ideal but about the need for solidarity with the poor, which means "a revolution in the social imagination."[21] The poor are not singled out because poverty is valuable in itself, but because God has a special closeness to those who are defenseless. And this says more about God than about the nature of poverty.[22] Poverty can be a means to get closer to God since it invites trust in God because of the sheer fact of absolute dependence. The first beatitude (Matt 5:3, "Blessed are the poor in spirit") can be read as a message about an undivided heart, a heart set on God and God alone, a simple heart that is not filled with many other concerns that would stand in the way of a relationship between a person and God. There is a special blessing for those who "lack" something, "thirst" for something, are "hungry" (Matt 5:3–4:6; Luke 6:20-21) and are thus open to what only God can give. Poverty is epistemically privileged in that it is an adverse condition that makes people thirst for transformation. Saturation is not a situation that brings about hunger or thirst. It is difficult to thirst for justice if one constantly experiences life as saturated. In this sense poverty can be seen as a condition that has the potential to free a person to follow Jesus, just like the disciples left their socio-economic security (at least in some sense) to follow Jesus. Clearly, poverty is not a value in itself but a form of life that can lead to spiritual wealth and strength. By way of analogy, wealth is not seen as intrinsically evil but as a social condition that could potentially be destructive to or beneficial for the common good.

Early Christian writings dealt with wealth and poverty in numerous places; these writings are instructive since they show a "first debate" on poverty. First debates are important; they can be compared

---

21. Peter Brown, *Poverty and Leadership in the Later Roman Era: The Menahem Stern Jerusalem Lectures* (Hanover, NH: Brandeis University Press, 2002), 1.

22. Donald Senior, "Religious Poverty and the Ministry of Jesus," *American Benedictine Review* 26, no. 2 (1975): 169-79, at 173.

to a first sentence in a book, which can be seen to establish a contract between author and reader.[23] Similarly, first debates on important issues provide points of reference, establish contracts of interpretation. Let us explore some aspects of these first debates on poverty and the church in this section.

Early Christian texts on wealth and poverty have to be read and studied within the context and economics of the Roman Empire[24] with its preindustrial economy (mainly local agriculture for subsistence) and just a few elements of "proto-capitalism" (trade, monetization). Wealth was based on land rather than productivity; the economy was "embedded in social institutions such as kinship, marriage," which also meant that the economy was governed more by social values than by economic rationality. Issues such as power, position, privilege, prestige, patronage played a major role. Special connections to the emperor were key; the support systems would have been be guided by standards of *honestas* and *liberalitas* (the generous person will give to the right person). Elites were few, the middle class weak, the vast majority of the population poor. Among the poor we find farming families, unattached widows, orphans, disabled persons, beggars, unskilled day laborers, prisoners. There were categories such as *inopes* (resourceless), *egentes* (needy), *pauperes* (poor), *humiles* (lowly), *abiecti* (outcast) constituting "the many" (*vulgus, turba, plebs*). The rise of the urban poor was due to rural flight (because of repeated crop failures and an influx of slave labor) and urbanization. Again, we find a world mostly dark and fearful. It was in this world that Christianity rose to social significance, an impressive rise in sheer numbers based on issues such as social capital and community building, an offer of a better future, a narrative to explain present conditions (famously spelled out in Augustine's *City of God*), better mechanisms to cope with crises such as natural disasters.[25] Rodney Stark also argues that any new religious movements will mainly draw their converts from the ranks of the religiously inactive and discontented

23. Amos Oz, *The Story Begins: Essays on Literature,* trans. Maggie Bar-Tura (New York: Harcourt Brace, 1999).

24. Rhee, *Loving the Poor, Saving the Rich,* 1-26.

25. Rodney Stark, *The Rise of Christianity* (Princeton, NJ: Princeton University Press, 1996).

and those affiliated with the most accommodated (worldly) religious communities, those with most skepticism vis-à-vis the established religion, that is, the middle and privileged classes. This could be a window into understanding the new theological challenges around poverty and wealth at that time (Christianity attracting people in need of a vision of a better life as well as people, such as intellectual elites, discontent with established religious systems). Furthermore, Christianity with its clear position against infanticide offered new roles for women, which may have led to a number of secondary conversions. The changing sociological nature of the Christian community is reflected in an array of approaches to the question of wealth and poverty.

Early Christian writings display a spectrum of positions regarding poverty and wealth. A comparison of four first- and early-second-century texts could illustrate this theological space. (1) The book of Revelation with its image of the beast (Roman Empire) as superpower against God, an evil that also produces social evil through exploitation, with the origin of poverty seen as lying in the imperial system; the poor should denounce wealth; the rich should divest. (2) Two key passages from the letter of James (James 2:1-7; 5:1-6), with its outright criticism of the social system, identify local elites as the origin of poverty and ask the poor to tolerate wealth and the rich to correct social problems. (3) The book of Acts, with its emphasis on communal property (Acts 2:42-45: 4:32-37), is silent on issues of economic injustice and does not provide any justification for the economic rationale of community life; it does not broach the origins of poverty but exhorts the poor to embrace the rich and the rich to support the church.[26] The example of the community in Jerusalem described in the book of Acts does not provide clarity. How do we deal with people who have given everything away, and what would shield them from destitution in times of a disaster?[27] Do we actually know whether

---

26. Luke Timothy Johnson claims that Luke described the Jerusalem community in general and probably idealized terms since they provide a piece of narrative art (Luke Timothy Johnson, *The Literary Function of Possessions in Luke-Acts* [Missoula, MT: Scholars Press, 1977], 1-28).

27. Cf. Barry Gordon, *The Economic Problem in Biblical and Patristic Thought* (Leiden: Brill, 1989), 79.

Barnabas (mentioned in Acts 4:37) really gave away all his worldly goods? We are told only that he sold "a field" and gave the proceeds to the apostles. "This narrative scene gives us no intellectual right to infer that Barnabas sold all his property, or even that he ceased to be well-off in comparison with average Israelites."[28] (4) The *Shepherd of Hermas* describes wealth as a gift from God that can bring difficulties and temptations, but these moral and spiritual risks can be curbed by helping the poor through individual acts of charity that will buy goods in heaven.[29] The book sees God and divine providence as the origin of poverty, asks the poor to depend on the rich and the rich to earn their salvation by almsgiving. These positions share the spiritual concerns and the recognition of interconnectedness. But there is no moral clarity about behavioral guidelines.

It is not surprising, then, that early Christian writings would basically oscillate between two readings on wealth: a "moral compromise and social harmony reading" and a "radical incompatibility reading." Both readings were based on "a pervasive mistrust of the material world."[30] Both readings had to take account of the "turn to the inner" in the Sermon on the Mount, where Jesus exhorts his audience to cultivate awareness of the *inner* rather than relying on *external* criteria in the observable social sphere: "You have heard that it was said, 'You shall not commit adultery.' But I say to you, everyone who looks at a woman with lust has already committed adultery with her in his heart" (Matt 5:27-28). Both readings were possible because of the hermeneutical openness of the Gospels. John the Baptist, for instance, expresses fairly moderate claims (Luke 3:10-14): people with surplus—the haves—should share in order to meet the basic needs of the have-nots ("Whoever has two tunics should share with the person who has none. And whoever has food should do likewise"); tax collectors should collect only what is owing, and soldiers should

---

28. John Schneider, *The Good of Affluence: Seeking God in a Culture of Wealth* (Grand Rapids, MI: Eerdmans, 2002), 203.

29. See the Second Similitude: "As the Vine is supported by the elm, so is the Rich Man helped by the prayer of the poor."

30. Rebecca H. Weaver, "Wealth and Poverty in the Early Church," *Interpretation* 41, no. 4 (1987): 368-81, at 369.

not practice extortion and should be content with their wages. Even though the first claim has the potential to be socially explosive, there is no evidence that more systematic and deeper political reforms were being suggested.

The first hermeneutical line has been largely influenced by Clement of Alexandria's treatise "Who Is the Rich Man That Shall Be Saved?"[31] This treatise works with the "open end" of the Mark 10:17-31 passage: "the question as to whether or not the rich person who enquired of Jesus how he might gain eternal life did in fact refuse to become a disciple is not answered within the synoptic narratives."[32] Clement of Alexandria, working in a wealthy context, was confronted with the question as to whether one could be rich *and* a Christian. Clement accepts the moral challenges of wealth (wealth can corrupt: I, II, XX) but states at the outset that the inheritance of the kingdom of heaven is not absolutely unattainable for the rich if they obey the commandments (III). He interprets the rich man of Mark 10 as a person lacking life, lacking the good (VIII, X); and then he makes the influential interpretative move to suggest that Jesus' exhortation to him to sell his possessions has to be understood metaphorically: Jesus "does not, as some conceive off-hand, bid him throw away the substance he possessed, and abandon his property; but bids him banish from his soul his notions about wealth, his excitement and morbid feeling about it, the anxieties, which are the thorns of existence, which choke the seed of life" (XI). Clement argues a nonliteral interpretation of this passage: "So that (the expression) rich men that shall with difficulty enter into the kingdom, is to be apprehended in a scholarly way, not awkwardly, or rustically, or carnally" (XVIII). This, then, is the decisive move, the key hermeneutical decision. Clement points out that the

31. I will use the following version: *Clement of Alexandria, Who Is the Rich Man That Shall Be Saved?* trans. William Wilson; Ante-Nicene Fathers, vol. 2; ed. Alexander Roberts, James Donaldson, and A. Cleveland Coxe (Buffalo, NY: Christian Literature Publishing Co., 1885).

32. Andrew D. Clarke, "'Do Not Judge Who Is Worthy and Unworthy': Clement's Warning Not to Speculate about the Rich Young Man's Response (Mark 10.17-31)," *Journal for the Study of the New Testament* 31, no. 4 (2009): 447-68, at 448.

renunciation of wealth can be for the wrong reasons (e.g., to impress) and can lead to the wrong results (e.g., to an intensification of the passions of the soul [XII]). He argues for the usefulness of wealth, which puts people in a position to assist others (XIII), which also means that "riches ... which benefit also our neighbors are not to be thrown away" (XIV). He also underscores the theological challenge of divine injustice if those rich through "involuntary birth in wealth" (XXVI) were to be excluded from the kingdom of God. The main criterion in each and every context outlined above is the state of the soul and its purity (XV): "into the impure soul the grace of God finds not entrance" (XVI). The key point is to be "rich in virtue" (XIX). Consequently, the most painful persecution is not social and external but internal, "which proceeds from each man's own soul being vexed by impious lusts, and diverse pleasures, and base hopes, and destructive dreams" (XXV).

One might say that Clement's interpretation does not do justice to the texts; it waters down the "thorniness" of the passage and does not do justice to the point of costly discipleship that the passage invokes: "Clement gladly widens the needle's eye to welcome the rich who generously give."[33] One might also say that Clement fell into the trap of "spiritualizing" wealth and poverty. This is an ongoing theological challenge. It is theologically dangerous in daring to lose credibility by spiritualizing matters of lifestyle too quickly, for example, in the discourse on a vow of poverty: "a life according to the Vow of Poverty without any likeness with a life in involuntary poverty should not be called a life in Poverty."[34] The question of poverty must remain a "thorn in the flesh" to prevent moral self-righteousness and spiritual complacency.

---

33. Elizabeth A. Clarke, *History, Theory, Text: Historians and the Linguistic Turn* (Cambridge, MA: Harvard University Press, 2004), 173; for a deeper exploration, see Annewies van den Hoek, "Widening the Eye of the Needle. Wealth and Poverty in the Works of Clement of Alexandria," in Susan R. Holman, ed., *Wealth and Poverty in Early Church and Society* (Grand Rapids, MI: Baker Academic, 2008), 67-75.

34. Jan G. J. Van den Eijnden, *Poverty on the Way to God: Thomas Aquinas on Evangelical Poverty* (Leuven: Peeters, 1994), 245.

It may also be interesting for hermeneutical reasons to compare Clement of Alexandria's reading with Archbishop Oscar Romero's reading of the same passage: In his homily on October 14, 1979, on "Three Conditions to Enter the Kingdom of God," related to the Gospel reading of the day, Mark 10:17-30, Oscar Romero was surprisingly close to Clement of Alexandria's interpretation. He reconstructed the young man's question, "Good teacher, what must I do to inherit eternal life?" as the existential key question and Jesus' point about goodness as the deep theological message: "God is the source of goodness. If there is something good on earth, it is because it reflects God." He sees a dialogue of goodness and stresses Jesus' look of love toward the young man, which also serves to point out that the church bears no grudge against rich people; it is not leading a campaign against wealthy people. And then Romero makes the point about the justifiability of wealth just like Clement of Alexandria:

> [Jesus] affirms that wealth is good and that happiness can be found in this world but none of these should be erected as an idol. . . . There is nothing wrong with having money but to place one's trust in money is to make money an idol when in fact we should place our trust only in the one true God. . . . Jesus is telling the disciples that one can have wealth, but this wealth must be used on behalf of love and justice, must be used to do good. This, however, is a miracle and only God is able to do this."[35]

Similar to Clement of Alexandria, Archbishop Romero preaches a spirit of detachment and, quoting the encyclical *Populorum progressio* 19, calls to mind the destructive force of avarice. He is also convinced

---

35. "Pero Cristo viene a poner las cosas en su puesto y a decir que si es verdad que es buena la riqueza y que existe la felicidad también en este mundo, no hay que endiosarla. . . . Tener dinero no es malo pero poner su confianza en el dinero es convertir el dinero en Dios, sólo en Dios hay que tener confianza. . . . Con esto está diciendo que puede haber riquezas, donde el hombre se convierta a usar las riquezas al servicio del amor, de la justicia, a hacer el bien. Pero esto es un milagro, sólo Dios lo puede hacer" (http://www.sicsal.net/romero/homilias/B/791014.htm).

that the *status animae* is the key point at stake, with the challenge of following Jesus wholeheartedly, unreservedly, with an undivided heart. The homily develops three conditions for the kingdom of God in conversation with the gospel: fulfill the commandments, cultivate a spirit of poverty and detachment, and follow Jesus. These points can be easily reconciled with the second-century treatise. Unlike Clement of Alexandria, however, Oscar Romero transfers the challenge of the gospel to a political level: "Let there be no doubt that El Salvador has separated itself from God and only by listening to Jesus' response to the young man can we find the path of salvation: fulfill the law of the Lord." Romero is aware that this can be painful "to those who make idols out of the things of this world." He uses the criterion of detachment as a criterion for proper political judgment: "Those who are poor in spirit can see the relationship between the present situation in El Salvador and the avarice of those who are wealthy. Those who lack this spirit of poverty do not have eyes that enable them to see that detachment provides them with great freedom and a great sensitivity to the economic and social problems of El Salvador."[36] Oscar Romero argues that wealth and Christian identity are compatible, as long as wealth is connected to the appropriate attitudes and these attitudes to the appropriate behavior, that is, to the use of wealth: He concluded his lengthy homily with an invitation to inclusive participation: "All the social classes in El Salvador can do much" ("Todas las categorías de El Salvador pueden hacer mucho").

Romero's reading illustrates the possibility of reconciling political responsibility with a non-antiwealth reading of Mark 10. Notwithstanding the criticism that Clement of Alexandria's interpretation of Mark 10 may have blunted the cutting edge of the message, it seems to be clear that (1) the inner criteria of the state of the soul invoked by Clement can be interpreted quite radically, and that (2) there is

---

36. "Nadie puede encontrar la relación que existe entre las desgracias actuales de El Salvador y esta avaricia de las clases poderosas, como el que tiene espíritu de pobreza. El que no tiene espíritu de pobreza no tiene ojos limpios para mirar que el desprendimiento concede una gran libertad y una gran sensibilidad para los grandes problemas económicos y sociales de El Salvador" (http://www.sicsal.net/romero/homilias/B/791014.htm).

a revolution in social perception in the sense that the poor matter to the rich. So even without systematic structural change there was the opening toward the transformation of the social imagination.

Another influential author struggling with the question of a possible social harmony between wealth and poverty was John Chrysostom, who wrote in the fourth century mostly in the socially divided city of Antioch with its overt display of the luxury of the rich and the reality of the misery and destitution of many. Chrysostom himself was a theological leader who had embraced extreme asceticism for a few years after renouncing the family wealth. He can be seen as a representative of the second hermeneutical line of understanding wealth, an "incompatibility reading." "He was convinced that God had not created one rich and the other poor. To be honorably rich was not possible."[37] However, he did not push for systematic structural reforms but presented the model of a harmonious city with mutual assistance and dependence: the rich need the poor to be saved; the poor need the rich to survive. Consequently, he stressed the virtue of humility and the importance of *eleēmosynē* (which is more than almsgiving, but points to a fundamental attitude of sharing that includes benevolence, hospitality, and charity). He used his sermons to win listeners over to mercy by appealing to human compassion, reminders of the smallness of the demand and the reward in heaven, by the thought of the common human nature of Christ and his hearers, by remembering Jesus' passion on the cross and the final judgment before the theater of all humanity. He used vivid descriptions (e.g., in his treatment of the Lazarus story, where he would compare the rich man to a wolf (rapacious), a lion (savage temper), a cobra (deceitful), or even a stone (merciless, shameless), and where he would applaud the patient silence of Lazarus and, more generally, of poor people (meekness, humility).[38]

---

37. Rudolf Brändle, "The Sweetest Passage. Matthew 25:31-46 and Assistance to the Poor in the Homilies of John Chrysostom," in Susan R. Holman, ed., *Wealth and Poverty in Early Church and Society* (Grand Rapids, MI: Baker Academic, 2008), 127-39, at 129.

38. Francine Cardman, "Poverty and Wealth as Theater: John Chrysostom's Homilies on Lazarus and the Rich Man," in Susan R. Holman, ed., *Wealth and*

In his homilies Chrysostom frequently made a stark distinction between "the inner" and "the outer" (inner wealth versus outer wealth, inner servitude versus outer servitude).[39] This juxtaposition allowed him to pursue a certain "anthropological egalitarianism" (if one were to consider that both rich and poor dimensions are equal in the sense that one group loses out on the other dimension). This would also motivate his idea of the harmony of different social strata within a community.[40] At the same time, however, John Chrysostom did follow a hands-on approach and set up charitable institutions in Antioch (hospitals, hostels for strangers, widows properly registered, to be supported by the church), thus professionalizing and institutionalizing charity. He was also one of the first influential writers to reflect on the dangers of a rich church that was busy with administering money. And he did make mention of the primacy of the alleviation of poverty over liturgical concerns ("The fellow human is a temple of God, and this temple is far more important than the temple of the church building"[41]) and about the questionable form of life of wealth, including the claim that it was not possible to be honorably rich.[42] The tone of his preaching is particularly provocative in the face of hunger and famine, and delivers the message that the rich should be held responsible for hunger since they are abusing available resources because of their misplaced values.[43] However, in a certain sense, there is an "appeasement approach" in John Chrysostom's writings. The main message could be that while there is no need to change estab-

Poverty in Early Church and Society (Grand Rapids, MI: Baker Academic, 2008), 159-75.

39. See especially Homily 90 on Matthew, Homilies 2 and 18 on Hebrews, and his sermons on Luke 16:19-31.

40. Nicu Dumitraşcu, "Poverty and Wealth in the Orthodox Spirituality (with Special Reference to St. John Chrysostom)," *Dialog: A Journal of Theology* 49, no. 4 (2010): 300-305, esp. 301.

41. Brändle, "The Sweetest Passage," 134. Brändle refers to Homily 50 on Matthew.

42. Ibid., 129. The statement is based on an understanding of wealth as having gold, silver, precious stones, or silks.

43. Hennie Stander, "Chrysostom on Hunger and Famine," *HTS Teologiese Studies / Theological Studies* 67, no. 1 (2011): Art. #880.

lished conditions, the frameworks that are given should be used in a morally and spiritually responsible way.

Around the time of the fourth century, however, the second hermeneutical line to discuss the relation between wealth and the gospel becomes clearly visible, a line more radical in that it challenges existing structures. This is a theology of decision based on complete disjunction: either God or Mammon. Aloysius Pieris argues for this reading by working with the hermeneutical principle that "in Jesus, God and the poor have formed an alliance against their common enemy: Mammon."[44] Jesus is clear about his judgment of an irreconcilable opposition between God and money (on the basis of Matt 6:24). Mammon is more than assets; it is an attitude of mind; it is "an acquisitive instinct driving me to be the Rich Fool that Jesus ridicules in the parable (Luke 12:13-21)."[45] The twofold thesis of (1) the connection between wealth and love of Mammon and (2) the mutual exclusivity of service to God and Mammon constitutes a basis for much more challenging questions with regard to the *status quo*.

The Cappadocian Fathers, especially Basil of Caesarea, show a commitment to this more radical way of viewing the relationship of poverty and the gospel. They argued for social equality; they pursued an "option for the insignificant," reminded wealthy Christians of the fundamental Christian obligation to share, based on the idea of the human person bearing the image of God, referring to Luke 16 and Matthew 25 as key passages, and based on a clear vision of God as judge and savior.[46] Again, as in the case of Chrysostom, humanitarian plights triggered these more radical positions. There are reasons to believe that events in the year 369, particularly a severe famine, triggered a substantial change in leadership style, a change in organized charity, a change in lived solidarity, and a change in the social imagi-

---

44. Aloysius Pieris, "To Be Poor as Jesus Was Poor?" *The Way* 24 (1984): 186-97, at 186 (text reprinted in A. Pieris, *An Asian Theology of Liberation* [Edinburgh: T&T Clark, 1988], 15-23).

45. Ibid., 187.

46. Brian Daley, "The Cappadocian Fathers and the Option for the Poor," in Daniel Groody, ed., *The Option for the Poor in Christian Theology* (Notre Dame, IN: University of Notre Dame Press, 2007), 77-88.

nation culminating in the belief that the dying poor are our concern.[47] The famine that struck the region was the point of departure for a new sense of responsibility. "Basil, bishop of the capital city, Caesarea . . . , immediately began to preach on the moral connection between the hyper-retentive lifestyle of the rich and the meteorological retention of a catastrophic seasonal drought that had caused disaster, particularly for the now-starving poor."[48] Poverty was not only the concern of the poor; it was, in part, caused by the rich. This new belief overcame hitherto prevailing indifference and made way for a new sense of solidarity.

Basil was deeply committed to social welfare.[49] In his funeral oration on Bishop Basil, Gregory of Nazianzus (Oration 43.34-36) describes the unbearable circumstances prevailing at the time: "The city was in distress, and there was no source of assistance, or relief for the calamity . . . the hardest part of all such distress is, the insensibility and insatiability of those who possess supplies. For they watch their opportunities, and turn the distress to profit, and thrive upon misfortune" (34).[50] Basil was able to persuade shopowners to open their stores, and he "gathered together the victims of the famine with some who were but slightly recovering from it, men and women, infants, old men, every age which was in distress, and obtaining contributions of all sorts of food which can relieve famine, set before them basins of soup and such meat as was found preserved among us, on which the poor live" (35). Basil succeeded in establishing charitable institutions (a complex for different groups of the poor, a "ptochotropheion"), and he succeeded in transforming the *sensus moralis* of his commu-

---

47. Susan Holman, *The Hungry Are Dying: Beggars and Bishops in Roman Cappadocia* (Oxford: Oxford University Press, 2001), 64-98.

48. Susan Holman, *God Knows There's Need: Christian Responses to Poverty* (Oxford: Oxford University Press, 2009), 51.

49. Cf. Susan Holman, "Rich City Burning: Social Welfare and Ecclesial Insecurity in Basil's Mission to Armenia," *Journal of Early Christian Studies* 12, no. 2 (2004): 195-215.

50. Gregory of Nazianzus, *Select Orations*, trans. Charles Gordon Browne and James Edward Swallow; Nicene and Post-Nicene Fathers, Second Series, vol. 7; ed. Philip Schaff and Henry Wace (Buffalo, NY: Christian Literature Publishing Co., 1894).

nity, thus shifting the boundaries of collective moral perception. He worked according to "syngeneis" ("kinship") to underline the egalitarian design of God's creation. Basil was particularly outspoken against avarice and usury, and he considered the vice of greed as destructive for the whole person.[51] Usury was identified as a particularly foul and nasty game because it exploited a state of emergency, characterized by anxiety and distress, added to the people's plight and privation by acting in a premeditated and purposeful way to achieve its own ends. At the same time we also find the following challenging question: Can you be a Christian and a businessman?[52] Business dealings in fourth-century Constantinople were generally eyed with suspicion because they were thought to obscure Christian identity and responsibilities; businesspeople were characterized by their "desire for gain," which created a spiritual challenge because this desire might well blur powers of judgment and perception. Poverty was depicted as a shield providing protection from avarice; efforts were made to include the poor in the scope of concern of Christian communities. In other words, a process of "painstaking" steps was clearly being taken to establish poverty as a thorn in the flesh of the rich.

However, we cannot really say that these centuries were paving the way for a Church of the Poor; a church was not being constructed that would put the perspectives and point of view of the underprivileged and disadvantaged center stage. In fact, the early church widely took social stratification for granted, with the *scandalon* of an organization that owned slaves, or the fact that Gregory the Great "ordered Vitalius, rector of Sardinia, to help Gregory's agent purchase local pagans as slaves for the church that these pagan slaves would then do the mundane and dirty relief tasks for a Roman parish ministry to the destitute poor."[53] This system of "clean hands" and delegation is definitely not Pope Francis's vision of a Church of the Poor. It may be

---

51. Brenda Llewellyn Ihssen, "Basil and Gregory's Sermons on Usury: Credit Where Credit Is Due," *Journal of Early Christian Studies* 16, no. 3 (2008): 403-30.

52. Rhee, *Loving the Poor, Saving the Rich,* ch. 6.

53. Holman, *God Knows There's Need,* 13.

difficult to find obvious traces of "cleanliness" in the early church. The key passages (Matt 25; Luke 16; Mark 10) were at the time interpreted more in terms of moral and social harmony with the poor, who were regarded less as epistemic agents than as "objects of works of mercy." Nonetheless, in those early years, some tough questions and some radical thoughts do emerge that continue to challenge the credibility of the church's lifestyle. The discussion of the real meaning of the "vow of poverty," for instance, echoes these concerns. Thomas Merton, to name a prominent example, saw collective poverty as a major challenge in this regard: a monk may be personally poor but still inclined to make excessive demands in his job asking for (and even expecting) extravagant and exorbitant payment to cover "so-say" costs incurred, seeking to satisfy selfish needs under the pretext of "working for the common good."[54] Poverty is a key issue in spiritual integrity: Merton (in his conferences as novice master) quotes Dom Delatte: "It is a matter of experience that apostasy begins almost always with violations of poverty."[55] That is why the ownership of community goods has to be clearly regulated; the monk must not take, retain, borrow, lend, give, destroy, or use without or beyond reasonable permission.[56] These normative ideas can also be applied (*cum grano salis*) to the use of personal private property in the light of its common-good orientation. I can use my private property but with morally informed prudence and wisdom-filled compassion. This is an ongoing concern; there is no way to establish a "system" that would make the question of proper use of property disappear. The question of the state, concept, meaning, and role of poverty and property is an ongoing criterion that has to be safeguarded and constantly assessed, re-assessed, and applied. It is a thorn in the flesh and must remain so: The accumulation of wealth is morally inacceptable from a Christian point of view as long as there are people whose basic needs have not been met.

---

54. Thomas Merton, *The Life of the Vows,* ed. Patrick F. O'Connell (Initiation in the Monastic Tradition 6; Collegeville, MN: Liturgical Press, Cistercian Publications, 2012), 381.

55. Ibid., 382.

56. Ibid., 401-6.

4.3 A Church of the Poor as Risky and Costly

A Church of the Poor is not only "bothered" ("bruised" to use Pope Francis's words) by the thorn in the flesh of poverty, it is actually shaped by it. This involves social, moral, and political as well as spiritual and theological risks. A turning point in the history of the perception of the riskiness of poverty was definitely Francis of Assisi embracing a life of poverty. He started a paradigm shift in the theology and spirituality of poverty in the early thirteenth century, a shift that could be and has been described as a move from generosity to solidarity.[57] He was systematically and methodically pursuing a Church of the Poor within the context of his community. This Church of the Poor was characterized by material poverty on an individual as well as on a communal level, by voluntary deprivation of property of all kinds, by a sense of dependence and vulnerability, as well as by the humility to beg, and by the commitment to work, especially manual labor.

The history of the Franciscans illustrates some of the risks and costs of a Church of the Poor; these struggles were a new phenomenon. Yes, there was and had been a vow-of-poverty culture within the monastic tradition for many years, but the main issue of the "role of material poverty" and "role of communal poverty" remained. The Benedictine tradition, with its principle of the primacy of the spiritual and its distinction between individual poverty and communal property, is based on the rule of Benedict, which does not see value in material poverty. There is no special chapter on poverty in the *Regula Benedicti* (RB); the rule wants monasteries to share their property with the poor and to realize a culture of hospitality.[58] Monks are to be content and should be provided for with material goods on the basis of a moderate and temperate interpretation of individual needs. "Necessities" define the monastic understanding of poverty.[59] The individual

57. Leonardo Boff, *Saint Francis: A Model for Human Liberation,* trans. John W. Diercksmeier (New York: Crossroad, 1982), 56.
58. Viktor Dammertz, "Poverty in the Rule of St. Benedict and Today," *American Benedictine Review* 35, no. 1 (1984): 1-16, at 6.
59. Cf. Joel Rippinger, "The Biblical and Monastic Roots of Poverty in the

consideration of needs (an exercise in listening as mutual obedience between abbot and monk) implies that avarice with its inclination toward comparison and a comparative or even competitive attitude should be curbed. This is most explicitly stated in the RB 33-34.[60] The economic administration must not be driven by greed (RB 31.12); sales of items produced in the monastery should be lower than usual (RB 57.7-8). The key point is the glory of God (RB 57.9). However, the rule does not discourage the amassing of monastic property or the accumulation of moderate forms of wealth. Due to an array of factors contributing to the well-documented economic success of Benedictine monasteries,[61] there were well-situated monasteries quite early on in the history of monasteries, with rich monasteries later on as well. The spirit of the "vow of poverty on an individual level within the context of proper supportive infrastructure or even institutional wealth" made it difficult to see a Church of the Poor emerging out of such a tradition.

The contrast between poor mendicant movements and a rich monastery is vividly and accurately described in Umberto Eco's novel *The Name of the Rose*. The novel is set in 1327 against the background of the debate about poverty. The English Franciscan theologian William of Baskerville is set the challenge of solving a case of murder in a rich Italian Benedictine monastery. The novel has the Benedictine abbot embody a church of the non-poor, a church suspicious of poverty and inimical to radical poverty movements.[62] In a key passage William of

---

Rule of Benedict under the Aspect of Koinonia," *American Benedictine Review* 27, no. 3 (1976): 321-31.

60. Terrence Kardong, "Poverty in the Rule of Benedict: Chapters 33 and 34," *Cistercian Studies* 20 (1985): 184-201.

61. See Emil Inauen, Bruno S. Frey, "Benediktinerabteien aus ökonomischer Sicht. Über die ausserordentliche Stabilität einer besonderen Institution," Working Paper No. 388. Institute for Empirical Research in Economics (Zurich: University of Zurich, 2008); Katja Rost, Emil Inauen, and Margit Osterloh, "The Corporate Governance of Benedictine Abbeys: What Can Stock Corporations Learn from Monasteries? *Journal of Management History* 16, no. 1 (2010): 90-115.

62. Umberto Eco, *The Name of the Rose*, trans. William Weaver (New York: Houghton Mifflin Harcourt, 2014), 161-63.

Baskerville explains the connection between poverty and politics to Adson, his inexperienced and aptly named companion:

> The kings are the merchants. And their weapon is money.... Money circulates everywhere.... And even priests, bishops, even religious orders have to take money into account. This is why rebellion against power takes the form of a call to poverty. The rebels against power are those denied any connection with money, and so every call to poverty provokes great tension and argument, and the whole city, from bishop to magistrate, considers a personal enemy the one who preaches poverty too much.[63]

Poverty is provocative if preached either as the result of injustice or as demanded by Christ. In both cases it demands societal and structural change. Naïve young Adson, who believes in the goodness of the human person, wonders why people are afraid of those who lived in poverty, asking himself whether it wasn't more understandable to fear those wishing to live in wealth and taking money from others.[64] These questions are at the core of the fight over poverty in the thirteenth and fourteenth centuries.

The life and teachings of Francis of Assisi serve as a key to the debate. St. Francis wanted to live a life of radical poverty; at the same time, however, he wanted to stay within the church. He did not claim that the form of life he chose after his conversion (radical material poverty and social insecurity) should be accepted as universal standards. He was not saying that everybody had to live the kind of life he chose to live. Notwithstanding, he was adamant that the movement that emerged from his foundational praxis should be committed to the idea of radical poverty. During the course of his lifetime he was forced to make certain concessions to appease the expectations and standard practice of the institutional church. The *bulla non regulata*, the nonratified rules, with their more radical ideas on poverty, had to be changed. The ratified version of his rule, the *Regula bullata*, contains three important sections on

---

63. Ibid., 136.
64. Ibid., 253.

poverty: In chapter 4 St. Francis commands that the brothers should not receive money, not even "through an interposed person." But there is a concession and at the same time a conundrum: "However for the necessities of the infirm and for the clothing of the other friars, only the ministers and the custodes are to conduct a sollicitous care, by means of spiritual friends, according to places and seasons and cold regions, as they see expedites necessity; with this always preserved, that, as has been said, they do not receive coins nor money." In other words, Francis recognizes situations that require institutional support, not motivated by any sense of personal or institutional greed or an improper way of seeking security, but born of solidarity and an attitude of caring. At the same time, however, and here we have the conundrum, Francis holds on to the "no money" ideal. Goods can be received and handed over only to friars in need, which does in fact complicate the situation, as one can imagine. Chapter 5 ("On the Manner of Working") exhorts friars to work faithfully and devotedly, not for wages, but in exchange for goods "for the necessity of the body," but again, they must not accept coins or money, as "followers of most holy poverty." Here again, the exchange situation Francis has in mind is not compatible with financial planning, let alone any idea of a cash economy. Exchange remains within the context of a subsistence economy, which is less flexible than economic agency based on money as a currency that translates goods into goods and values into values.

Given the above-mentioned challenge of living poverty as a community we reach a culmination with respect to poverty in chapter 6 of the *Regula bullata*, where Francis is clear about a strictly nonproperty policy: "Let the Friars appropriate nothing for themselves, neither house nor place, nor any thing. And as pilgrims and exiles (cf. 1 Pet 2:11) in this age let them go about for alms confidently, as ones serving the Lord in poverty and humility." He further exhorts the friars to reveal to one another their respective needs. "And, if any of them should fall into infirmity, the other friars should care for him, as they would want to be cared for themselves." Here again we find the conundrum intensified. How can institutional support be given without an institution?

The scriptural passage used in chapter 6 of the *Regula bullata*, 1 Peter 2:11 ("Beloved, I urge you as aliens and sojourners to keep away from worldly desires that wage war against the soul") is also quoted in Francis's testament, where we read a eulogy of "the holy poverty, which we have promised in the Rule, always dwelling there as strangers and pilgrims" (cf. 1 Pet 2:11). Pilgrims depend on others, may not have money on their person, in the same way as the seventy-two disciples Jesus sent out in Luke 10 ("Carry no money bag" [Luke 10:4]) had no money. Thus, Francis left his community with a conundrum: be a community but one without property. This conundrum lies at the heart of the very question of a Church of the Poor. How can a church be poor and still be a community that serves and provides? In the face of such a challenge it seems worthwhile to explore some aspects of medieval debates. Soon after Francis's death spiritual, theological, and communal tensions mounted. Two camps emerged. While some friars ("Zelanti") lived in strict observance of Francis's testament, in isolation and seclusion, other friars, a number of them in urban convents ("Conventuals"), lived a life reflecting the need for liturgical, institutional, and study aids, in short, a life in need of an infrastructure. Urbanization and the monetization of economic life added to the existing pressure. One could, of course, see both camps as reflecting Christian values. The Zelanti cheerfully embraced the hardships of material poverty and renounced comfort and convenience for the sake of gaining inner freedom and and a life of credible discipleship; the Conventuals expressed a desire to serve and the humility to do so by accepting the human condition (sanctified in a new way through Christ's incarnation), a condition that requires "flesh," that is, a material dimension to human endeavors. After the general council in 1230, Pope Gregory IX (who had solemnly canonized St. Francis on July 16, 1228) issued the bull *Quo elongati* (September 28, 1230) at the request of the Franciscans; he declared that the Franciscans were not bound by the testament, and that the friars had the mandate to have a *"nuntius"* and *"spiritual friends"* in order to provide for their daily needs. However, the friars were not to possess anything and were only allowed *"usus pauper,"* that is, use of all the things given to them in accordance with the vow of poverty.

Pope Innocent IV gave the Franciscans permission to appoint "procurators" to buy, sell, and administer goods given to them. Nicholas III issued a clarifying bull, *Exiit qui seminat,* in 1279 that tried to reach and confirm a compromise. He reminded the friars of their meek and docile spirituality rooted in poverty and humility (2), and confirmed—an important point for later on!—that the Franciscans were to love and fully embrace Christlike poverty:

> Since the rule itself expressly contains that the friars may appropriate nothing to themselves neither house nor place nor any thing, and [thus] has it been declared by the same predecessor, Pope Gregory IX, and by not a few others, that this ought to be observed not only individually but also in common. . . . We say that the abdication of this kind of property over all things not only individually but also in common is in the sight of God meritorious and holy, which Christ showing the way to perfection both taught by word and strengthened by example (7).

Franciscan poverty is an expression of trust in divine providence (8); section 13 clarifies the respect for the "non-use of money" clause: it is legitimate for the Franciscans to nominate someone (a procurator) to take care of monetary matters:

> [I]t is lawful for the friars to make known and specify and manifest their necessities to the aforesaid person and to beg him to fulfill them. They can even exhort and induce the same person to conduct himself faithfully in the matter committed [to his care]; and to take care of the salvation of his soul in the execution of the matter committed to himself, to this extent, that the friars abstain entirely from all administration or dispensation of this money and from [all] action or judicial prosecution, as has been said, against the aforesaid person.

The bull did, however, not resolve the intra-party conflict. Clement V's 1312 bull *Exivi de paradiso* failed to appease the community as well. Pope John XXII then took the matter into his hand in an ongoing situation where some of the "Spirituals," preaching radical poverty, were disseminating their vows in open confrontation with the established church. In 1317, John XXII condemned one particularly radical branch of this group, the "Fraticelli." In 1322 he commissioned a group of theological experts to look into the issue of radical communal poverty and the theology of the poverty of Christ. In May of the same year, the general chapter of the Franciscans held in Perugia underlined that it was true to claim that Jesus and the apostles possessed nothing, neither individually nor communally, and that they did not have right of ownership and dominium. The pope reacted with an influential document in December 1322, the bull *Ad conditorem canonum,* which deconstructed the existing provisions as legal fictions and imposed the burden of ownership on the Franciscans. He built his case by listing the following arguments against Nicholas III's ruling: in spite of these regulations the brothers have not been freed from solicitude; they have not been made poorer; the arrangements have even damaged the church as being too troublesome. The main argument that the use of consumables without ownership is impossible is stated in section 4:

> For what sane person could believe that it was the intention of
> so great a father to keep the lordship for the Roman Church,
> and the use for the Brothers, of an egg, or a cheese, or a crust
> of bread, or other things consumable by use, which are often
> given to the Brothers themselves to consume on the spot?

An even harsher statement was made less than a year later when John XXII declared in his short bull *Cum inter nonnullos* (November 12, 1223) that "the opinion, which asserts, that Christ and His disciples had nothing, and in regard to those things, which they did have, they had no right, is erroneous and heretical." After that, the conflict escalated with Michael of Cesena, the general of the Franciscans; and a significant number of monks of the same order, directly challenged the pope on this question of poverty. They sided with Louis the Bavarian in 1324, and the conflict reached a new and hitherto unknown level of politicization.[65]

---

65. See the well-written article on this matter by Brian Hamilton: B. Hamilton, "The Politics of Poverty: A Contribution to a Franciscan Political Theol-

A sober voice in heated debates is always, if I may say so, St. Thomas Aquinas. Living in the thirteenth century, he would be witness to the ongoing debates. Moreover, he found himself in a position to articulate a theological position on the issue in question.[66] Aquinas defines poverty as "*privatio omnium facultatum*," as privation of possessions,[67] and discusses community property as well. He underscores the difference between an individual's and a communal situation. Excessive riches in any "common" situation are an obstacle to perfection:

> though not absolutely incompatible with it; while it is not an obstacle to religious perfection to have enough external things, whether movables or immovables, as suffice for a livelihood, if we consider poverty in relation to the common end of religious orders, which is to devote oneself to the service of God. But if we consider poverty in relation to the special end of any religious order, then this end being presupposed, a greater or lesser degree of poverty is adapted to that religious

---

ogy," *Journal of the Society of Christian Ethics* 35, no. 1 (2015): 29-44. Hamilton gives a deep and insightful account of the debate about the "vita apostolica" challenging established mainstream church life culminating in the provocative theological claim "that Christ was poor, that his followers ought to imitate his poverty, and that one could claim his authority only on the basis of such imitation" (ibid., 32). Hence, the whole structures of authority were challenged: "In their embrace of poverty, these movements were not affirming instability, social stigma, or material need in themselves; but what they affirmed was inseparable from these things. The movements caught fire precisely because they revalued the actual conditions being forced on a growing portion of the population. Because they identified the apostolic life with real poverty, and not just the chosen asceticism of an elite class or an existential posture that anyone might in principle assume, they exacerbated the risk of romanticizing a dehumanizing condition. But only on this basis is it possible to say that the movements offered a plausible political rendition of the traditional connection between poverty and freedom. For this poverty to be liberating, it had to be simultaneously identified with and opposed to the poverty that was a form of bondage and servility" (ibid., 38).

66. Cf. Van den Eijnden, *Poverty on the Way to God*, chs. 2 and 3.
67. STh II-II, 188,7, resp.

order; and each religious order will be the more perfect in respect of poverty, according as it professes a poverty more adapted to its end.[68]

In other words: the point of a religious community is to serve; different religious communities and orders have different ways of rendering this service. Thus there will be different ways of living credible discipleship even with regard to the question of poverty. Aquinas explicitly introduces active and contemplative orders and mentions orders cultivating a service of hospitality that requires an appropriate infrastructure. Aquinas emphasized the importance of withdrawing from worldly things in the quest for spiritual perfection, thus seeing voluntary poverty as an important means to follow Jesus in the light of Matthew 19:21.[69] Perfection, however, does not consist in poverty itself as state or experience; it lies in following Christ, which means that "true" discipleship is not the pursuit or practice of poverty alone. It does not suffice since it is neither a value *in* itself or *by* itself.[70] In a central passage in the *Summa contra gentiles*, Aquinas expresses a differentiated view on poverty: poverty is praiseworthy insofar as it frees a person from wealth-related vices and riches-based solicitude. However, not everyone can or will develop morally if the solicitude that comes with responsibility (including financial responsibility) is taken away. Aquinas quotes Gregory on this point in his example of a person in a postretirement situation: some individuals may fall into even worse traps. Furthermore, wealth enables people to assist others, and here we find a striking statement: "In so far as poverty takes away the good which results from riches, namely, the assisting of others and the support of oneself, it is purely an evil."[71] Poverty, and this cannot be stressed

---

68. STh II-II, 188,7, resp.; cf. John D. Jones, "Poverty and Subsistence: St. Thomas and the Definition of Poverty," *Gregorianum* 75, no. 1 (1994): 135-49, esp. 140-42.

69. STh II-II, 186,3, resp.

70. STh II-II, 188,7, resp.

71. Cf. John D. Jones, "Poverty as *Malum simpliciter*: A Reading of Aquinas' *Summa contra gentiles* 3.11," *Philosophy and Theology* 13, no. 2 (1999): 213-39;

enough from a poverty research perspective, can be a *malum simpliciter*, can be purely evil. It is evil not to be able to support oneself; it is evil not to be able to assist others.[72] "Decent life" and "integrity," we could say, are at stake in the discussion of poverty as well as of wealth. The ultimate role model to contextualize poverty is Christ: Christ did not live a solitary life but associated with others: "therefore it was most fitting that Christ should conform to others in the matter of eating and drinking."[73] But Christ did live a life of poverty in this world, as an itinerant and credible preacher living out a kenotic existence.[74] This kenotic existence is the foundation for a theology of a Church of the Poor; the challenge to the spirit of wordliness with its cheap answer to the compatibility of wealth and discipleship does not go away. What does it mean to have a kenotic church? Could this credibly happen without a dimension of material poverty?

4.4 The Church of the Poor and Epistemic Practices

During the Second Vatican Council a Church of the Poor was challenged, as mentioned above, to develop a theological vision consistent with the tradition and broad enough to incorporate the diversity of the experiences of poverty.[75] Jon Sobrino has characterized a Church of the Poor as "the ecclesial setting of Christology because it is a world shaped by the poor."[76] Precisely this view was admonished by the

---

see as well for the possibility of poverty as *malum simpliciter* in Aquinas: Stephen Pope, "Poverty and Natural Law," in William A. Galston and Peter H. Hoffenberg, eds., *Poverty and Morality: Religious and Secular Perspectives* (Cambridge: Cambridge University Press, 2010), 265-84.

72. John Jones argues in his reconstruction of Aquinas's position "that poverty is unqualifiedly evil in reference to humans so far as it is a privation of our activity to gather together or procure things such that we are unable to sustain ourselves and assist others" (Jones, "Poverty as *Malum simpliciter*," 231).

73. STh III, 40,2, resp.

74. STh III, 40,3, resp.

75. See Planellas I Barnosell, *La iglesia de los pobres*, 125-34.

76. Jon Sobrino, *Jesus the Liberator: A Historical-Theological Reading of Jesus of Nazareth* (Maryknoll, NY: Orbis Books, 1993), 31.

Congregation for the Doctrine of Faith: "The ecclesial foundation of Christology may not be identified with 'the Church of the poor,' but is found rather in the apostolic faith transmitted through the Church for all generations. The theologian, in his particular vocation in the Church, must continually bear in mind that theology is the science of the faith. Other points of departure for theological work run the risk of arbitrariness and end in a misrepresentation of the same faith."[77] There are major challenges in developing a theology of a Church of the Poor.

I would like to take a closer look at two main themes that take center stage facing this challenge: the theological concept of kenosis and the ethical concept of vulnerability. Both amalgamate and unite in their key concern to overcome a spirit of worldliness. Jesus lived out a kenotic existence and calls us to be his disciples. God himself "can be said to be poor in so far as He can be said to be marginal in the world as the poor are. God is overlooked as easily as the poor."[78] A marginal existence is not compatible with a high-profile way of life. A marginal existence expects to be overlooked in the same way as God is overlooked and that Jesus was overlooked for most of his life.

This then is the main point, the main risk, and the main cost of a Church of the Poor, to live a kenotic existence. Kenosis means "forgoing privileges"; so what does it mean for a church to forgo privileges? Privileges are special rights that put the holder in an advantageous position over and against others. Privileges cannot be separated from power. A Church of the Poor calls for an explicit reflection on power; such reflection will challenge existing patterns of power distribution and power execution. One important element of this power is epistemic power. If we perceive a "poor church" as one committed to the poor, perceiving the poor as the prophetic leaven and acknowledging them to be agents of *sensus fidelium* and thus the object of apostolicity, this could well have an impact on the way we perceive orthodoxy. Obviously, there are social privileges and there are epistemic privileges; both types of privileges have to be scrutinized. There are also

---

77. CDF, "Notification on the Works of Father Jon Sobrino, SJ," (2006), 2.
78. Van den Eijnden, *Poverty on the Way to God*, 245.

social privileges connected to epistemic privileges. Being addressed by revelation is an epistemic privilege; the church hierarchy has social privileges in terms of the control over institutional aspects of the church; the position of judgment on the *depositum fidei* is a social and epistemic privilege. A Church of the Poor will rethink concepts and realities of privilege. Could it mean the challenge of forgoing the privilege of infallibility and of taking epistemic risks? Could we not say that the social encyclicals, in talking about signs of the times and not only perennial truths, were beginning to make steps in this direction?

A Church of the Poor cannot *not* be self-effacing, since kenosis and institutional humility are inextricably linked and cause the additional challenge of avoiding triumphant language or language without penitential elements in the church. A Church of the Poor will be empty, so that the church can be filled by the Spirit. In a morning meditation on the widow who placed the two coins she possessed in the temple treasury Pope Francis reflects on the great virtue of the church, namely, that the church is not the "shining of her own light" but rather reflects "the light that comes from her Spouse." Especially since "over the centuries, when the Church wanted to have her own light, she was wrong." It was for good reasons that the church had been compared to the moon, and that the church was described as *mysterium lunae*. Jorge Mario Bergoglio had used this image in his pre-conclave remarks on March 9, 2013, in Rome. When the church is humble and poor, Francis concluded his morning meditation, and even "when the Church confesses her misfortunes—we all have them—the Church is faithful." We could explore a paradox here. Being "full" of faith is still an obstacle to the emptiness that gives way to the Spirit. Simone Weil was very attentive to this call for "detachment"—detachment from material but also from epistemic and spiritual foundations to make room for the absolute.[79] Are we treading dangerous territory here? Can one pursue the question whether Simone Weil's concerns for honoring God in detachment could also be relevant for institutional and communal realities or even the mystical reality of the Bride of Christ?

---

79. Simone Weil, "Detachment," in Simone Weil, *Gravity and Grace* (London: ARK Paperbacks, 1987), 12-15.

In any case, a Church of the Poor will change epistemic practices. It will recognize new types of epistemic goods, such as the experience of poverty, the experience of dependence and vulnerability, as a privileged perspective from which to do theology; and it will ask the question about the proper access to and distribution of epistemic goods. Epistemic goods are the *bona* inherent in the praxis of knowing and understanding, goods such as "judgments," "distinctions," "concepts," whereby truth is the highest epistemic good there is. Poor people are epistemic agents with a special access to special epistemic goods, especially insights into the condition of vulnerability, which give rise to deep insights into the human condition and what it means to be created by God and depending on God. How can a person obtain a deep understanding of her creatureliness without a deep experience of vulnerability? How can a person have a deep understanding of the term "salvation," if she does not know struggle and torment of the soul? The encounter between Jesus and Nicodemus outlined in Chapter 2 reminds us of the connection between epistemic goods and salvation; people have to "understand" something, they have to "believe" something, they have to "know" something in order to be a disciple of Jesus, the Christ. Pope Francis underlines the "special place of the poor in God's people" and reminds us of the testimony of Christ who lived his life among the poor, a sign they would always have a special place in God's heart: "This is why I want a Church which is poor and for the poor. They have much to teach us. Not only do they share in the *sensus fidei*, but in their difficulties they know the suffering of Christ. We need to let ourselves be evangelized by them" (*Evangelii gaudium* 198). We may find ourselves in the role of Nicodemus, who seeks a nocturnal conversation with the poor. Nicodemus, however, was also the poor seeking counseling and instruction as spiritual works of mercy. He had access to epistemic goods.

Poverty can also mean deprivation of access to epistemic goods. It cannot be taken for granted that underprivileged people have access to epistemic goods such as the joy of the gospel. Bryant Myers gives the following example: "Sitting at a campfire in the Kalahari Desert, I heard a San woman say, in response to hearing the news that the Son of God had died for her sins, that she could believe that God would let his Son die for a white man, and that maybe she could believe that God might let his Son die for a black man, but she could never accept the idea that God would let his Son dies for a San woman."[80] I would suggest that one aspect of a Church of the Poor is respect for the universal destination of precious epistemic goods, as expressed at the end of the Gospel of Matthew: "Make disciples of all nations, baptizing them in the name of the Father, and of the Son, and of the holy Spirit, teaching them to observe all that I have commanded you" (Matt 28:19).

The well-established principle in the Catholic Social Tradition of the universal destination of goods means that every single individual should have "access" to "well-being necessary for his full development." This requires "common effort" for favorable conditions to be created; it also means that everyone can and must make a contribution to a better world for everyone.[81] The principle "of the universal destination of goods requires that the poor . . . should be the focus of particular concern."[82] If we were to summarize the "theory of goods" within Catholic Social Teaching we could mention the following points:

1. The goods of the earth serve a general purpose to which there is a universal right of use.
2. The use and employment of goods are closely knit with the context in which they are employed.
3. The purpose of goods are firmly embedded in the human order of coexistence in which the principles of subsidiarity and solidarity play a key role.
4. Resources can be acquired through the application of exertion and intelligence, which is also the basis of private property.
5. Private property is not an absolute in itself and needs to be set within a wider context orientated to the common good.
6. The general provision and purpose of goods means that special care and concern must be given to poor.

---

80. Bryant L. Myers, *Walking with the Poor* (Maryknoll, NY: Orbis Books, 2011), 129.
81. *Compendium of the Social Doctrine of the Church* 172 and 175.
82. *Compendium*, 182. This concern has to do with material but also cultural and religious poverty (*Compendium*, 184).

7. The key categories of Christian thinking (truth, life, grace, justice, love, peace) provide the framework within which resources must be "seized."

A Church of the Poor will make sure that epistemic goods are properly redistributed in the spirit of the universal destination of goods. Now, if we then transfer this doctrine to epistemic resources, we could make the following observations:

(1) Epistemic goods (such as true judgments, true cognizance) all serve a universal purpose and as such are not goods through which possession alone can make us contented as human beings; there is an obligation to share those goods. The universal purpose of epistemic goods may perhaps not go down well with the elitist learned thinking of Pharisees (cf. Luke 10:21). Jesus preached not only in synagogues but also outside in the open air, on mountains, beside lakes and in private homes. The universal purpose of epistemic goods corresponds to the idea of a universally accessible God, as was highlighted during the First Vatican Council, who "can be known with certainty by the natural light of human reason from created things" and the idea of a natural theology based on a natural capacity to understand the same.

(2) Epistemic goods such as "theological wisdom" or "spiritual counsel" have to be respectful of the local context with its specific demands and signs of the times and signs of the space. There are grounds to argue for local epistemologies in the sense that different contexts will honor—by accepting commitments to accepting constitutive elements of the human condition and the idea of universal truth—different normative sources (local traditions, local language, and local epistemic habits). Even universal truth claims have to be expressed in a way that does justice to the hermeneutical demands of a local context. "Inculturation" is also "inculturation in local epistemic practices."

(3) Epistemic resources are created and administered by and within an epistemic community; the individual "knower" is a member of a community of knowers and seekers. This social aspect of epistemology is connected to the principles of solidarity and subsidiarity. The principle of solidarity exhorts us to share epistemic resources; the principle

of subsidiarity reminds us to assign a maximum of epistemic freedom and epistemic responsibility at the lowest possible level. It may also point to issues such as Ockham's razor in the construction of theological responses to questions or to the commitment to simplicity in epistemic practices following, among others, the idea that "whatever can be said in simple language should be said in simple language."

(4) Epistemic goods such as doctrinal truths are to be appropriated within the church, have to become part of one's intellect and will, have to become "personal knowledge," a kind of knowledge that will guide the individual and provide orientation in life's journey, in other words, knowledge put into practice.[83] A good example of this appropriation would be Karl Rahner's short text on the experience of grace in which he gives clear pointers as to what it means when we claim that we experienced grace. Rahner suggests questions such as the following: "Have we ever kept quiet, even though we wanted to defend ourselves when we had been unfairly treated? Have we ever forgiven someone even though we got no thanks for it and our silent forgiveness was taken for granted? Have we ever obeyed, not because we had to and because otherwise things would have become unpleasant for us, but simply on account of that mysterious, silent, incomprehensible being we call God and his will? Have we ever sacrificed something without receiving any thanks or recognition for it, and even without a feeling of inner satisfaction?"[84] These are invitations to appropriate theology on a personal level, a commitment to making theological truths, to making the Word of God, available and accessible. But there is also the insight that in theology the epistemic work needed to acquire certain resources is, according to John 15:4, less reliant on the cognitive processes of *thinking* and *understanding* than on *prayer*.

(5) Epistemic resources are oriented toward the good of the community. Truth is a key contributor to community building. A true conversation is an expression of a commitment to "shared

83. Michael Polanyi, *Personal Knowledge: A Post-Critical Philosophy* (Chicago: University of Chicago Press, 1962).

84. Karl Rahner, "Reflections on the Experience of Grace," in Karl Rahner, *Theological Investigations III*, trans. Karl-Heinz and Boniface Kruger (London: Darton, Longman & Todd, 1967), 86-89, at 86.

ownership" and to a "common-good orientation." Truth manifests itself in and through conversation: "without genuine conversation, no manifestation."[85] Any conversation—dialogue—presupposes that not just our own individual questions be allowed or authorized to take the stage.[86] It is not surprising that Pope Francis underlines the importance of dialogue in the epistemic culture of the church.

(6) The orientation of epistemic resources to the well-being of the community goes hand in hand with a special mindfulness for the poor; epistemic resources need to be distributed in such a way as to make them easily accessible to the socially deprived and underprivileged. The Gospels make powerful reading if they are read against the background of the experience of poverty and pain.[87] A particular way of life will give access to particular examples and concerns. Poverty is often linked to epistemic deprivation, to a deprivation of epistemic resources, to a lack of access to epistemic goods. A Church of the Poor will be committed to honor the experience of poverty as an epistemic good and to make the epistemic goods of the church available also to those who suffer from deprivation of capabilities. The poor have so much to teach us because the experience of poverty creates depth of understanding, freshness, and rawness. Just imagine a poor person praying the Lord's Prayer with its petition "Give us today our daily bread." What does it mean to pray for "our" daily bread in a situation without food security? What does it mean to pray for daily bread with sincerity when there is food security, when the bread along with the hundred and one other things consumed in the course of a day are taken for granted? The poor have so much to teach; material poverty is a severe teacher.

(7) The core categories of Christian thinking (truth, life, sanctity, grace, justice, love, and peace) make up the framework within which epistemic resources are to be perceived and understood. "Discern-

85. David Tracy, *Plurality and Ambiguity: Hermeneutics, Religion, Hope* (San Francisco: HarperSanFrancisco, 1987), 28.

86. Cf. David Tracy, *Dialogue with the Other: The Inter-religious Dialogue* (Louvain: Peeters Press, 1990), 95.

87. A classic example: Ernesto Cardenal, *The Gospel in Solentiname* (Maryknoll, NY: Orbis Books, 2010).

ment" does not take place in isolation but is part of the wider journey toward sanctity; discernment requires the grace of God as a constant companion. Discernment is a form of love, and here we might speculate on the epistemic power of love, for example, discernment as encounter, or indeed on the connection between epistemic and social justice.[88] Working out the ideal setting, context, and content for dialogue to take place is a major theological challenge, and the content of dialogue is a core concern of Catholic Social Teaching. Human life and relationships cannot exist in a morally neutral space; politics cannot be enacted, and economic business of any kind cannot take place (including processes or realization and discernment) in a sterile vacuum, which means that justice and solidarity, proper conduct in life, and the role of love are absolutely essential in the context of doxastic praxis.

This brings us ultimately to the challenge of rethinking orthodoxy in social and communal terms. We could ask, are not proper subject and agent of orthodoxy the relational and social person and, in a certain sense, then, the community?

88. Cf. Clemens Sedmak, "Strukturen epistemischer Gerechtigkeit," in *Salzburger Jahrbuch für Philosophie* 46/47 (2001/2): 139-52.

Chapter 5

Orthodoxy in a New Key: Faith in Practice

Thus far, we have looked into the idea of joyful orthodoxy expressed in *Evangelii gaudium* (EG) as a relationship with God grounded in the experience of being loved by God, and we have explored some aspects of the gospel of joy and Jesus' way of changing epistemic practices and encouraging healing faith. We have reflected on the ethical significance of the wound of knowledge, the experience of poverty inflicting such a wound, and the implications of this wound for human knowing and understanding. And we have discussed the concept of a Church of the Poor in the light of church documents and tradition with special reference to the fourth and the fourteenth centuries. Poverty, as we have approached it, is first and foremost an experience of raw vulnerability; this experience can lead to a singular openness to words of salvation and healing. A Church of the Poor will find key resources in this openness that beg for recognition of poor people as "doctors of the church" in a particular sense and way. "Orthodoxy," then, is at its core the right relationship with God; this relationship, however, cannot be right (in the light of, among other passages, Matt 25:31-36) if there is not a "right" relationship with the poor. Now, in this final chapter, we explore the concept of orthodoxy in more depth.

"Transforming orthodoxy," as the title of this book suggests, is about a "right" relationship with God, a relationship that transforms us from within, as the result of an experience of transfiguration, as a process of ongoing renewal. If we now view this relationship through the lens of a concern for a Church of the Poor, the concept of orthodoxy is transformed. In general, orthodoxy as "rightness of opinion" can be understood as the condition of being orthodox. The term cannot be found in the New Testament and emerged only in late Antiquity; it works best in an epistemic space that allows for the authoritative administration of clear distinctions between right and wrong, that is, in a space that is characterized by clear and distinct epistemic commitments. Augustine characterizes orthodox Christians as "custodians of integrity" (*integritatis custodes*), those who preserve the purity of doctrine without allowing it to be corrupted.[1] We are tempted (and frequently tend) to use the theological language of Paradise and the Fall in this context: orthodoxy is the epistemic state of "being in paradise"; a heresy as sinful fall ends with the expulsion from paradise. The temptation of using language to express black-and-white images of either absolute perfection or downright corruption leads to a further temptation, namely, the idea of using such language to describe those who are saved and those who are lost. Ironically, the temptation for "the orthodox ones" and "the fallen ones" is the same: pride. It is the pride of the praying Pharisee, on the one hand, and it is the pride of the person not accepting the spiritual authority of a faith community, on the other.

In this chapter we will look at the idea of propositional orthodoxy (5.1), the political dimension of orthodoxy understood as institutional orthodoxy (5.2), the existential dimension of orthodoxy (5.3), and the orthodoxy of pilgrims (5.4). The epilogue following on from this chapter will consider what I identify as the key question at stake: what does it mean to love God?

5.1 Propositional Orthodoxy

Doctrinal orthodoxy (being "sound" with regard to the understanding and acceptance of doctrine, being conscious of and faithful to the church's teaching) inevitably shows aspects of propositional orthodoxy. The Catholic tradition has explicitly developed a body of texts that help us gain insights into the "logic of religion," into the

---

1. Augustine, *De vera religione* V,9.

organization of a set of beliefs into a coherent body of propositions.[2] Propositions are truth bearers; and, within the Catholic understanding, "correspondence with the real" ("the divine order") as well as "coherence of propositions with the set of accepted propositions" can be taken to be truthmakers. Doctrines are expressed by way of propositions. Orthodoxy, as said in the introduction, can at its most basic level be described as the acceptance of certain propositions as true; these are propositions that have been declared true by the authority of the church. "To use an image, these truths are like precious coins, paintings, and books, given by the great benefactor in the sky, now kept in a Vatican vault."[3] The quintessence of orthodoxy lies in the church affirming the truth of the binding doctrines it teaches and repudiating any doctrine incommensurate with its commitment to a doctrine of truth. Fundamentally speaking, denying the truth of an orthodox statement or maintaining the truth of a misconception is a violation against orthodoxy at its simplest level. Thus seen, orthodoxy engenders accordant modes of monitoring, which display aspects of coherence theory (testing the coherence of the proposition p taking S as the sum of propositions accepted as true). The procedure employed to assess the doctrinal accuracy of a text is comparative; an authority compares a text with a set of established texts (statements, documents) and confirms its compatibility or incompatibility on the basis of this comparison. To use an example: on December 13, 2004, the Congregation for the Doctrine of the Faith deemed it necessary to issue a Notification on "erroneous positions" in Father Roger Haight's book *Jesus Symbol of God*; the core issue of contention—that "one can no longer claim . . . Christianity as the superior religion, or Christ as the absolute center to which all other historical mediations are relative. . . . It is impossible in postmodern culture to think . . . that one religion can claim to inhabit the center into which all others are to be drawn"—was rejected as being untenable with Christ's universal mis-

---

2. Joseph M. Bochenski, *The Logic of Religion* (New York: New York University Press, 1965); this book makes the claim that each and every religion can be reconstructed as a set of beliefs.

3. Edward Collins Vacek, "Orthodoxy Requires Orthopathy: Emotions in Theology," *Horizons* 40, no. 2 (2013): 218-41, at 227.

sion of salvation; the Congregation backed its argument with normative sources: (1) the Holy Scriptures[4]; (2) official teaching texts and accounts[5]; and (3) the universal truth of the mission of the church.[6]

The full spectrum of normative sources can be and must be considered when assessing the status of a position (always facing the challenge of justifying the selective use of sources); the method is the same: comparing a proposition or position with an established set of propositions. The *tertium comparationis* is the creed. This method, of course, works best if the same ground is covered by the incriminated position and the available set of normative propositions. It is more difficult if new territory is being entered, as can and does happen in moral theology regarding questions related to new biomedical technologies. In such cases, it is a matter of the "application" of teachings to new situations, and an application is never a mechanical process. That is why the procedure has to be regulated and proper authority established. The procedure for determining orthodoxy requires particular regulative practices, and these were compiled and arranged in the document *Agendi ratio in doctrinarum examine* on June 29, 1997. These are institutional realities that ensure a level of procedural justice and also reflect the institutional framework for the discourse on orthodoxy.

Assessing the status of propositions is an epistemological challenge for many reasons. Let me mention a few. (1) There is the "depth grammar" of propositions, which means a level beyond their face value. It takes a lot of semantic labor, working in the mines of meaning, to do reasonable justice to a text "after Babel."[7] (2) There is the challenge of "holism," in the sense that one can only assess the status

---

4. Acts 4:12; 1 Tim 2:4-6; John 14:6; Matt 28:19; Mark 16:15; Eph 3:8-11.

5. Innocent XI, *Cum occasione* 5: DH 2005; Holy Office, *Errores Iansenistarum* 4: DH 2304; Vatican II, *Lumen gentium* 8; *Gaudium et spes* 22; *Ad gentes* 3; John Paul II, *Redemptoris missio* 4-6; Congregation for the Doctrine of the Faith, *Dominus Iesus* 13-15.

6. *Lumen gentium* 13, 17; *Ad gentes* 7; *Redemptoris missio* 9-11; *Dominus Iesus* 20-22.

7. George Steiner's idea on the impossibility of translation are also ideas about the impossibility of understanding; George Steiner, *After Babel: Aspects of Language and Translation* (Oxford: Oxford University Press, 1998), esp. ch. 1.

of a proposition within a set of propositions (Duhem-Quine thesis). (3) There is the question of the available categories of judgment: orthodoxy and heterodoxy are not to be boxed as neat opposites with clear boundaries; we are confronted with a wide spectrum of "nuances and degrees of error." In the light of these subtleties, I want to make two main statements about propositional orthodoxy: (1) propositional orthodoxy is not enough; and (2) the concept of propositional orthodoxy is indispensable for the church. Let us explore this in more depth.

The discourse on orthodoxy cannot be reduced to propositional orthodoxy. Propositional orthodoxy (i.e., accepting doctrinal statements) will lead to doctrinal orthodoxy and what could be called "positional orthodoxy," the acceptance of standpoints in line with official and formal Catholic teaching (e.g., regarding contraception, homosexuality). Propositional orthodoxy can be separated from community and form of life. Edward Collins Vacek suggested an interesting exercise. "Envisage a great systematic theologian who brilliantly understands and organizes each major item of the *Catechism of the Catholic Church*. This scholar, however, no longer believes any of these Catholic claims. He still teaches orthodox positions, but he has been alienated from Christianity."[8] Of course, in practice, it would be difficult to sustain this cognitive dissonance, but it is not unheard of.[9] Propositions have to be appropriated; they have to be affectively apprehended. Such personal and emotional investment requires personal experience and personal language. Certain propositions can be appropriated more easily than others; some are a struggle, while others are a life experience changing one's position on a moral question such as the indissolubility of marriage.

Thus seen, propositional orthodoxy is not enough. After mentioning subjective gnosticism as a source for worldliness, Pope Francis goes on to talk about the "self-absorbed promethean neopelagianism" of those "who ultimately trust only in their own powers

---

8. Vacek, "Orthodoxy Requires Orthopathy," 219.

9. See Dennett's and LaScola's exploration of clergy who have lost faith, based on thirty-five interviews; some tragic stories emerge. See Daniel C. Dennett and Linda LaScola, *Caught in the Pulpit: Leaving Belief Behind* (Durham, NC: Pitchstone, 2015).

and feel superior to others because they observe certain rules or remain intransigently faithful to a particular Catholic style from the past. A supposed soundness of doctrine or discipline leads instead to a narcissistic and authoritarian elitism, whereby instead of evangelizing, one analyzes and classifies others, and instead of opening the door to grace, one exhausts his or her energies in inspecting and verifying" (EG 94). The pope also clearly states that a person who adopts this positon is not really concerned with Jesus Christ. Propositional orthodoxy is compatible with a life of indifference, with "dead orthodoxy."

Karl Rahner distinguishes between the printed and the unprinted catechism, and the two major mistakes that are often made: underestimating the unprinted catechism or underestimating the printed one:

> When you ask the orthodox Christian for his beliefs, he will refer you to the Catechism, where all the truths of faith which have been expressed most explicitly and in an existentially clear manner in the history of the Faith up to date, have kept their unchanged place. The orthodox Christian seldom stops to realize that the unprinted catechism of his heart and religious life has quite a different distribution of materials from his printed Catechism, and that in the former many pages of the latter are missing completely or have become quite faded and illegible.[10]

The unity of Cartesian logic looking at the coherent body of doctrines with the *logique du coeur* is of preeminent importance here. But it is also epistemically irresponsible to ignore the printed catechism: "The 'unorthodox', the one who has leanings towards heresy, and the 'heretic', open their internal catechism as it were reflectively: whatever they do not find clear in it, they would then like to see removed from both the printed and unprinted Catechism. They say: whatever we

---

10. Karl Rahner, "The Resurrection of the Body," in Karl Rahner, *Theological Investigations II*, trans. Karl Heinz Kruger (London: Darton, Longman & Todd, 1963), 203-16, at 203-4.

grasp today quickly and clearly, vitally and comfortingly in our heart and life, should not weigh down the memory and mind of the Christian of today."[11] "Inconvenience" is a plausible attribute of orthodoxy if we were to take costly discipleship seriously. It may be inconvenient to wait for the meaning of a proposition to emerge; it may be inconvenient to accept the *Sitz im Leben* of doctrinal clarifications that amount to the insight: doctrinal orthodoxy understood as firm acceptance of propositions is not enough. Can one claim to have accepted a deep statement without inner engagement and a transformation of life?

Yes, doctrines are indispensable guideposts; they have to have the kind of "spiritual clarity" that enables a person to build her life on that doctrine, and this clarity cannot be reached by way of narratives alone. There has to be the defining capacity of a proposition. Doctrines are indispensable in upholding the expressions of truth in a propositional form; they are an expression of love of God and loyalty to the gospel—"the integrity of the Gospel message must not be deformed" (EG 39). Gospel sentences are much more than single words strung together; they are Word of God. Doctrinal statements are also much more than just "sentences." They are "important propositions," in Bernard Bolzano's sense, as outlined in Chapter 3. They are propositions that influence our lives as a whole and therefore, too, our systems of virtue and happiness. If we maintain that only those epistemic resources are relevant for salvation that govern our powers of judgment, convictions, and knowledge acquired, then the question as to modes and possibilities of access and distribution of epistemic resources acquires theological relevance. Doctrines have to be lived so that they can come alive in another person: "We need to remember that all religious teaching ultimately has to be reflected in the teacher's way of life, which awakens the assent of the heart by its nearness, love and witness" (EG 42). In his book on teachers George Steiner sees the teacher as a messenger who was a hearer of the Word and is now in a position to pass it on, because she has made the received teaching her own.[12] The teaching of doctrine, then, is a testimony of life. The sheer

---

11. Ibid., 204.
12. George Steiner, *Lessons of the Masters* (Cambridge, MA: Harvard University Press, 2003).

acceptance of dogmatic propositions without pastoral commitments and the commitments called for by the Catholic Social Tradition is not enough.

John McSweeney underscored the limits of "doctrinal orthodoxy" ("propositional orthodoxy," "positional orthodoxy") in a comment on the so-called Murphy Report by the Irish government on child abuse within the archdiocese of Dublin. The report, chaired by Yvonne Murphy, was issued in 2009.[13] McSweeney identified section 1.55 of the report as key to understanding the situation. Here the report states:

> The Church is not only a religious organisation but also a human/civil instrument of control and power. The Church is a significant secular power with major involvement in education and health and is a major property owner. As an organisation operating within society, it seems to the Commission that the Church ought to have some regard to secular requirements in its choice of leader. The Archbishop is the manager of the Archdiocese as well, of course, as being its spiritual leader. The Church is not a democracy and does not have transparent selection procedures so it is not known what criteria are used when Archbishops are being chosen. Appointments to positions as Archbishops and bishops seem to have been made primarily on the basis of doctrinal orthodoxy.

In this last sentence McSweeney is reflecting on the twofold challenge that arises from such an understanding of orthodoxy: (1) "'Doctrinal orthodoxy' seems a reasonable standard for an aspiring leader in the Church. The trouble is, however, that in recent years the orthodoxy required, especially for archbishops, includes some moral rulings that many of the *Christifideles* would not fully embrace."[14] It would be all too easy to say that this was solely a problem of the theologically uneducated and morally defective faithful. The question is whether

---

13. John McSweeney, "Doctrinal Orthodoxy," *The Furrow* 61, no. 5 (2010): 306-8.
14. Ibid., 306.

orthodoxy is to be framed in terms of "if a statement is an authentic doctrine of the community, then it is true or right" or rather in terms of "if a statement is true or right, then it is an authentic doctrine of community."[15] Doctrinal orthodoxy is not necessarily transforming; it can be safe, preserving and conserving without an element of existential transformation and without attending to the signs of the times. A certain understanding of orthodoxy made the bishops, as the report states in 1.30, adjust priorities in the sense that "the highest priority was the protection of the reputation of the institution and the reputation of priests." For good reason, McSweeny favors spiritual leadership based on "listening," on consideration of community and congregation, which amounts to a more relational understanding of orthodoxy.

Because propositional orthodoxy clearly has limits I suggest embracing the idea of discursive minimalism, as articulated by Pope Francis: "Saint Thomas Aquinas pointed out that the precepts which Christ and the apostles gave to the people of God 'are very few.' . . . Citing St. Augustine, he noted that the precepts subsequently enjoined by the church should be insisted upon with moderation 'so as not to burden the lives of the faithful' and make our religion a form of servitude, whereas 'God's mercy has willed that we should be free'" (EG 43). The pope refers to STh I-II,107,4, where we can see how Aquinas discusses the Old Law prescribing ceremonies and putting a heavier burden on us than the New Law, which "added very few precepts to those of the natural law. . . . Even in these Augustine says that moderation should be observed, lest good conduct should become a burden to the faithful" (STh I-II,107,4 resp.). Aquinas, however, also states that the precepts of the New Law are more burdensome than the precepts of the Old Law with regard to the inner life and the emphasis on interior acts. This thought could be translated into the implications of emphasizing love in the sense that the personal commitment to a living relationship with the living God is more challenging (requiring more depth) than the acceptance of propositions or the carrying out of ceremonies.

---

15. Kathryn Greene-McCreight, "Feminist Theology and a Generous Orthodoxy," *Scottish Journal of Theology* 57 (2004): 95-108, at 100-101.

Discursive minimalism also makes practical sense since over-complexity cannot be administered. These questions gain in significance when set against the self-referential terminology of church documents and texts that construct an increasingly impervious web of discursive commitments.[16] How can we reconcile the pressure of "thick coherence" with divine creativity and with the poor? May this not also demand a switch from perfectly polished "prepared" phrases to a more rough and ready, "raw" approach and mode of expression? Would a language that is acceptable to the poor be the same as the one used among theological and ecclesiastical elites?[17] *Evangelii gaudium* argues for a pluralism and freshness of expression and warns us not to think "that the Gospel message must always be communicated by fixed formulations" (EG 129). These are grounds to think about the limitations of propositional orthodoxy.

There is an undeniably existential dimension to orthodoxy even in its propositional form; even the concept of propositional orthodoxy was developed in conversation, although probably among a few intellectuals. Christopher Celenza made an acute sociological observation that the focus in the debate about orthodoxy should be shifted "away from religion in the abstract and onto small communities of intellectuals and the manner in which they receive and generate new ideas."[18] The discourse on orthodoxy reflects both a process of consensus building and networks of power. The propositional form of creeds condenses debates as well as negotiations. The core issue here seems to be that a set of propositions with identity-conferring power, thus establishing a framework for orthodoxy, has emerged in conversations to fend off heresies. Augustine concedes that the church

---

16. Cf. Robert Brandom, *Making It Explicit: Reasoning, Representing and Discursive Commitment* (Cambridge, MA: Harvard University Press, 1994), esp. 141-98.

17. Gerald Cohen has introduced the interpersonal test to ask "whether the argument could serve as a justification of a mooted policy when uttered by any member of society to any other member" (Gerald Cohen, *Rescuing Justice and Equality* [Cambridge, MA: Harvard University Press, 2008], 42).

18. Christopher S. Celenza, *The Lost Italian Renaissance: Humanists, Historians, and Latin's Legacy* (Baltimore: Johns Hopkins University Press, 2006), 82.

learned from dealing with errors, that is, from conversations with heresies.[19] Assaults of heresy can contribute to the vitality and clarification of faith and can serve as testing grounds for the faithful.[20] James Sosnoski sees the concept of orthodoxy as a response to an accepted set of beliefs (which he calls *doxa*) being challenged.[21] This defensive understanding depicts the developing process of orthodoxy as a form of social bonding. And this brings us to a second dimension of orthodoxy: institutional orthodoxy.

5.2 Institutional Orthodoxy

The actual term *orthodoxy* developed out of the gradual institutionalization of church and dogma. According to historian Hans-Georg Beck, the word was not used before the fourth century.[22] In his *Nicomachean Ethics* (7.9), Aristotle used the term *orthodoxeō* (but not *orthodoxia*) to underline the correct philosophical school of thought. References to orthodoxy in early Christian texts usually use it in the sense of existential, that is, in connection with hope and love, or in stressing the need to cling to faith no matter what, or again in connection with the fruits of faith, such as peace.[23] The term *orthodoxy* itself then undergoes a twofold transformation in its philosophical and its

---

19. Augustine, *De vera religione* VI,10.

20. Based on these consideration John Henderson reflects on the providentiality of heresy (John Henderson, *The Construction of Orthodoxy and Heresy* [Albany: State University of New York Press, 1998], 171-77).

21. "Orthodoxy is a defense of beliefs once taken for granted by the members of an organization instituted by a commitment to an aim justified by the beliefs in question" (James J. Sosnoski, *Token Professionals and Master Critics: A Critique of Orthodoxy in Literary Studies* [Albany: State University of New York Press, 1994], 104) (the entire quotation is in italics in the original). Sosnoski's notion of "doxa" (beliefs taken for granted) reminds us of Thomas Kuhn's concept of a paradigm that will also be more explicitly expressed if challenged.

22. Hans Georg Beck, *Das byzantinische Jahrtausend* (Munich: Beck, 1978), 87. "Orthodoxy" could originally have been a Christian term, since "pagan grace" was not commonly used.

23. *Epistle of Barnabas*, ch. 1; *Didache*, ch. 16; *Shepherd of Hermas*, ch. 8; Clement's *First Letter to the Corinthians*, ch. 22.

existential meaning. First, it becomes the benchmark representing a way of life that stands in sharp contrast to its philosophical use; this is a practical bias through which life is perceived as a whole with all its facets and elements and thus gains in importance and meaning. Second, the term "theoretical" is upgraded and moves from *pistis* to *doxa*. *Doxa,* unlike *pistis,* is not subjective in meaning and relies on validation for essence and value; "the δόξα has to be correct."[24] Perceiving *orthodoxy* as a "correct school of thought" demands a benchmark of conformity against which prevailing doctrine can be measured Such norms avail themselves of legal language and juridical mechanisms. It can be argued that orthodoxy is embedded in discursive formations devised by legal scholars who base their judgment on the literary genre of creeds understood as a set of beliefs.[25] It has also been argued that certain types of organization will elicit heresies, especially organizations with strict and universal claims.[26]

These were the circumstances in which the emerging Christian church found itself. A council was needed to oversee and supervise exactly this: to agree upon and draw up unequivocal guidelines of best-practice standards, so to speak, provide an incentive to set principles and doctrines down in writing, a medium that allowed and demanded a higher degree of objectivity than the spoken word. Stelios Chiotakis maintains that orthodoxy suggests an intellectual processing of faith and implies that pneumatic-charismatic church structures have been adapted or adjusted to suit everyday needs and have been transformed into ecclesiastical norms and doctrines guaranteed and upheld by the written constitution. In the course of time, stereotyping and institutionalizing routine have replaced an understanding of orthodoxy as spontaneous faith through conformity of belief administered by prevailing sovereign powers.[27]

---

24. Beck, *Das byzantinische Jahrtausend,* 87.

25. Norman Calder, "The Limits of Islamic Orthodoxy," in Farhad Daftary, ed., *Intellectual Traditions in Islam* (London: Tauris, 2000), 66-86, at 83.

26. Randall Collins, *Weberian Sociological Theory* (Cambridge: Cambridge University Press, 1986), 218.

27. Stelios Chiotakis, "Der Sinn der Orthodoxie—Herrschaftsstrukturen

This process of institutionalization indicates the shift from ortho-doxy as dogma to orthodoxy as a political phenomenon with doctrinal links and implications. This shift can probably be seen most clearly in the phenomenon of heresies. Wrong beliefs lead to "wrong practices," and because of that to a disruption of "communities of practiced faith." Roman authorities applied the term "sect" to St. Paul's com-munity (Acts 24:5; 28:22), implying that Paul's activities would lead to "dissension among Jews all over the world"; the Romans also stated that "this sect is denounced everywhere." The doctrinal aspect cannot be separated from the social and political aspects.

Damaging orthodoxy in a theological understanding violates the integrity of the body of Christ; it wounds the unity of Christ's body.[28] Orthodoxy not only guarantees a proper relationship with God but also a proper harmony within the community of faith. The concept of heresy has to be distinguished from concepts of apostasy (total repu-diation of the Christian faith) and schism (refusal of submission to the Roman pontiff or of communion with the members of the church subject to him), even though they all share the built-in dynamism of eroding unity and communal integrity. Heresy, according to Catholic teaching, is "the obstinate post-baptismal denial of some truth which must be believed with divine and catholic faith, or it is likewise an obstinate doubt concerning the same."[29] The concept of heresy pre-supposes fundamental Christian commitments; it is brought forward by a Christian believer; it generally refers to a theological truth that is not open to non–revelation-based debates; it contains an element of pertinacity, which is a morally but also epistemically relevant cat-egory, a category opposed to "prudence," which involves "*docilitas*."[30] An act of heresy can only be identified if it fulfills three conditions: (1) there is a fundamental truth of faith expressed in a proposition; (2) there are clearly identifiable and applicable criteria in determining the degree of deviation and divergence; (3) there is the claim and the

und Orthodoxie in Byzanz und Griechenland," in M. N. Ebertz and R. Schützei-chel, eds., *Sinnstiftung als Beruf* (Wiesbaden: VS, 2010), 71-85, at 71.

28. *Catechism of the Catholic Church*, 817.

29. Ibid., 2089.

30. See Aquinas, STh II-II, 48,1.

power structure to sanction established deviation. This third point is closely linked with the principle of sovereignty as outlined above by Chiotakis. Rome established itself as the center of Christianity from the second century onward;[31] after this, the struggle for orthodoxy characterized the Christian community, partly because of the challenges of "seeking and finding itself," and partly because of the specific theological as well as social institutionalization.[32]

Insights into the discourse on heresies as political challenges can be found in Umberto Eco's novel *The Name of the Rose*, which was mentioned in the previous chapter in connection with the medieval dispute over poverty. Eco establishes a link between poverty and heresy, thus embracing a social theory of heresy that he puts in the mouth of William of Baskerville: "I think the mistake is to believe that the heresy comes first, and then the simple folk who join it (and damn themselves for it). Actually, first comes the condition of being simple, then the heresy."[33] Social and political exclusion will lead to epistemic and spiritual exclusion. Eco reconstructs orthodoxy in

---

31. Walter Bauer, *Rechtgläubigkeit und Ketzerei im ältesten Christentum* (Tübingen; J. C. B. Mohr, 1964), 231.

32. Paul Asveld underlines the uniqueness of this dynamics: "Le souci d'orthodoxie et la lutte contre hérésie caractérisent donc le christianisme dès la deuxième moitié du premier siècle. Nous ne découvrons rien de comparable ni dans le monde greco-romain, ni même dans le monde juif. La raison essentielle de ce phénomène reside dans le fait qu'y faisait défaut l'idée d'une orthodoxie canonisée, l'idée d'une dogmatique comme norme de la foi à une révélation jugée decisive, formulae en une confession de foi obligatoire, amenant à vouloir distinguier le vrai du faux dans le detail et à dépister les deviations doctrinales" ("The concern for orthodoxy and the fight against heresy thus characterize Christianity in the second half of the first century. There is nothing comparable, neither in the Greco-Roman world, nor even in the Jewish world. The primary reason for this phenomenon lies in the absence of the following: a canonized orthodoxy, dogma as a standard of faith in a revelation deemed decisive, formulae in a mandatory confession of faith, leading to a capacity for distinguishing right from wrong in detail and to detect deviations in doctrine") (Paul Asveld, "Orthodoxie et hérésie," in Christiane d'Haussy, ed., *Orthodoxie et hérésie* [Paris: Didier-Érudition 1993], 17-24, at 22).

33. Umberto Eco, *The Name of the Rose*, trans. William Weaver (New York: Houghton Mifflin Harcourt, 2014), 215.

terms of power, as a strategy of a dominant and powerful group, a "church of the powerful and wealthy." Orthodoxy is presented within a particular organizational framework and a certain type of social regulation that directs members' behavior as well as beliefs.[34] Consequently, Eco's novel draws a picture of heresy as social discontent. The historical context anchored in Eco's novel is particularly ideal for addressing issues related to maintaining power, promoting unity and community, and the ensuing emergence and role of heresy.[35] It is worthwhile mentioning that the novel, set in 1327 and featuring William Ockham, discusses the rightness of faith in close connection with rights and issues of power. Historically, William Ockham questioned the established authorities to assess the status of a theological position; he expressed his conviction that the pope himself had fallen into heresy, and he emphasized the importance of epistemic authority (i.e., authority based on expertise) and its priority over deontic authority (i.e., authority based on position and status).[36] In his *Dialogus*, Ockham challenged the reduction of heresy to a legal category and defined heresy in the strict sense as "an assertion that was not consonant with Scripture." He also differentiated between different modes of heresy beyond contradicting Scripture, namely, to oppose the unwritten doctrine of the apostles; to deny what has been revealed to the church since the time of the apostles; to contradict

---

34. This understanding of orthodoxy would bring the discourse close to the discourse on ideology and the exercise of power through ideological means. Cf. Jean-Pierre Deconchy, *Orthodoxie réligieuse et sciences humaines* (La Haye: Mouton, 1980), 272-73.

35. Christoph Auffarth, for instance, discusses the construction of heresy with the aim of constructing identity using Catharism by way of example. See Christoph Auffarth, "Das Ende der Katharer im Konzept einer europäischen Religionsgeschichte," in Kocku von Stuckrad and Brigitte Luchesi, eds., *Religion im kulturellen Diskurs—Religion in Cultural Discourse: Festschrift für Hans G. Kippenberg zu seinem 65. Geburtstag* (RGVV 52; Berlin: de Gruyter, 2004), 291-305.

36. One could see the year 1277 as the first clash of Magisterium and academic theology, also as a conflict between those two types of authority; see Kurt Flasch, *Aufklärung im Mittelalter? Die Verurteilung von 1277* (Mainz: Dieterich, 1989).

the approved chronicles, histories, or oral traditions; to contradict the sources of catholic truth. "In short, heresy was defined as a contradiction of either Scripture or the extrascriptural sources of Christian doctrine."[37] The point of the heresy, then, is not a verdict by an authority but the deviation from normative sources. In other words, it has to be evidence based.

And this is the point where things can become murky and muddled; heresy as a social conflict is easier to understand than heresy as doctrinal error. If questions of orthodoxy and heterodoxy were reduced to power issues and power relations, it would be possible to reconstruct Christian orthodoxy without reference to Jesus Christ. Clearly, there is an indispensable theological element that calls for subtle distinction and nuanced judgments. Judging a position to be heretical requires theological depth and even *finesse* because heresies presuppose common ground. Only in a very wide understanding of the word can religions be considered as being heretical to each other; normally, a heresy is placed within the dynamics of a shift from a right to an erroneous belief, but not from belief to unbelief. Aquinas's definition of heresy is based on this understanding of common ground as "a species of disbelief, attaching to those who profess faith in Christ yet corrupt his dogma."[38] We have people with firm and fervent beliefs—the opposite of the lukewarm Christians rejected in Revelation 3:16—and these firm believers who really care about matters of faith and theological commitments challenge established beliefs. "The person who deviated from the larger group did so in the overwhelming conviction that he was right and the others were wrong."[39] In other words, a religious community interested in believers with robust concern about Christianity will run a higher risk of heresy formation than a community of more thoughtless and more carefree

---

37. Takashi Shogimen, "William of Ockham and Conceptions of Heresy, c. 1250–c. 1350," in Ian Hunter, John Christian Laursen, and Cary J. Nederman, eds., *Heresy in Tradition: Transforming Ideas of Heresy in Medieval and Early Modern Europe* (Hants, UK: Ashgate, 2005), 59-70, at 65.

38. Aquinas, STh II-II, 11,1, resp.

39. Rufus M. Jones, *The Church's Debt to Heretics* (New York: George H. Doran, n.d.), 11.

Christians. The boundaries and distinctions between heretics, martyrs, and witnesses of truth may not always be clear. A person seeking to do God's will and not to conform to a "spirit of worldliness" may pose a high epistemic and social risk factor. A spirit of worldliness may deem it prudent to abstain from conflict of any kind and from upsetting communal structures. Real problems are caused by the people who care and not by the indifferent and lukewarm members of a community. People who care will see the existential implications of "propositional orthodoxy"; they will see that it is "not just words" that could be changed and adjusted.

Karl Rahner has deepened our understanding of this first paradox.[40] A heresy is, spiritually speaking, very dangerous; it threatens the foundations of one's spiritual existence. A heretic is a person who cares, not a person who has fallen into the heresy of "dead orthodoxy," which is "merely the result and expression of an inner indifference towards truth."[41] A heresy can be an expression of a terrible error, terrible for the person in the erroneous state, terrible for the affected community. There is a lot at stake. A person can love God and still be in error. But this is the key point: the love of God. I see no theological grounds to question this.

There is a second paradox: a heresy presupposes common ground. A heresy distinguishes itself from an apostasy in that it is not so much a falling *out* of a community than a falling *within* a community. "Historically effective and powerful heresies are not simply assertions deriving from stupidity, obstinacy and inadequate information. Rather they are rooted in an authentic and original experience moulded by some reality and truth."[42] Given these caveats, it seems that a Church of the Poor with its institutional humility and commitment to dialogue and encounter would be willing to accept the learning challenge from positions that can be qualified as heresies, at least in terms of the effort to make sense of the experience leading to

---

40. See Karl Rahner, *On Heresy* (New York: Herder & Herder, 1964).

41. Karl Rahner, "What Is Heresy?" in Karl Rahner, *Theological Investigations V*, trans. Karl Heinz Kruger (London: Darton, Longman & Todd, 1966), 468-512, at 508.

42. Rahner, *On Heresy*, 38.

the position. There is always a story, always a history; no one wakes up one morning and "decides" to be a heretic. There is a communal dimension to heresy with social and relational aspects. This is where Ockham's account is reductionist.

An act of heresy is thus a subjective and a personal act of faith with both moral and social aspects; it cannot be separated from the moral dimensions of dialogue or from the public ripple effect on communal life, including the disruption of a *communion* or the splitting apart of a segment of this community. The moral aspects of a lack of orthodoxy are traditionally reconstructed as pertinacity, stubbornness, unwillingness to subordinate self and beliefs to the authorities in power. Heresy thus becomes not only a dogmatic but also a moral and political affair that impinges on personal character traits and the public sphere. Notifications made by the Congregation for the Doctrine of the Faith on publications lacking in orthodox principles provide us with a history of the debate and steps undertaken to combat it, as becomes apparent in, for example, the introduction to the Notification of March 30, 2012, on Margaret Farley's book *Just Love: A Framework for Christian Sexual Ethics*. We find not only references to documents justifying the judgment on the theological status of the incriminated text but also references to interactions similarly providing, we could say, implicit or explicit judgments on relevant relationships or even the spiritual and moral status of the author. The same dynamics can be observed in the wording of the Notification (January 2, 1997) by the Congregation for the Doctrine of the Faith about Tissa Balasuriya's book *Mary and Human Liberation*, a harsh dispute that eventually led to the temporary excommunication of the Sri-Lankan theologian. The discourse on orthodoxy and heterodoxy, then, reflects the quality of a person's relationship to the relevant authorities (entrusted with monitoring and guarding, as it were, the foundations of orthodoxy); it goes without saying that psychological aspects of social skills as well as sociological aspects of power negotiations come into play as well.

A learning church would monitor these aspects and reflect on possible entry points for sinfulness. Institutional humility should be reflected on in compassionate language, together with a commitment to "try to make sense":

It can be tempting to regard Church orthodoxy as automatically demonstrating scholarly competence. It can imagine that the great questions of God and the world have been discussed enough and that all that is required is to pass on the sacred formulas like an inheritance of ancient and precious jewels; it can harden its heart and not see behind the opponent's false assertions the deep distress of a fellow man; it can forget that not all talk about truth is automatically done in love, although this ought to be the case. It is possible for theology to be carried on in a sinful manner. This is because the theologians are themselves sinners.[43]

We might want to think about a closer conceptual link between orthodoxy and sinfulness, especially since "sin" is a category that characterizes a relationship, a relationship between God and the human person. Orthodoxy as a term makes statements about a relationship rather than about an epistemic situation. It is the relationship between a person and God, on the one hand, and the relationship between a person and her faith community, on the other hand, that is at stake. This second dimension, the communal aspect of orthodoxy, confronts us with the concept of conscience, with issues of humility, of proper obedience, and with listening skills. Orthodoxy in this second regard has a lot to do with "obedience." Obedience is first and foremost openness to listening; a faithful member will listen carefully to her community and the community's leadership. The famous opening word in the Prologue of the *Regula Benedicti* is the following exhortation: *Obsculta.* Listen! The word *obsculta* points to an active "stretching out towards the source." The image of the "inclination of the ears of the heart" points to a deep understanding of listening as allowing something to enter one's innermost being. Orthodoxy is in its communal aspect primarily a spiritual task of listening.

And this is not only an invitation to "the faithful as the flock" but also for the "shepherds leading," who are also responsible leaders in

---

43. Karl Rahner, "The Historicity of Theology," in Karl Rahner, *Theological Investigations IX*, trans. Graham Harrison (London: Darton, Longman & Todd, 1972), 64-82, at 76.

a context that values "orthodoxy" (right relationships to sisters and brothers in the light of a right relationship with God). In the *Regula Benedicti* the imperative of listening is not only relevant for simple monks; it is also constitutive for monastic leadership. The *Rule of Benedict* mentions the practice of "listening willingly to holy reading" as an instrument of good works; "obedience" to God is the key for exercising the abbot's responsibility.[44] The abbot must be a hearer of the Word; "the abbot should never teach, prescribe, or command (God forbid!) anything contrary to the laws of the Lord; but his commands and teaching should be instilled like a leaven of divine justice into the minds of his disciples."[45] A person has a right relationship with God as a hearer of the Word if these listening skills are reflected in the person's readiness and capability to listen to the people of God and the *sensus fidelium*, and to sources of normativity inspired by God, such as the Sacred Scriptures, the tradition, and the Magisterium. Orthodoxy in this understanding is not so much the ability to speak as the ability to listen.

This commitment to a "listening orthodoxy" is also part of the "teaching for teachers" of Vatican II: According to the council, the teaching office is based on "listening devoutly" to the Word of God (*Dei verbum* 10). Members of religious orders are reminded that their key calling is listening to the words of Christ (*Perfectae caritatis* 5). The priest is warned against becoming an empty preacher of the Word of God; he should be a listener inwardly (*Dei verbum* 25). The document on priestly training emphasizes the fostering of capabilities such as "the ability to listen to others and to open their hearts and minds in the spirit of charity to the various circumstances and needs of men" (*Optatam totius* 19); the priest is admonished "to willingly listen to the laity" (*Presbyterorum ordinis* 9). Bishops are encouraged to

---

44. "Lectiones sanctas libenter audire" (RB 4,55). The abbot is reminded to listen to the council of his confrères ("audiens consilium fratrum"; RB 3,2), but his entire leadership is based on fear of God and obedience to the *Regula* (RB 3,11).

45. "Ideoque abbas nihil, extra praeceptum domini quod sit, debet aut docere aut constituere vel iubere, sed iussui eius vel doctrina fermentum divinae iustitiae in discipulorum mentibus conspargatur" (RB 2,4-5).

"listen more attentively to laymen who are outstanding for their virtue, knowledge, and experience" (*Christus Dominus* 10). The bishop should also be "ready to listen" to the priests (*Christus Dominus* 16), even "gladly listen" to them (*Presbyterorum ordinis* 7), and should, in general, "not refuse to listen to his subjects" (*Lumen gentium* 27). Similarly, religious superiors are instructed to "gladly listen to their subjects" (*Perfectae caritatis* 14). Orthodoxy within a community is based, as we can see, on the virtue of listening; I would suggest that we understand listening as a virtue, integrating in itself aspects of patience (an attitude of "waiting" and also "vulnerability because of the risks involved in being spoken to"), aspects of humility (openness and commitment to reality), aspects of courage (accepting the risks that come with the exposure to the word). "Listening" is a particular trait of presence, of being present in a situation, of being attentive and open. If the bishops exercising the ordinary Magisterium are called to listen, to listen also to the *sensus fidelium*, then this culture of listening is part of a Church of the Poor, a church that listens to the poor, a church whose Magisterium is shaped by this listening to the cry of the poor. This cry may demand changes not only in language but also in practices, not only in "pastoral application" but also in moral considerations.

This concept of "listening orthodoxy" will play a major role in tackling the challenges involved although, at the same time, it cannot be denied that there are institutional risks linked to the concept and practice of orthodoxy. Andrew Cameron identifies "costs" of orthodoxy such as the connection between "zeal for orthodoxy" and "proneness to religious violence," the development of repressive legislation, and the direction of Christian writing "into what may well seem sterile."[46] It is safe to say that zeal for orthodoxy has led to the emergence of polemical writing that may not always help the cause of the credibility

---

46. Averil Cameron, "The Cost of Orthodoxy," *Church History and Religious Culture* 93 (2013): 339-61, 352 and 359, respectively. Rahner had made a similar point: "dogmatic theology today is very orthodox. . . . But it is not very vividly alive" (Karl Rahner, "The Prospects for Dogmatic Theology," in Karl Rahner, *Theological Investigations I*, trans. Cornelius Ernst [London: Darton, Longman & Todd, 1961], 1-18, at 13).

of Christian love of the other, let alone love of the enemy. And this is where we reach the existential dimension of orthodoxy.

5.3 Existential Orthodoxy

"There must be a conscious and intense orthodoxy in the field before there can be a standard that can be used to differentiate and determine heresy."[47] Quaker theologian Rufus Jones, who made this comment, was critical of the development of the discourse on orthodoxy, which he felt was moving away from what he called "Galilean Christianity":

> If by any chance Christ Himself had been taken by His later followers as the model and pattern of the new way, and a serious attempt had been made to set up His life and teaching as the standard and norm for the Church, Christianity would have been something vastly different from what it became. Then "heresy" would have been, as it is not now, deviation from His way, His teaching, His spirit, His doctrine. Love and Life—not doctrine—would have been the sacred words, the spiritual realities for a Christian.[48]

Existential orthodoxy precedes doctrinal orthodoxy; the latter presupposes the former and remains the point of reference as well as the *telos*. The simple message of the gospel as the main point of orientation underlines the discursive minimalism suggested—with primacy in some respect given to the pastoral dimension over the doctrinal one. Pope Francis is inviting his "listeners" to a pastoral (existential) approach in questions of orthodoxy when he states, "Pastoral ministry in a missionary style is not obsessed with the disjointed transmission of a multitude of doctrines to be insistently imposed" (EG 35). In other words, ministry, including the academic ministry of theology, serves; it serves the purpose of helping people to serve God, to be disciples, to grow in love. The Magisterium can be seen to be primarily a therapeutic institution charged with concern for those who need the doctor,

---

47. Jones, *The Church's Debt to Heretics*, 12.
48. Ibid., 15f.

charged with the healing of relationships and the healing of the wounds of error. The very name Pope Francis chose for himself underlines his commitment to a Franciscan tradition, a tradition that would see theology as practical. The thirteenth- and fourteenth-century Franciscan tradition of theology expresses this concern beautifully. Bonaventure perceived theology to be a discipline engendering wisdom, that knowledge necessary for life and allowing that fine line between knowing and doing to be crossed. Seen thus, theology is about changing people; in other words, we pursue theology "ut boni fiamus" (so that we may be good).[49] It is knowledge and understanding that bring about change in the lives of human beings.[50] Theology is about elevating the human intellect toward its intrinsic desire and need to reunite with God, and wisdom is exactly this condition of complete fulfillment: it is knowing the right path to take in life. This thread was taken up by John Duns Scotus, the Doctor Subtilis, who explicitly debated the question whether theology was practical.[51] Scotus describes praxis as the object of practical knowledge, and cognition and as an act of the will rather than the intellect whereby the will naturally "follows" the intellect and has to conform to right reason in order to be right.[52] Scotus

---

49. Bonaventure, In Sent I, Prooem., q 3, resp. See Bonaventure, Commentaria in quatuor libros Sententiarum Magistri Petri Lombardi, vol. 1 (Opera Omnia 1; Ed. Quaracchi, 1882), 13.

50. Realizing that Christ died for us and similar theological messages should move humankind to believe. In comparison, realizing that the diagonal of a square cannot be the same as the length of its sides does not and will never impact one's way of life: "Nam haec cognitio, quod Christus pro nobis mortuus est, et consimiles, nisi sit homo peccator et durus, movet at amorem; non sic ista: quod diameter est asymeter costae" (ibid.).

51. John Duns Scotus, Prologus, quaestio 3; Supplementum epigraphicum graecum 28-43; cf. Vladimir Richter, "Duns Scotus' Text zur Theologie als praktischer Wissenschaft," Collectanea franciscana 60 (1990): 459-74.

52. Johannes Duns Scotus, Über die Erkennbarkeit Gottes (Texte zur Philosophie und Theologie. Lateinisch-deutsch; ed. and trans. Hans Kraml, Gerhard Leibold, and Vladimir Richter; Hamburg: Meiner, 2000), 31; "Dico ergo quod praxis ad quam cognitio practica extenditur est actus alterius potentiae quam intellectus, naturaliter posterior intellectione, natus elici conformiter rationi rectae ad hoc ut sit rectus" (ibid., 30).

adds that the proper approach is paramount. Proper approach is the inner desire and willingness to employ all powers of reasoning for this purpose of orientation.[53] Theology accepts speculative thinking as a practical discipline only insofar as it serves the purpose of attaining practical knowledge and as such is subservient to praxis.[54] Speculative thinking in theology must, above all, recognize the "the guiding force of praxis" (*ad praxim dirigendam*).[55] Scotus rejects the idea that faith could be anything but practical. "Just as Faith is not a speculative habit and believing is not a speculative act, beatific vision is not a speculative act, but a practical one. For beatific vision must according to her nature proceed within intellect which is created so that true devotion can develop proportionately."[56] Faith is a habit, an act of doing; discerning God is part of a greater praxis, which precedes the *fruitio,* devotion to God which gives that ultimate peace in God. Faith, then, encompasses the individual in her entirety; it impacts action and the way we live our lives overall; it impacts the ultimate goal. If we understand theology as working within a practical framework, it is the theologically minded individual and her life that become the focus of attention.

A Church of the Poor will pay special attention to the experience of poverty, which will make it difficult to conceive of orthodoxy without orthopraxy and orthopathy.[57] Propositional orthodoxy is in a sense the tip of the existential iceberg; there are identity issues involved. The search for what was considered orthodox ("right belief") started

---

53. Ibid., 32; Scotus is citing Aristotle's *Nicomachean Ethics* (6.3–1139a 22-25), in which the right choice is required to be able to attain the right insight. He expands upon this idea to include the rightness of wanting, "quia ipsa requirit rationem rectam cui conformiter eliciatur" (ibid.).

54. Cf. ibid., 41: "Illa cognition est practica in qua non determinatur de speculabilibus magis quam eorum cognition pertineat ad praxim vel cognitionem practicam" (ibid., 40).

55. Ibid., 40.

56. Ibid., 43: "Fides non est habitus speculativus nec credere est visio speculativa, sed practica. Nata est enim ista visio esse conformis fruitioni et prius naturaliter haberi in intellectu creato ut fruitio recta illi conformiter eliciatur" (Ad argumenta principalia, ibid., 42).

57. R. Paul Stevens, "Living Theologically: Toward a Theology of Christian Practice," *Themelios* 20, no. 3 (1995): 4-8.

very early on within Christianity. The Christological debates during the first five centuries reflect this existential struggle to be Christians in the proper sense and to be disciples of Jesus Christ worthy of the name. It is important "to remember that all parties at all times in the patristic period considered themselves to be orthodox and never referred to themselves otherwise than as orthodox tells us something of the deep problems involved, and indeed is a pointer to the fact that more than reason was at stake."[58] We are dealing with existential issues rather than positional conflicts within a community of faith. This can clearly be traced if we were to look at key texts of the patristic era. If we rely on the early Christian literature of the period, for example, Eusebius of Caesarea's *Ecclesiastical History*, Theodoret of Cyrus's *History of the Monks of Syria* and his *History of the Church*, we are faced with the following complex views of orthodoxy.[59]

In the first half of the fourth century, Eusebius examines the task of preserving the purity of apostolic orthodoxy (3.38). He insists that for a text to be worthy, it must fulfill the prescriptive criterion of being in *harmony* with the apostolic ideal and tradition, which means it must refer directly back to a live encounter with Christ for it to be considered worthy of being classified as orthodox literature (3.31). The way in which orthodoxy is discussed and perceived is well illustrated by an exchange of letters between Dionysius, the bishop of Corinth, and Pinytus, the bishop of Knossos. Pinytus employs the image of wholesome, nutritious food versus a diet of milk to emphasize that people can and indeed must be given something to chew on (and over), to digest, so as not to spiritually fade and wither (4.23). This image depicts the (ever-increasing) levels of spiritual growth, in which an understanding of and for the divine becomes essential. Orthodoxy is seen in the

---

58. Cameron, *The Cost of Orthodoxy*, 344.

59. The following references are based on the carefully translated and annotated German versions of the texts: Eusebius, *Ausgewählte Schriften Band II: Kirchengeschichte*, trans. Philipp Häuser, Bibliothek der Kirchenväter 2 Reihe, Band 1 (Munich: Kösel, 1932); Theodoret von Cyrus, *Mönchsgeschichte*, trans. K. Gutberlet, Bibliothek der Kirchenväter, 1 Reihe, Band 50 (Munich: Kösel, 1926); Theodoret von Cyrus, *Kirchengeschichte*, trans. A. Seider, Bibliothek der Kirchenväter 1 Reihe, Band 51 (Munich: Kösel, 1926).

context of "the Spirit of the Church" (5.27), which reflects the spirit of the Holy Bible. Repeated reference is made to the fact that orthodoxy must be continually tried and tested. Eusebius expands on this line of thought in his example of the young man Origen. On the death of his father, we are told, Origen was taken in and then adopted by a noble woman whose husband belonged to a group of heretics centered in Alexandria at this time. Origen was thus forced to live under the same roof as this man, but was careful never to pray or be moved to pray together with him (6.2). This extract reflects the conviction that false faith can contaminate orthodoxy, which must be kept *pure* at all costs. The matter becomes even more subjective when we discover a few lines later that Origen *abhors* heretical teachings of any kind. Here we see the rejection of impure practices expressed in highly personal and emotional tones, that is, in the sense of it being in "bad taste." Orthodoxy is not perceived as a rigid adherence to a code of doctrines or principles but as keeping well away from impure—toxic—influences.

Theodoret of Cyrus is more interested in providing a perspectival description than a factual reconstruction of ecclesial history, which is why his detailed explanations can perhaps shed light on orthodoxy as terminology.[60] Eusebius's rather passionate outburst reflecting his orthodox "feelings" pointedly echo Theodoret's position. In his essay, *History of the Monks of Syria,* Theodoret describes Marcianus's strong sense of orthodoxy, which "abhors the blasphemous thoughts of Arius," as well as the "unsound arguments" and "dangerous doctrines" of Apollinarius, and regards the Euchites as his greatest enemy (3). All the emotional ammunition imaginable is rolled out to describe the zeal and industry Marcianus invests to defend orthodoxy. This emotional dimension of orthodoxy becomes even more apparent in his *History of the Church,* in which those attacking orthodoxy are portrayed as being "fraudulent" (4.29), "tyrannical," and "mercenary," and as such are lacking in moral values (1.4). They know and show no fear of God and even spurn divine judgment. "Fear of God" is seen to be a benchmark for assessing orthodoxy and the proper balance between what is human and what is divine. It is not surprising that in this context

---

60. Cf. Ferdinand Prostmeier, "Christliche Paideia. Die Perspektive Theodorets von Kyrrhos," *Römische Quartalschrift* 100 (2005): 1-29.

wisdom is linked with *orthodoxy* (4.7)—and even an ascetic disposition, which neither seeks nor finds value in worldly ways (4.32). Theodoret, too, employs the motive of the ethics of memory in orthodoxy, describing it as an inheritance to be preserved "untouched" (2.4; 2.33; 5.13). In a similar vein to Eusebius, Theodoret describes the dynamics of defilement that spread themselves by means of false beliefs, "smuggled in secretly" (2.8), or as infectious "diseases of the mind" (4.7). Orthodoxy by contrast is seen to be a "healthy attitude of mind" (4.8). One particularly telling text on the need for a pure understanding of intransigence in matters of orthodoxy is to be found in book 4 of his *History of the Church* and illustrated in an encounter between Basil, the bishop of Caesarea, Modestus the prefect, and Valens, who after his baptism by Eudoxius of Antioch displayed Arian-friendly views. The emperor wanted to put an end to the Arian ideology conflict and, according to Theodoret, had his prefect tell Basil "not to forsake so many churches on account of minor matters of accuracy pertaining to issues of dogma" (4.19). Such claims clearly indicate that it is not worth splitting hairs over a few small points. Theodoret goes on to express Basil's reaction to the issue in no uncertain terms. "They who are nurtured by divine words will not suffer so much as a syllable of the divine creeds to be let go" (4.19). *Orthodoxy* is about the words of doctrine, but not just any sort of doctrine; it is about those fundamental propositions that express the Divine himself and our understanding of the relationship between God and humankind: an absolute, nonnegotiable, no-go area, regardless of whether it be petty or not.[61]

---

61. At the same time, Theodoret describes how Ephrem the Syrian kept the original tune of a well-known melody and inserted an "orthodox" text in order for it to have a soothing and beneficial effect on his listeners (IV,29). This underlines the importance of getting across the message of orthodoxy in which the medium used is key, and the scope the message provides and projects which, if wholly subject to the strict rules and standards of uncontaminated doctrines, would not be feasibly possible. One could compare the dynamics at work here with the missionary work of Robert de Nobili, who modified his presentation to suit the needs of the listener without compromising the content or message of true Christian faith; see Cody C. Lorance, "Cultural Relevance and Doctrinal Soundness: The Mission of Roberto de Nobili," *Missiology* 33, no. 4 (2005): 415-24.

Orthodoxy can be characterized by attributes such as "strict" or "pure" or in aesthetic categories such as "beautiful."[62] Orthodoxy as an attitude and state of mind needs to be both nourished and practiced;[63] orthodoxy can be adapted and defended with much fervor and enthusiasm. It is the expression of a decision taken on how one wants to lead one's life, a way of life that is incommensurate with aspects of living. Thus, orthodoxy is an attitude of mind that governs one's approach to life. This is not a matter of changing the wording of propositions. It is a life-or-death matter. The early church is very clear on that. The ceaseless striving for orthodoxy is so much intertwined with the reality of martyrdom that no one can claim that issues of orthodoxy are primarily a dispute about the style and register or propositions. Those propositions that really matter should be treated with the utmost urgency and gravity: the divine being of God, eternal salvation, divine truth, sanctity, and divine will. These propositions express the truth of God and as such leave no room for compromise whatsoever.

This, then, is the image of orthodoxy that might be gleaned from early Christian writings. We see different conceptualizations of orthodoxy developed during this period, an understanding of orthodoxy as a "given" that finds itself challenged and sometimes even threatened by heterodox positions or an understanding of orthodoxy that sees orthodoxy as emerging from different competing versions. What was at stake was the idea of unity, both synchronically as well as diachronically, the unity of the existing community but also the union with tradition. Scriptural evidence and apostolicity, the unbroken line to the apostles, were the main patristic truth-tests used to establish the rightness of belief. We can read these texts as telling us the following: no orthodoxy without identity; no orthodoxy without accepting the truths of faith as existential, identity-conferring truths. No orthodoxy without existential commitments; in other words, the epistemic commitments entered by accepting, for example, statements of the creed, are existential commitments. A proposition of faith cannot be isolated from a form of life, and the core concern of orthodoxy must

---

62. Cf. Theodoret von Cyrus, *History of the Church* 5.3 (focusing on the "ugliness of Arian heresy").

63. Cf. ibid., 5.39—"sustaining orthodox piety."

be the way in which God's love is experienced and responded to. In an anonymous letter to Diognetus written in the second century we find an interesting description of orthodoxy as coming to "love the Logos" (chapter 11), which in the context of orthodoxy can be interpreted as that meaningful second-person perspective, that love given and received in a filial relationship with Logos.

As practical, theology is connected to questions of the good and proper life. The existential dimension of orthodoxy, especially relevant for a Church of the Poor, may invite new ways to think about "falling away from the church." Alberto Moira gives an account of extraordinary events that point in this direction:

> On 21 May 1986, a "Communication to the People of God" from the 11 bishops of the Brazilian state of Maranhão caused a disturbance throughout the country and far beyond. Ecclesiastical and political circles were astonished by the measure announced by the bishops. The Christian population and the press were officially informed that the Governor of Maranhão . . . its Chief of Police . . . and the newspaper publisher of the Federation of Landowners . . . "have cut themselves off from the community of the Church. There is no point if they show no signs of conversion in the true meaning of the Gospel."[64] This excommunication is astonishing since it was not based on schism or traditional heresy or blasphemy, but on what could be called "political or social offences.[65]

Construction of structural injustice and denial of justice to the poor were at the core of the understanding of orthodoxy that was being applied in this situation. Seeking orthodoxy, then, is seeking a proper relationship with God, a relationship that unfolds on our human journey, on our pilgrimage to see the face of God.

---

64. Alberto Moreira, "Orthodoxy for the Protection of the Poor?" in Johann-Baptist Metz and Edward Schillebeeckx, eds., *Orthodoxy and Heterodoxy* (Edinburgh: T&T Clark, 1987), 110-15, at 110.

65. Ibid., 111.

5.4 Orthodoxy of Pilgrims

We are pilgrims in the middle of a journey. Propositional orthodoxy opens new doors for moral and doctrinal temptations, such as the moral temptation of self-righteousness and the doctrinal temptation to see revelation as a possession that can be fully controlled. It is theologically and spiritually challenging to claim that one is in possession of the truth, and it is similarly challenging to claim that one could overcome every aspect of the "indeterminacy of orthodoxy." There is a sense in which the indeterminacy of orthodoxy has to be respected. We can distinguish at least three limits to the determinability of orthodoxy: (1) the dividing line between doctrine and God; (2) the limits of our individual personal perception of *doctrine*, that is, the dividing line between doctrine and person, between appropriation and doctrine; and (3) the boundaries that exist between nonpropositional aspects of faith and faith as way of life—as lived.

The first limitation has been expressed by the Fourth Lateran Council. "Inter creatorem et creaturam non potest tanta similitudo notari, quin inter eos maior sit dissimilitudo notanda" ("Between Creator and creature no similitude can be expressed without implying a greater dissimilitude").[66] Karl Rahner, who reflected on the central role of this dogmatic statement in his final theological reflections a week before his death, translates this point: "The Fourth Lateran Council clearly stated that from the perspective of this world, that is from any starting point we might conceive of based on human knowing, nothing substantial of a positive nature about God can be stated without, at the same time, perceiving the radical inadequacy of such affirmative statements."[67] That this "gap" or "distance" ("dissimili-

---

66. Denzinger 806.

67. Karl Rahner, "Experiences of a Catholic Theologian," in Declan Marmion and Mary E. Hines, eds., *The Cambridge Companion to Karl Rahner* (Cambridge: Cambridge University Press, 2007), 297-310, at 299. Joseph Ratzinger (Pope Benedict XVI) uses the same motif from the Fourth Lateran Council in his preface to the 2004 edition of "Introduction to Christianity" (Joseph Ratzinger, *Introduction to Christianity* [San Francisco: Ignatius Press, 2004], 23) and as Pope Benedict in his "Regensburg lecture" on September 12, 2006.

tude") between doctrine and the divine must not be closed or bridged has far-reaching implications for institutional humility as well. The second limitation is discussed in hermeneutics: What does it mean to understand one's understanding of a text? What does it mean to appropriate a text so that it can become "personal knowledge"? Graham Greene, with the characteristic freedom of fiction, alludes to aspects of this imitation when in his novel *The Heart of the Matter* he announces, "The Church knows all the rules, but it doesn't know what is going on in a single human heart."[68]

The insight into the inexhaustibility of the individual ("individuum est ineffabile") holds true for all entities, but especially for the individual human person with her depth. Pope Francis has echoed this same point in *Evangelii gaudium*: "One who accompanies others has to realize that each person's situation before God and their life in grace are mysteries which no one can fully know from without" (EG 172). Respect for the person expresses itself, among other things, in a certain abstinence from passing judgment. The third limit reminds us of the slightly elusive relationship between propositional, institutional, and existential orthodoxy, of the fact that there are limits to what a concept of propositional orthodoxy can achieve.

These three limits constitute aspects of "the indeterminacy of orthodoxy." Recognizing these aspects of an indeterminacy of orthodoxy will lead to cautious, slow, and humble approaches to judgments about orthodoxy, always respecting eschatological reservation. These limits are not "epistemic diseases"; they express our epistemic vulnerability as much as our need for companionship and correction. One of the main healing forces of orthodoxy the pope employs is the means of dialogue; this is the response we can give to the question of how to deal with the limits of the determinacy of orthodoxy outlined above. Orthodoxy is dialogical; orthodoxy is, in fact, relational in two ways: it concerns the relationship with God and it concerns social relationships. "In many places an administrative approach prevails over a pastoral approach" (EG 63); ignoring the depth and weight of these relation-

---

68. Graham Greene, *The Heart of the Matter* (New York: Penguin, 1971), 272. The church, of course, takes a pastoral approach in many contexts and thus differs from secular courts.

ships is a sign of loss of orthodoxy: "This practical relativism consists in acting as if God did not exist, making decisions as if the poor did not exist, setting goals as if others did not exist, working as if people who have not received the Gospel did not exist. It is striking that even some who clearly have solid doctrinal and spiritual convictions frequently fall into a lifestyle" (EG 80). Solid doctrinal and spiritual convictions will not guarantee that we do not fall into the trap of practical relativism, the idea of "orthodoxy as if God did not exist." Practical relativism administers church and theology "as if God did not exist." Studies of bureaucracy confirm that a main element in administration is standardization, the introduction of uniform procedures that provide the grounds for accountability (monitoring, evaluation) as well as for professionalization. A church without God may be—given the teachings on divine creativity—even more convenient, more comfortable, and more controllable. Dostoevsky's Grand Inquisitor captures this intuition well. Orthodoxy based on propositions is more easily administrated than orthodoxy based on relationships. As a relational category, orthodoxy is open to nuanced judgments; orthodoxy can gradually lose its righteousness—step-by-step orthodoxy can be transformed into "grey pragmatism" (EG 83).[69] It is healing to think of orthodoxy in relational terms, because it gives ownership to the (interpersonal truth of the) relationship rather than the (objectified truth of the) text. If one emphasizes the relationship with God, theological language can be understood to serve the purpose of transforming us ever more into becoming more and more aware of signs of God.[70]

Dialogue is healing, because dialogue enables us to address aspects of nonresolution without being disturbed by it. Dialogue can ensure

---

69. Pope Francis quotes a 1996 statement by Cardinal Joseph Ratzinger: "And so the biggest threat of all gradually takes shape: 'the gray pragmatism of the daily life of the Church, in which all appears to proceed normally, while in reality faith is wearing down and degenerating into small-mindedness'" (EG 83). There is another instance when Pope Francis makes the point of a living area turning grey: "Once we separate our work from our private lives, everything turns grey and we will always be seeking recognition or asserting our needs" (EG 83).

70. Cf. Susannah Ticciati, *A New Apophaticism: Augustine and the Redemption of Signs* (Leiden: Brill, 2013), esp. 217-46.

relational integrity and enable positional disagreement at the same time. One element of orthodoxy (based on a proper relationship with God) is its social dimension, that is, orthodoxy in its fullness is manifest in the ability to uphold relationships of dialogue (maybe even of prophetic dialogue[71]) with people who are not like minded and like spirited: "Even people who can be considered dubious on account of their errors have something to offer which must not be overlooked" (EG 236). This statement is relevant to the project of a Church of the Poor: yes, the homeless person may look "dubious," because he lacks proper clothing and proper language, but he has something to offer; yes, the investment banker may look "dubious," with her lifestyle and subjective justification of the remuneration she receives, but she has something to offer. Dialogue is a face-to-face encounter; it is an encounter of one person in the presence of another person looking and listening to her attentively. A state of "facelessness," a state lacking direct, personal encounter, can with all theological accuracy be described as "hell."[72]

When we meet someone face to face, when we "touch" the real face of that person, we see and sense so many more facets than those perceived by way of language or judgment. In order to fully understand and appreciate what people have to offer, we need to adopt a particular hermeneutic attitude, namely, "principles of charity." These are hermeneutical principles that commit a person to interpret another person as holding true beliefs wherever it is plausible to do so.[73]

---

71. Cf. Stephen B. Bevans and Roger P. Schroeder, *Constants and Context: A Theology of Mission for Today* (Maryknoll, NY: Orbis Books, 2004), 348; Stephen B. Bevans and Roger P. Schroeder, *Prophetic Dialogue: Reflections on Christian Mission Today* (Maryknoll, NY: Orbis Books, 2011); Stephen Bevans and Cathy Ross, eds., *Mission on the Road to Emmaus: Constants, Context and Prophetic Dialogue* (London: SCM, 2015).

72. Abbas Macarios, a desert father, had a vision of hell as a state where it is not possible to see anyone face to face; the face of one suffering person is fixed to the back of another suffering person. Hell is a place where people do not see each other (Benedicta Ward, ed., *The Sayings of the Desert Fathers: The Alphabetical Collection* [Kalamazoo, MI: Cistercian Publications, 1984], section 38, pp. 136-37).

73. Cf. Donald Davidson, "Radical Interpretation," *Dialectica* 27 (1973): 314-28.

Principles of charity set the default position for listening and interpreting; the basic assumption is that the other person is reasonable, well informed and of good will; one holds on to this assumption as long as possible. Without principles of charity it is impossible to learn a foreign language or make significant epistemic progress beyond familiar grounds. Principles of charity express a fundamental affirmation of the other person as a meaningful contributor and an epistemic agent. If a person makes a statement we accept this statement as a truthful basis for further statements and actions in the light of principles of charity. If you are learning a foreign language and you are told that *"fromage"* means "cheese," you will work with this information unless you have strong reasons to mistrust the translation.

But principles of charity are not enough; we need to go beyond that and embrace what I would call "epistemic mercy." Mercy has been defined as "the willingness to enter into the chaos of others."[74] Epistemic mercy is the willingness to patiently endure the chaos of another, to humbly await revelation and insight through the chaos of another. Mercy is the readiness to forgive, the readiness to make allowances, the readiness to make the effort to understand a person's overall situation beyond the obvious and the spoken. Mercy is the basis for proper judgment. EG 193 quotes James 2:12-13 ("So speak and so act as people who will be judged by the law of freedom. For the judgment is merciless to one who has not shown mercy; mercy triumphs over judgment"). In other words: there is no proper judgment without mercy. Jesus built the Church of the Poor on mercy and a heart moved by pity (Matt 14:14; 15:32), which enabled him to provide a gentle yoke (Matt 11:28-30) and to move beyond too strict an understanding of Sabbath laws (Matt 12:7, 10; Luke 6:5; 13:10-17; 14:1-5) with an ultimate commitment to well-being and goodness: "Is it lawful to do good on the sabbath rather than to do evil, to save life rather than destroy it?" (Mark 3:4). A commitment to mercy emerges in Jesus' way of dealing with sinful behavior, for example, in the encounter with the adulterous woman in John 8. The central value of mercy says a lot about the understanding of orthodoxy. There are many forms of

---

74. John F. Keenan, *The Works of Mercy: The Heart of Catholicism* (Lanham, MD: Rowman & Littlefield, 2008), 4.

joy in the gospel, but there is the special "joy of the Father who desires that none of his little ones be lost, the joy of the Good Shepherd who finds the lost sheep and brings it back to the flock" (EG 237).

Epistemic mercy is an aspect of the spiritual work of mercy of counseling and instructing, but also of the humility to accept counseling and instruction from unusual voices, especially people on the margins. Epistemic mercy is the willingness to allow the chaos of reality to shape one's thinking. It is an attitude that allows for transformative dialogue. Dialogue and encounter will lead to the discovery of differences; true encounters change the person. This attitude is important not only with outsiders but also within the church, in the dialogue among pilgrims with a strong sense of orthodoxy. Epistemic mercy is an attitude that accepts the lack of chaos as well as the lack of order in a person's belief system, shaped by her life. Forms of life matter epistemically. The situations a person has lived through will shape the categories and available exemplifications of that person; a person's biography will shape her theological judgments, which always imply a moment of "taste." And the conceptual clarification of "taste," according to Kant's *Critique of Judgment*, has to make use of indeterminate concepts. There will be limits as to what arguments can achieve.

Different persons will develop different theological tastes, will treasure different passages from the Holy Scriptures, will have different favorite dogmatic formulas. Each human person is called to her personal way of holiness. The uniqueness of the human person with her (unique) biography and her (unique) personality leads to the development of different spiritual and, consequently, different theological styles.[75] This difference in theological "tastes" and "styles" matter in our discussion of transforming orthodoxy since there are ample ways of mercilessness to enter the grounds of debates on orthodoxy. Existential orthodoxy asks us to appropriate revelation and the church's teaching in a personal way.

This personal way is unique. A human person develops her own spiritual style. "Spiritual style" is a distinctive way of living the faith; it is a spiritual "fingerprint." It is telling that St. John Paul II's episcopal

---

75. Cf. Robert J. Nogosek, *Nine Saints for Today: Different Spiritualities for Different Personalities* (Notre Dame, IN: Corby Books, 2015).

motto was "*Totus tuus,*" which expressed his commitment to Mary in words taken from St. Louis Marie Grignion de Montfort's *Treatise on True Devotion to the Blessed Virgin.* It is telling that Pope Benedict's episcopal motto was "*Cooperatores veritatis*" (collaborators of the truth); in his autobiography from 1997 he explained:

> As my episcopal motto I selected the phrase from the Third Letter of John "Co-workers of the truth." For one, it seemed to be the connection between my previous task as teacher and my new mission. Despite all the differences in modalities, what it involved was and remains the same: to follow the truth, to be at its service. And, because in today's world the theme of truth has all but disappeared, because truth appears to be too great for me and yet everything falls apart if there is no truth, for these reasons this motto also seemed timely in the good sense of the word.[76]

The motto Jorge Bergoglio chose was taken from Venerable Bede, *Homily* 21 (CCL 122.149-151), on the Feast of Matthew, where it said: "*Vidit ergo Jesus publicanum, et quia miserando atque eligendo vidit, ait illi, 'Sequere me'*" [Jesus therefore sees the tax collector, and since he sees by having mercy and by choosing, he says to him, "follow me"]. "By having mercy and by choosing" (*Miserando atque eligendo*) became his three-word motto. There are biographical notes to these selections of episcopal mottos that beg mention. Karol Wojtyła lost his mother when he was not yet nine years old; Joseph Ratzinger was struggling with relativism in Germany; Jorge Bergoglio had an experience of divine love and mercy on the Feast of St. Matthew in 1953.

One motto does not "contradict" another motto; there is a lot of space for healthy pluralism and spiritual nuance. But it cannot be denied that a motto reflects a particular "appropriation" of a tradition and a spirituality beyond "rule following"; and this appropriation with particular emphases will have an influence not only on forms of life but also on theological judgments. Persons develop specific

---

76. Joseph Ratzinger (Pope Benedict XVI), *Milestones* (San Franciso: Ignatius Press, 1997), 153.

spiritual and theological styles. And here we face a challenge to our understanding of orthodoxy in the sense that different spiritual styles lead to different ways of "doing" theological reflection and to "making" different theological judgments; these differences cannot be fully bridged by way of arguments, even though theological debate matters and arguments count. But unlike (most) theological models (many) spiritual styles do not follow patterns of argumentative justification. We are not only speaking about a limited number of different spiritual styles such as the distinction between cognitive and word centered; emotional and heart based; social and action centered; imaginative and symbol centered styles.[77] We are talking about personal styles that lead to a particular way of reading and connecting a person's inner experience with her social environment and the political context. It makes a difference whether a person draws inspiration from "nature" (like Malwida von Meysenbug, quoted by William James in *The Varieties of Religious Experience*, Lecture 16) or from "culture" (like Thomas Merton, as told in his autobiography, *The Seven Storey Mountain*). It makes a difference whether a thick understanding of divine providence is placed at the center of one's spiritual life, as we can see in the lives of Brother Lawrence or Jean Pierre de Caussade. It makes a difference which "foundational form of life" a person accepts, for example, a Benedictine, Franciscan, or Ignatian form of life.

Again, there are no "contradictions" between a Benedictine and a Franciscan way of life; but there are clearly "incompatibilities'" or "incommensurabilities." I am sure it is possible to be a more Franciscan and a less Franciscan Jesuit. I am sure it is possible to be a more Ignatian and a less Ignatian Benedictine. So again, there is space for healthy pluralism not only within the spectrum of communal charisms but also in the way a person chooses to live out a particular charism. Timothy Radcliffe defended this healthy pluralism in a memorable address to the U.S. Conference of Major Superiors for

---

77. Cf. Joyce E. Bellous et al., *Spiritual Styles: Assessing What Really Matters* (Edmonton: Tall Pine, 2009); Tobin Hart and Catalin Ailoae, "Spiritual Touchstones: Childhood Spiritual Experiences in the Development of Influential Historic and Contemporary Figures," *Imagination, Cognition and Personality* 26, no. 4 (2006–2007): 345-59.

Men (CMSM) on August 8, 1996. The address, entitled "The Identity of Religious Today," used the image of ecological niches for the many religious communities, traditions, and charisms.[78] "According to Mary Douglas, a healthy society is one that has all sorts of counterbalancing structures and institutions that give a voice and authority to different groups so that no one way of being human dominates and no single map tells you how things are. Perhaps what we want is not to reproduce the homogenized desert of the consumer world but to be more like a rain forest which has all sorts of ecological niches for different ways of being a human being." This was explicitly meant not as a plea for "less hierarchy" but as a plea for "more hierarchy."

Finding one's spiritual style is a deeply personal matter, inextricably linked to a person's story and history. Sharing religious experience and stories goes deeper than entertaining a theological exchange. According to *Dialogue and Proclamation* (from the Pontifical Council for Interreligious Dialogue), the exchange of religious experience is the deepest way of encounter.[79] The common ground can be slowly built on respectfully shared space even though there may then be the painful realization that the building of that common ground will fail or has failed. This calls for a capacity that can only be developed, I would argue, on the basis of epistemic mercy: the capacity of not understanding. It may be an expression of epistemic mercy to embrace the gift of entering the chaos of not understanding.[80] This attitude is important because God leads every human person in a unique way. We are pilgrims; there is one goal, but unique journeys.

Dialogue and encounter have been suggested as the proper responses to the indeterminacy of orthodoxy. Dialogue is risky because it must be based on trust (and there cannot be trust without risk since trusting means "handing over"). Entering a dialogue is based on the trust that we can expect transformation through the other. We have seen that dialogue is based on "principles of char-

---

78. http://www.dominicans.ca.
79. See *Dialogue and Proclamation* 42d; http://vatican.va.
80. Z. D. Gurevitch, "The Power of Not Understanding: The Meeting of Conflicting Identities," *Journal of Applied Behavioral Science* 25, no. 2 (1989): 161-73.

ity" and "epistemic mercy." The dialogue outlined above is dialogue between people who learn and need one another for correction and companionship. It is the dialogue between those who accept that the human person cannot shake off certain questions. "Some people think they are free if they can avoid God; they fail to see that they remain existentially orphaned, helpless, homeless. They cease being pilgrims and become drifters, flitting around themselves and never getting anywhere" (EG 170).

We are pilgrims; and as pilgrims we are called to humility. Orthodoxy on earth is different from orthodoxy in heaven (an intriguing theological question!); there is a difference between a pilgrim's orthodoxy and the orthodoxy of one "who has arrived." One of the most serious temptations of being a Christian is the temptation to think that one has arrived, the temptation to conclude from the termination of revelation that we "possess" it. In his 2006 J. H. Walgrave Lecture at the Katholieke Universiteit Leuven Archbishop Bruno Forte reminded his audience of the importance of the pilgrim's attitude:

> When human beings ask the deepest questions about their inevitable vulnerability to pain and death, they do this not as people who have already arrived, but as searchers for the distant homeland, who let themselves be permanently called into question, provoked and seduced by the furthest horizon. Human beings who stop, who feel they have mastered the truth, for whom the truth is no longer Someone who possesses you more and more, but rather something to be possessed, such persons have not only rejected God, but also their own dignity as human beings.[81]

These are strong reminders of how to properly appropriate the truth, of how to live the truth. Living the truth as a pilgrim will always have a tentative aspect to it; there may even be a paradox here: the more I am rooted in my faith, the deeper my insights into my sinful-

81. Bruno Forte, "Theological Foundations of Dialogue within the Framework of Cultures Marked by Unbelief and Religious Indifference," *Louvain Studies* 31 (2006): 3-18, at 13.

ness, the firmer my trust in God, the clearer my view of my (spiritual, moral, and epistemic) fragility. Pope Francis has underlined the image of the pilgrim: "We must never forget that we are pilgrims journeying alongside one another. This means that we must have sincere trust in our fellow pilgrims, putting aside all suspicion or mistrust, and turn our gaze to what we are all seeking: the radiant peace of God's face" (EG 244). We are pilgrims, and as pilgrims we are seekers, and as seekers we embrace orthodoxy in a particular way.

Orthodoxy is, on the one hand, an epistemic state to be in (propositional orthodoxy and one's position vis-à-vis those propositions) and, on the other hand, an existential state in some kind of connection with the epistemic state (living one's life on the basis of one's beliefs). But there is also orthodoxy on a meta-level, orthodoxy as an attitude toward one's epistemic state. In other words, it is one thing to believe that the Son is consubstantial with the Father, and it is another thing to be grateful for this belief or proud of this belief. Insofar as orthodoxy is "practical," one's estimation and valuing of one's belief are also relevant for one's state of being orthodox. Self-righteousness, for instance, or Pharisean complacency, cannot be proper attitudes vis-à-vis the grace of faith. I would suggest we distinguish between first-order orthodoxy (being faithful to the teachings of the church) and second-order orthodoxy (being a faithful disciple of Jesus Christ in the way one's first-order orthodoxy is embraced). This somewhat clumsy distinction points to questions about the different ways of "living one's orthodoxy." There are different ways of being a *conditio possidentis*. If a person has property this property can, as early church writers liked to point out, be used for prideful display, using one's possessions as instruments to establish social differences and to consolidate social distinctiveness. There is a temptation to "possess" and to be acutely aware of one's possessions. There is also a temptation to treat one's possessions as alien objects that can be replaced, without a relationship of responsibility or care. This is a way to possess without really appropriating one's possessions. Similarly, there is the question of being in possession of some understanding of the *depositum fidei*. Is "possessing as if we did not possess" a proper way to honor the invitation to detachment mentioned in the last chapter?

How orthodox is a person who accepts doctrinal statements and is filled with a feeling of "having arrived" rather than a feeling of "being on a pilgrimage"? Notwithstanding the question whether the concept of orthodoxy can regulate its own application and realization[82] we can argue that the application (realization, "living out") of orthodoxy is itself a case of orthodoxy. One can be orthodox yet still fall into the trap of pride. First-order orthodoxy and second-order orthodoxy can be separated.

We have seen that pride has been identified as an element in the standard reading of heresies. The same can be said about the heresy of being orthodox without humility. John Cassian writes in no uncertain terms about the spiritual dangers of pride in his *Institutes*, book 12. He describes pride as "an evil beast … chiefly trying those who are perfect."[83] Pride is more destructive than the other principal faults of the soul; it was pride that made Lucifer fall; it is pride that gives the incentive to all sins, paradigmatically shown in the sin of the Fall. Pride is "the cause and fountain head of evils"[84]; it is to be remedied with humility, the deep insight that no one can obtain virtue by one's own strength alone. Pride is vicious, because it may be the result of living a moral life (and becoming proud of one's moral integrity); it may be the result of orthodoxy (and becoming proud of one's doctrinal soundness). You may make impressive moral progress, you may show wonderful spiritual growth, but then you become proud of it and lose everything. Dag Hammarskjöld, Secretary General of the United Nations from 1953 to 1961, mentions in his reflections a fairy tale: "once upon a time, there was a crown so heavy that it could only be worn by one who remained completely oblivious to its glitter."[85]

---

82. Onora O'Neill, when discussing the limits of contracts that always need a basis of trust since a contract cannot fully define its application, makes a similar point (Onora O'Neill, *A Question of Trust* [Cambridge: Cambridge University Press, 2002]).

83. John Cassian, *Institutes* 12.1.

84. Ibid., 12.8.

85. Dag Hammarskjöld, *Markings*, trans. Leif Sjöberg and W. H. Auden; new preface by Jimmy Carter, 1964; foreword by W. H. Auden (New York: Vintage, 2006), 64.

Let us translate that: the crown of orthodoxy must be worn by one who is oblivious of its glitter. And then, of course, a truly orthodox person will not be able to claim to be orthodox; she may suffer the same fate as Peter, who confirmed his faithfulness prior to his three-fold betrayal. "Absolute certainty about *one's own inmost* orthodoxy in the sight of God (which would be the presupposition of such absolute certainty) seems to me to be as impossible and as un-Catholic as absolute certainty about one's own justice in the sight of God," wrote Karl Rahner in his *Questions of Controversial Theology on Justification*.[86]

The church "exists concretely in history as a people of pilgrims" (EG 111). As pilgrims we live in a "messy" world that does not always encourage us to make clear judgments or to reconstruct our experience in clearly delineated and neatly defined categories. There is messiness and there is chaos—which is why we need epistemic mercy: the idea of having orthodoxy as "straightened opinion ... restoring the primal state of innocence of doxa"[87] may lack humility and honesty to the real.

One consequence of the image of the pilgrim implying imperfection and transitoriness is the recognition of a need for growth, moral growth, spiritual growth, but also epistemic growth. Even the

---

86. Karl Rahner, "Questions of Controversial Theology on Justification," in Karl Rahner, *Theological Investigations IV*, trans. Kevin Smyth (London: Darton, Longman & Todd, 1966), 189-218, at 196; and similarly in another text: "As has been said already, no one can know with absolute and reflex certitude whether he really believes. For no one can give a final account as to whether the propositions of faith which he is certainly willing to accept as his own, are also accepted by him in his free theoretical consciousness with such depth and existential power of free decision (and without such a free 'agreement' there can be no faith, but at the most a sympathizing with recognized propositions) that these propositions have a sure theoretical and practical validity governing all those other norms and ideals which everyone also inevitably possesses" (Karl Rahner, "What Is Heresy?" 497).

87. Pierre Bourdieu, *Outline of a Theory of Practice* (Cambridge: Cambridge University Press, 1977), 169. Bourdieu's analysis may be helpful when looking at the messiness of local social realities; see Jacques Berlinerblau, "Toward a Sociology of Heresy, Orthodoxy, and Doxa," *History of Religions* 40, no. 4 (2001): 327-51.

church is called to this growth; even the church needs to grow, as we have seen before: "The Church is herself a missionary disciple; she needs to grow in her interpretation of the revealed word and in her understanding of truth" (EG 40). The question of epistemic growth within the church and of the church leads to the question of (epistemic) vulnerability. What are the implications of the idea that "the obedient Jesus becomes most fully one with God in increasing human powerlessness"[88]? Is the church, we could ask, epistemically vulnerable? Vulnerability has been identified as the key aspect of poverty. A Church of the Poor will develop a particular relationship to vulnerability. "Spiritual vulnerability has been a very attractive doctrine to many Christians."[89] Is this an expression of a longing for openness to God, so that divine creativity, as Pope Francis develops the notion in *Evangelii gaudium*, can transform the face of the earth?

---

88. William C. Placker, *Narratives of a Vulnerable God: Christ, Theology, and Scripture* (Louisville, KY: Westminster John Knox Press, 1994), 16.

89. Timothy P. Jackson, *Love Disconsoled: Meditations on Christian Charity* (Cambridge: Cambridge University Press, 1999), 145.

Epilogue

On Loving God

Joyful orthodoxy, generous orthodoxy, bruised orthodoxy, listening orthodoxy, pilgrim's orthodoxy . . . all these terms are about the one important point, the point of life: the love of God. In the *Apophthegmata patrum*, a collection of wisdom of the desert fathers and desert mothers, we learn about the meaning of the right relationship with God:

> It was said concerning Abba Agathon that some monks came to find him having heard tell of his great discernment. Wanting to see if he would lose his temper they said to him "Aren't you that Agathon who is said to be a fornicator and a proud man?" "Yes, it is very true," he answered. They resumed, "Aren't you that Agathon who is always talking nonsense?" "I am." Again they said "Aren't you Agathon the heretic?" But at that he replied "I am not a heretic." So they asked him, "Tell us why you accepted everything we cast you, but repudiated this last insult." He replied "The first accusations I take to myself for that is good for my soul. But heresy is separation from God. Now I have no wish to be separated from God." At this saying they were astonished at his discernment and returned, edified.[1]

Heresy is separation from God; it is a severing of the ties with God; it is like a "divorce," or at least an act of unfaithfulness, doctrinal

---

1. Benedicta Ward, ed., *The Sayings of the Desert Fathers: The Alphabetical Collection* (Kalamazoo, MI: Cistercian Publications, 1984), 20-21.

adultery, running after idols, worshiping the golden calf. Orthodoxy cannot be separated from the idea of fidelity;[2] it is connected to faithfulness: "We should not be concerned simply about falling into doctrinal error, but about remaining faithful to this light-filled path of life and wisdom" (*Evangelii gaudium* [EG] 194). In the same passage Pope Francis quotes the instruction *Libertatis nuntius* (XI,18), issued by the Congregation for the Doctrine of Faith, with the words: "Defenders of orthodoxy are sometimes accused of passivity, indulgence, or culpable complicity regarding the intolerable situations of injustice and the political regimes which prolong them." If we take an analogy from the discourse on marriage, in which faithfulness is an attitude as much as a *modus operandi*, we see that it is concerned with big lines as well as small details; there is faithfulness "in the small things" and faithfulness in "the major decisions." Faithfulness to one's spouse will affect choices at every level of life. This is not to say that there may not be mistakes or failures, but the commitment to faithfulness constitutes the horizon within which mistakes happen and forgiveness is possible. There is, nevertheless, still the possibility of making poor judgments, but the foundations are firm. Similar to marriage, faithfulness to God manifests itself in many ways, and these ways cannot be separated from one another. Faithfulness to God is not compatible with social inertia if we take the fruits of the genuine relationship with the living God seriously.[3] A Church of the Poor will not encourage an understanding of orthodoxy without embracing too the social dimension. It will be an orthodoxy with "dirty hands," an orthodoxy with "feet on the ground," an orthodoxy that clings to reality: "It is good that we are here" (Matt 17:4).

---

2. Cf. EG 102, where the document talks about lay persons with a deeply rooted sense of community and great fidelity to the tasks of charity, catechesis and the celebration of the faith" (EG 102).

3. "The *kerygma* has a clear social content: at the very heart of the Gospel is life in community and engagement with others. The content of the first proclamation has an immediate moral implication centred on charity" (EG 177). Our redemption has a social dimension as well. My redemption is linked to your redemption, your redemption is linked to my redemption; redemption is a cooperative and not a competitive good. We do not believe that there is a limited number of rooms in the Father's House (cf. John 14:2).

Orthodoxy is about proper relationship with God. The Gospels provide insight into the nature of this relationship. The central issue of the Gospels is the invitation to respond to the God of love: "If this invitation does not radiate forcefully and attractively, the edifice of the Church's moral teaching risks becoming a house of cards, and this is our greatest risk. It would mean that it is not the Gospel which is being preached, but certain doctrinal or moral points based on specific ideological options. The message will run the risk of losing its freshness and will cease to have 'the fragrance of the Gospel'" (EG 39). The freshness of a text is part of this "fragrance." Living in a particular way will create a "fragrance" as a living expression of an experience. And this experience cannot be "delegated." "There are people," Charles Taylor observed, "who have an original, powerful religious experience, which then gets communicated through some kind of institution; it gets handed on to others, and they tend to live it in a kind of second-hand way. In the transmission, the force and intensity of the original tend to get lost, until all that remains is 'dull habit.'"[4] Well, orthodoxy cannot be tenable with a second-hand relationship with God.

Religious persons who live within a tradition of theism will conduct their lives in the second person singular; in other words, they will conduct their lives constantly in the presence of God (cf. Ps 139:7-10). Rowan Williams describes this close relationship to God, of our being "the object of God's non-historical regard," as assurance that both status and involvement make up that relationship, one in which "we are always 'addressed.' That is to say, our time can be apprehended by us as a question, or a challenge, as something to be filled. To sense my future as being a question to me is to sense that what I can receive, digest and react is not yet settled or finished."[5] We are always being addressed by God. Matthew 25:31-46 tells us that the poor enable, empower us to encounter the Lord; a Church of the Poor will bear witness to this belief of living in a second-person perspective, as a pilgrim moving closer to God and encountering the poor by faith in God. And it is this

---

4. Charles Taylor, *Varieties of Religion Today: Revisiting William James* (Cambridge, MA: Harvard University Press, 2002), 5.

5. Rowan Williams, "Interiority and Epiphany," in Rowan Williams, *On Christian Theology* (Oxford: Oxford University Press, 2000), 239-64, here 249.

perspective of the second person singular that changes the epistemic situation: such a relationship creates a new understanding of God. John Henry Newman points this out when he distinguishes between a "notion" and a "real image" of God. "The proposition that there is One Personal and Present God may be held in either way, either as a theological truth, or as a religious fact or reality. The notion and the reality assented-to are represented by one and the same proposition, but serve as distinct interpretations of it."[6] This differentiation between an existential and affective true picture of God and a mere notion is of pivotal concern in our understanding orthodoxy.

The book of Job illustrates this point by depicting Job as embracing a second-person perspective and talking *to* God, whereas his "comforters" operate on the basis of a third-person perspective in talking *about* God. God does not take issue with Job's wrestling with him; God does not take issue with Job being in doctrinal error, as it were; but God does take issue with those who did not say anything wrong, were doctrinally in the right, were able to "speak their faith," but were unable to live it. Here is the main trap of a propositional reductionism of orthodoxy. "Once revelation becomes propositional—which in itself is wholly appropriate because we are persons with intellects—we can learn the propositions without having the personal encounter with Ultimacy. We can know about God without loving God."[7]

And this is the key point: the love of God. What does it mean to love God? Again, the basis for this question is a relationship, a relationship between God and the human person. There is the wider relationship of God with "humanity" and "the world," and there is the specific relationship of God with each and every individual person. The way God relates to us as individuals may, in the first instance, be a relationship between creator and creature. We are creatures, and this means our identity is "given," rather than "constructed," "negotiated," or "achieved." We believe in the Christian tradition that God affirms the existence of each person, that there is a fundamental blessing in

---

6. John Henry Newman, *An Essay in Aid of a Grammar of Assent* (Notre Dame, IN: University of Notre Dame Press, 1979), 108.

7. Edward Collins Vacek, "Orthodoxy Requires Orthopathy: Emotions in Theology," *Horizons* 40, no. 2 (2013): 218-41, at 229.

each person's "natality," to apply Hannah Arendt's philosophical term. Christians understand the relationship between creator and created as a relationship of love expressed in "the gift of life." We believe that God loves a human person and a human person loves God. "Faith also means believing in God, believing that he truly loves us, that he is alive, that he is mysteriously capable of intervening, that he does not abandon us and that he brings good out of evil by his power and his infinite creativity" (EG 278). Orthodoxy is in an important sense the recognition of the truth that "God truly loves us." If we wholly understand this, we will have but one response—to love God back. "You shall love the Lord, your God, with all your heart, with all your soul, and with all your mind" has been named "the greatest and the first commandment" in the gospel (Matt 22:37-38). A proper relationship with God is shaped by this love.

What does it mean to love God? Let me at the end of this enquiry mention four points.

First, as we have seen, to love God means to recognize the truth that we are loved by God. This recognition can be painful. Consider, for example, Leopold, a paranoid person with trust issues. His friends would like to prepare a surprise party for his birthday, carefully thinking about ways to withhold information from Leopold and to plan the surprise in secrecy. This raises Leopold's suspicion. He finds out that friends have been meeting behind his back and he feels betrayed. He confronts them angrily and tells them in no uncertain terms that friendship is no longer an option; he cancels all ties of friendship. Sadly, they tell him what the meetings "behind his back" had been for and about what they were planning. How will Leopold feel? Probably utterly ashamed and embarrassed. It can be painful to find out that one has made a terrible mistake. Then consider Bertha, who makes her own life's dream come true by splurging and spending all the money she has ever saved on a cruise. She has so little money left that she does not dare join the other guests at meal times; she lives on the simple food she has brought with her in her cabin throughout the cruise. Only on the last evening does she put on her best dress, take her purse, and join the other guests for dinner. She has a wonderful meal and when she asks for the bill she is told, "This is all included in the price, Madam." How does she feel when she realizes the mistake she has made—that this was how it was meant to be and could have been all along?

Just imagine if the following were to happen to you and me. We face the final judgment, vividly described in Matthew 25, and proudly present our "lists" of true beliefs, our lists of good works, lists of heroic sacrifices, lists of healthy habits, lists of spiritual achievements, only to find out that this isn't what life is or was about at all: it is not about achievements, but about relationships, especially our living relationship with the living God, especially our relationships with the most disadvantaged. It is not about achievements; it is about recognizing our need for mercy. Imagine a tax collector in the temple next to the spiritually impressive Pharisee; he can only offer his humble and contrite heart rather than the Pharisee's "lists" of ascetic and altruistic achievements (cf. Luke 18:13-14).

If we find out what it was all about we will be ashamed, and we can understand why. This is how life was meant to be! If we take another look at the book of Job, we might now appreciate an important point. Job's friends were propositionally orthodox, and they said all the right things; Job was wrestling with God and said, we might say, some "raw things" about God (not dissimilar to C. S. Lewis's wrestling with God after the loss of his wife). Job may not have found the right words by the standards of propositional orthodoxy, implying, for instance, a divine injustice; but he spoke from his heart, and he spoke to God, whereas his friends seem only to have spoken about God. At the end of the book we read to our astonishment, "the Lord said to Eliphaz the Temanite, 'My anger blazes against you and your two friends! You have not spoken rightly concerning me, as has my servant Job'" (Job 42:8). This is truly astonishing, given the undeniable fact that there were no doctrinal errors on the side of Job's friends, no violations of standards of propositional orthodoxy. The book seems to suggest that you can say the right things at the right time, but if you do not say them in the right way they are wrong. Orthodoxy is not *talking about* loving God, but *about loving* God.

To love God means to accept that God loves us. Admittedly, the love of God can be experienced as "severe mercy," as harshness even. If we accept commitments to truth we have to accept that love is not only or always kindness.[8] Love is not primarily about making another person's life easier through seeming kindness; perhaps the opposite is required: love creates depth and vulnerability. When we look at the way Jesus showed his love in some instances, we find sternness and rebuke. A prominent example would be his rejection of Peter (Matt 16:23) before the transfiguration and right after Peter's statement of faith in Matthew 16:16. Jesus tells Peter that he is "thinking not as God does, but as human beings do." He is rejecting the "worldly spirit" that Peter embraces, and it is this idea that goes against our own grain and makes things difficult. We may want to have theological clarity that "the world" is to be rejected and that there is a clear dichotomy between "the world" and "the divine"; however, the incarnation and years of unobtrusive everyday life as well as Jesus' enjoying the fruits of the earth and the "fruits" of culture make it difficult to set clearly defined boundaries between world and spirit.

A second point about the question of what it means to love God: it means responding to God's love by loving God. We can gain a deeper understanding of what it means to love God from a Christian perspective when we turn to the Gospels for insight. What does it mean to love Jesus, according to the Gospels? An answer can be found in those Gospel passages in which Jesus approves of a person's interactions and relationship with him. He appreciates the fact that his disciples have clearly made a fundamental decision (cf. Matt 10:37-39) and left everything to follow him (Matt 19:27). To love Jesus means to understand who Jesus is (Matt 16:16) and to be prepared to be led (John 21:18). Jesus appreciates insights into a person's need for healing (Matt 9:12-13; Luke 5:31-32); he appreciates support given to the most disadvantaged (Matt 10:42; 18:5); he appreciates faith as trust, not "blind trust" but trust with judgment, as seen in the negotiations with the centurion (Matt 8:10; Luke 7:9) and the Canaanite woman (Matt 15:28). Mary's unshakeable trust in her own words, "Do whatever he tells you" (John 2:5), can also be read as a way of loving Jesus.

---

8. Peter Kreeft, *The God Who Loves You* (San Francisco: Ignatius Press, 2004), 54-55.

Two scenes, however, stand out: the anointing scenes (Matt 26:6-13; Mark 14:3-9; John 12:3), which depict a moment of abundance and waste, a moment of breaking social expectations, a moment of tenderness and physical closeness; they constitute memorable acts of love of which Jesus clearly approves: "She has done a good thing for me" (Mark 14:6); and the scenes of closeness with Mary and John (Luke 10:38-42; John 13:23-25), which depict a person delighting in the presence of Jesus and allowing Jesus to be present to them. Martha's sister, Mary, is sitting at Jesus' feet listening to him speak (Luke 10:39); Martha complains about that, but Jesus calls her sister's action "the better part"; it is a matter of choice. Mary chooses to be close to the Lord, to rejoice in his presence without "doing" or "serving." Mary moves Jesus to tears by her own tears (John 11:33). Again we can find her at his feet, close to him. Similarly, we find "the one whom Jesus loved" "reclining at Jesus' side" (John 13:23). He "leaned back against Jesus' chest" to ask Jesus about the betrayer, that is, to elicit deep sharing through Jesus (John 13:25).

To love Jesus means to trust Jesus and to be willing to commit self to costly discipleship; to love Jesus means to seek Jesus' presence and to rejoice in his presence, in the "being with him," in "abiding." To love God, we could tentatively say, means to rejoice in God's presence, to seek God's presence, to "waste yourself" in God's presence, to give to God an "overflowing presence of oneself." Obviously, we reach limits of language here and would need to resort to poetic language. St. Bernard of Clairvaux, in his beautiful treatise *On Loving God,* distinguished different degrees of the love of God, moving from a selfish love of God to loving God for God's sake and then—a fourth and final degree of love of God—to love oneself only in God. "In the beginning man loves God, not for God's sake, but for his own. It is something for him to know how little he can do by himself and how much by God's help, and in that knowledge to order himself rightly towards God, his sure support" (chapter 9). In the beginning people seek the gifts rather than the giver, and at the end they find that their whole identity rests in God. In the beginning of the relationship people love God out of selfishness and fear; both lead to isolation and bondage (chapter 12). In the end the same people keep nothing back for themselves. This fourth degree of love of God is illustrated with the beautiful image of a drop of water

poured into wine so that it loses itself, and takes on the color and fla-
vor of wine (chapter 10). Love of God is responsive; in this sense "our
love is not a gift, but a debt" (chapter 6). Love of God can be described
as an ever-increasing longing for the presence of God, resting sweetly
in the contemplation of God (chapter 4). Bernard of Clairvaux talks
about the capacity for loving as a gift from God (chapter 6): "He hath
endowed us with the possibility of love" (chapter 8). In other words,
we can pray to God to increase the gift of the capacity of love. And this
prayer is already an expression of love; there is "a paradox, that no one
can seek the Lord who has not already found Him" (chapter 7). Love
of God, then, is not "construed" or "forced," but flows, we could say,
naturally out of the human soul. To love God means to abide in God
and to allow God to dwell in oneself.

A third point: what else does it mean to love God? To love Jesus
means to love him "with hair and tears," as we have seen. Now, if a
human person loves God she will love God "in the real," as a creature of
flesh and blood; she will love God in a way that honors the incarnation.
An understanding of incarnation is expressed in Jesus' claims about
his identity as offering a new "tangibility" of the divine; the "bread-
of-life discourse" in John 6 challenges the established reading of the
hidden God whose paths are beyond human grasp (e.g., Job 9:10),
on the one hand, and human ignorance, on the other. The "transcen-
dence" and "intangibility" of God, properties liturgically protected by
the prohibition against creating images of God, are challenged by new
accessibility of God (John 14:10). A new understanding of the material and the immaterial rings through in Jesus' authority to forgive sins
when he asks the paralytic to rise, pick up his mat, and go home (Mark
2:11). It is the same authority that heals the soul and heals the body;
this is good news to the poor indeed. We see Jesus after his resurrection eat fish to show that he is "real" (Luke 24:43). Real love of God
shows real commitments; there is dedicated space, there are dedicated
times, there are dedicated resources. A life filled with prayer is a good
indication of being happy to spend time with God; making a real effort
in time, energy, and space is a sign of God's love.

A fourth point in understanding the love of God is this: we need
to explore human, personal love. We tend to think of God in terms
of personhood, so it seems an obvious conclusion to ask: What does

it mean to love a person? Personal love can be characterized as an intentional and responsive act to promote overall well-being,[9] well-being in terms of "redemption," we could add from a Christian point of view. Love is concerned with the well-being of the beloved. We can claim that we can love God. Thomas Jay Oord points to some of the theological presuppositions of our claim to being called to love God for God's sake. "This means we have the capacity to promote God's own well-being. God rejoices when we rejoice and mourns when we mourn. We make a genuine difference to God."[10] And the belief in this difference is constitutive for a relationship that serves two purposes: interaction and reciprocity.

Personal love can be read as consenting to the other as a subject and as unique.[11] Personal love can mean seeing a value in the beloved person that others do not see; personal love can mean showing care and robust concern for the beloved. To love a person is to be engaged in a wholehearted encounter, an encounter shaped by "wholehearted-ness." Ultimately, to love another person is capacity, discipline, and willingness to be pierced to the heart by the one we love.

Let us return to Pope Francis's encounter with Vincio Riva, described on the first page of this book. There is here a moment of tenderness, a moment of self-forgetfulness, a moment of holding and risking. Jesus uses the image of the house with many dwelling places to talk about the love of the Father (John 14:2). To love a person can be understood as offering hospitality to another person in the house of one's life, to "make room" for the other person, to lead the other person into the protected sphere of one's trust-seeking and trust-depending intimacy. "Waiting on" the other as an expression of hos-pitality is the result of allowing the other to enter one's house of life. To love a person can also mean to accept the invitation of the other to enter her house, to "wait" at the threshold of the other's house of life, respectfully and patiently waiting for the invitation to enter, wait-

---

9. Thomas Jay Oord, *The Nature of Love: A Theology* (St. Louis: Chalice Press, 2010), 17.

10. Ibid., 81.

11. Cf. John Cowburn, *The Person and Love: Philosophy and Theology of Love* (Staten Island, NY: Alba House, 1967), 112.

ing for instructions about which rooms the guest can enter. To love a person can also be understood as the joint and shared effort to build a house of life together. It is not simply allowing the other to furnish a room with experiences, emotions, beliefs, and memories but to truly build a home together, a place to stay and cohabit, a place to grow and be transformed. Love, then, is not only about being host and guest, but about being co-owner and then co-designer and co-builder. The house of love will be wider and more hospitable if it is based on true encounter with those who are different. An option for the poor can also be read as an option for those who are different. A Church of the Poor recognizes the encounter with the poor as a privileged place to see the face of God (Matt 25). A Church of the Poor will build a house with many dwelling places. A Church of the Poor will see the love of God in seemingly unlikely circumstances. "Everyone needs to be touched by the comfort and attraction of God's saving love, which is mysteriously at work in each person, above and beyond their faults and failings" (EG 44).

A final point: it is a theological task, perhaps a key task, to administer orthodoxy, to identify misleading forms of the love of God, or forms that are "not right." A "theology of false love of God" could identify traps and potholes and "relationship errors," such as over-familiarity, undue distance, lack of trust, lack of wholeheartedness. A "theology of love of God" may want to reflect on paradoxes of love, such as the paradox of "selfless love" and, at the same time, "loving as being your true self and becoming truly oneself."

Love is the key to proper relationships, the key to a proper relationship with God. A person's ability to love affects all other abilities;[12] the ability to love affects the ability to live the faith, the ability to live with the chaos of another, the ability to live as a pilgrim with fellow pilgrims. Even the gift to comprehend all mysteries and all knowledge, even the gift of "all faith" is void if there is no love: "if I have the gift of prophecy and comprehend all mysteries and all knowledge; if I have all faith so as to move mountains but do not have love, I am nothing" (1 Cor 13:2).

---

12. Ílham Dilman, *Love: Its Forms, Dimensions and Paradoxes* (London: Macmillan, 1998), 38.

Bibliography

Abraham, William J. "The Epistemology of Jesus: An Initial Investigation." In Paul K. Moser, ed., *Jesus and Philosophy*. Cambridge: Cambridge University Press, 2008, 149-68.

Anovil, Gilles. *The Poor Are the Church: A Conversation with Father Joseph Wresinski*. Mystic, CT: Twenty-Third Publications, 2002.

Arendt, Hannah. *The Human Condition*. Chicago: University of Chicago Press, 1958.

Asveld, Paul. "Orthodoxie et hérésie." In Christiane d'Haussy, ed., *Orthodoxie et hérésie*. Paris: Didier-Érudition, 1993, 17-24.

Atkisson, Alan. "The lagom solution." In Cecile Andrews and Wanda Urbanska, eds., *Less Is More: Embracing Simplicity for a Healthy Planet, a Caring Economy and Lasting Happiness*. Gabriola Island, BC: New Society Publishers, 2010, 101-6.

Auffarth, Christoph. "Das Ende der Katharer im Konzept einer europäischen Religionsgeschichte." In Kocku von Stuckrad and Brigitte Luchesi, eds., *Religion im kulturellen Diskurs—Religion in Cultural Discourse: Festschrift für Hans G. Kippenberg zu seinem 65. Geburtstag*. RGVV 52. Berlin: de Gruyter, 2004, 291-305.

Bailey, James. *Rethinking Poverty: Income, Assets, and the Catholic Social Justice Tradition*. Notre Dame, IN: University of Notre Dame Press, 2010.

Bailey, Warner M. "'I was hungry. . . .' The Bible and Poverty." *Journal of Presbyterian History* 59, no. 2 (1981): 181-96.

Bassler, J. M. "Mixed Signals: Nicodemus in the Fourth Gospel." *Journal of Biblical Literature* 108, no. 4 (1989): 635-46.

Bauer, Walter. *Rechtgläubigkeit und Ketzerei im ältesten Christentum*. Tübingen; J. C. B. Mohr, 1964.

Beck, Hans Georg. *Das byzantinische Jahrtausend*. Munich: Beck, 1978.

Belk, Russell W. "Possessions and the Extended Self." *Journal of Consumer Research* 15, no. 2 (1988): 139-68.

Bellous, Joyce E., et al., *Spiritual Styles: Assessing What Really Matters.* Edmonton: Tall Pine, 2009.

Beltrán, Ginés García. "La dimensión social de la evangelizacion en la exhortación apostólica *Evangelii gaudium.*" *Scripta theologica* 46 (2014): 461-80.

Berlinerblau, Jacques. "Toward a Sociology of Heresy, Orthodoxy, and Doxa." *History of Religions* 40, no. 4 (2001); 327-51.

Bevans, Stephen B. "The Apostolic Exhortation *Evangelii gaudium* on the Proclamation of the Gospel in Today's World." *International Review of Mission* 103, no. 2 (2014): 297-308.

———, and Roger P. Schroeder, *Constants and Context: A Theology of Mission for Today.* Maryknoll, NY: Orbis Books, 2004.

———, and Roger P. Schroeder, *Prophetic Dialogue: Reflections on Christian Mission Today.* Maryknoll, NY: Orbis Books, 2011.

———, and Cathy Ross, eds., *Mission on the Road to Emmaus: Constants, Context and Prophetic Dialogue.* London: SCM, 2015.

Beyers, J. "The Effect of Religion on Poverty." *HTS Teologiese Studies/ Theological Studies* 70, no. 1 (2014): art. #2614.

Bloomberg, Craig L. "The Globalization of Biblical Interpretation: A Test Case John 3–4." *Bulletin for Biblical Research* 5 (1995): 1-15.

Bochenski, Joseph M. *The Logic of Religion.* New York: New York University Press, 1965.

Boff, Leonardo. *Saint Francis: A Model for Human Liberation.* Translated by John W. Diercksmeier. New York: Crossroad, 1982.

Bolzano, Bernard. *Lehrbuch der Religionswissenschaft.* Teil I. Stuttgart: Frommann-Holzboog, 1994.

Bourdieu, Pierre. *Outline of a Theory of Practice.* Cambridge: Cambridge University Press, 1977.

Boyle, Gregory. *Tattoos on the Heart.* New York: Free Press, 2010.

Brändle, Rudolf. "The Sweetest Passage. Matthew 25:31-46 and Assistance to the Poor in the Homilies of John Chrysostom." In Susan R. Holman, ed., *Wealth and Poverty in Early Church and Society.* Grand Rapids, MI: Baker Academic, 2008, 127-39.

Brown, Peter. *Poverty and Leadership in the Later Roman Era: The Menahem Stern Jerusalem Lectures.* Hanover, NH: Brandeis University Press, 2002.

Bunge, Gabriel. *Despondency: The Spiritual Teaching of Evagrius Ponti-cus on Acedia.* Yonkers, NY: St. Vladimir's Seminary Press, 2012.

Calder, Norman. "The Limits of Islamic Orthodoxy." In Farhad Daftary, ed., *Intellectual Traditions in Islam.* London: Tauris, 2000, 66-86.

Cameron, Averil. "The Cost of Orthodoxy." *Church History and Religious Culture* 93 (2013): 339-61.

Cardenal, Ernesto. *The Gospel in Solentiname.* Maryknoll, NY: Orbis Books, 2010.

Cardman, Francine. "Poverty and Wealth as Theater: John Chrysostom's Homilies on Lazarus and the Rich Man." In Susan R. Holman, ed., *Wealth and Poverty in Early Church and Society.* Grand Rapids, MI: Baker Academic, 2008, 159-75.

Carel, Havi. *Illness: The Cry of the Flesh.* Durham, NC: Acumen, 2013.

———, and Ian James Kidd, "Epistemic Injustice in Healthcare: A Philosophical Analysis." *Medicine, Health Care and Philosophy* 17, no. 4 (2014): 529-40.

Carson, D. A. *The Gospel According to John.* Grand Rapids, MI: Eerdmans, 1991.

Celenza, Christopher S. *The Lost Italian Renaissance: Humanists, Historians, and Latin's Legacy.* Baltimore: Johns Hopkins University Press, 2006

Chambers, Robert. *Rural Development: Putting the Last First.* Harlow: Longman, 1983.

Cherry, Mark J., and Pope Francis. "Weak Theology, and the Subtle Transformation of Roman Catholic Bioethics." *Christian Bioethics* 21, no. 1 (2015): 84-88.

Chiotakis, Stelios. "Der Sinn der Orthodoxie—Herrschaftsstrukturen und Orthodoxie in Byzanz und Griechenland." In M. N. Ebertz and R. Schützeichel, eds., *Sinnstiftung als Beruf.* Wiesbaden: VS, 2010, 71-85.

Chroust, Anton Hermann, and Robert J. Affeldt, "The Problem of Private Property according to St. Thomas Aquinas." *Marquette Law Review* 34, no. 3 (1950–51): 151-82.

Clifford, Catherine. "Pope Francis' Call for the Conversion of the Church in Our Time." *Australian eJournal of Theology* 21, no. 1 (2015): 33-55.

Christian Aid, *Report on Poverty*. London: Christian Aid, 2009.

Clarke, Andrew D. "'Do Not Judge Who Is Worthy and Unworthy': Clement's Warning Not to Speculate about the Rich Young Man's Response (Mark 10.17-31). *Journal for the Study of the New Testament* 31, no. 4 (2009): 447-68.

Clarke, Elizabeth A. *History, Theory, Text: Historians and the Linguistic Turn*. Cambridge, MA: Harvard University Press, 2004.

Cohen, Gerald. *Rescuing Justice and Equality*. Cambridge, MA: Harvard University Press, 2008.

Collins, Randall. *Weberian Sociological Theory*. Cambridge: Cambridge University Press, 1986.

Conant, James. "The Method of the Tractatus." In E. Reck, ed., *From Frege to Wittgenstein: Perspectives in Early Analytic Philosophy*. Oxford: Oxford University Press, 2002, 374-462.

Conant, James, and Cora Diamond, "On Reading the Tractatus Resolutely." In M. Kölbel and B. Weiss, eds., *The Lasting Significance of Wittgenstein's Philosophy*. London: Routledge, 2004, 46-99.

Congar, Yves. *Mon journal du Concile II*. Paris: Cerf, 2002.

Cotterell, Peter. "The Nicodemus Conversation: A Fresh Appraisal." *The Expository Times* 96, no. 8 (1985): 237-42.

Cowburn, John. *The Person and Love: Philosophy and Theology of Love*. Staten Island, NY: Alba House, 1967.

Cox, Damian, Marguerite La Caze, and Michael P. Levine, *Integrity and the Fragile Self*. Aldershot: Ashgate, 2003.

Daley, Brian. "The Cappadocian Fathers and the Option for the Poor." In Daniel Groody, ed., *The Option for the Poor in Christian Theology*. Notre Dame, IN: University of Notre Dame Press, 2007, 77-88.

Dammertz, Viktor. "Poverty in the Rule of St. Benedict and Today." *American Benedictine Review* 35, no. 1 (1984): 1-16.

Darwall, Stephen. *The Second-Person Standpoint: Morality, Respect and Accountability*. Cambridge, MA: Harvard University Press, 2006.

Davidson, Donald. "Radical Interpretation." *Dialectica* 27 (1973): 314-28.

Davies, Oliver. *Theology of Transformation*. Oxford: Oxford University Press, 2013.

Deconchy, Jean-Pierre. *Orthodoxie réligieuse et sciences humaines.* La Haye: Mouton, 1980.

de Jesus, Carolina Maria. *Child of the Dark. Quarto de despejo.* London: Penguin, 2003.

de Lubac, Henri. *Méditation sur l'église.* Paris: Aubier, 1953.

———. *The Splendour of the Church.* Translated by Michael Mason. Glen Rock, NJ: Paulist Press, 1963.

———. *Carnets du Concile I.* Paris: Cerf, 2007.

de Santa Ana, Julio. *Good News to the Poor: The Challenge of the Poor in the History of the Church.* Maryknoll, NY: Orbis Books, 1979.

———. *Towards a Church of the Poor.* Maryknoll, NY: Orbis Books, 1981.

Diamond, Cora. "Throwing Away the Ladder." *Philosophy* 63, no. 243 (1988): 5-27.

Dilman, İlham. *Love. Its Forms, Dimensions and Paradoxes.* London: Macmillan, 1998.

Dorling, Daniel. *Injustice. Why Social Inequality Still Persists.* Bristol: Policy Press, 2015.

Driscoll, Jeremy. "Penthos and Tears in Evagrius Ponticus." *Studia monastica* 36 (1994): 147-63.

Dumitraşcu, Nicu. "Poverty and Wealth in the Orthodox Spirituality (with Special Reference to St. John Chrysostom)." *Dialog: A Journal of Theology* 49, no. 4 (2010): 300-305.

Eco, Umberto. *The Name of the Rose.* Translated by William Weaver. New York: Houghton Mifflin Harcourt, 2014.

Edin, Kathryn J., and H. Luke Shaefer. *$2.00 a Day: Living on Almost Nothing in America.* Boston: Houghton Mifflin Harcourt, 2015.

Farmer, Paul. "Health, Healing, and Social Justice. Insights from Liberation Theology." In Dan Groody and G. Gutiérrez, eds., *The Option for the Poor beyond Theology.* Notre Dame, IN: University of Notre Dame Press, 2013, 199-228.

Ferry, Luc. *On Love: A Philosophy for the Twenty-First Century.* Translated by Andrew Brown. Cambridge: Polity, 2013.

Flasch, Kurt. *Aufklärung im Mittelalter? Die Verurteilung von 1277.* Mainz: Dieterich, 1989.

Formosa, Paul. "The Role of Vulnerability in Kantian Ethics." In C. Mackenzie et al., eds., *Vulnerability.* Oxford: Oxford University Press, 2014, 88-109.

Forte, Bruno. "Theological Foundations of Dialogue within the Framework of Cultures Marked by Unbelief and Religious Indifference." *Louvain Studies* 31 (2006): 3-18.

Frankfurt, Harry. *The Importance of What We Care About.* Cambridge: Cambridge University Press, 1998.

Frankfurt, Harry. *The Reasons of Love.* Princeton, NJ: Princeton University Press, 2004.

Füssel, Hans Martin. "Vulnerability: A Generally Applicable Conceptual Framework for Climate Change Research." *Global Environmental Change* 17 (2007): 155-67.

Gauthier, Paul. *Consolez mon people.* Paris: Cerf, 1965.

Genova, Lisa. *Still Alice.* New York: Simon & Schuster, 2009.

Goodin, Robert. *Protecting the Vulnerable.* Chicago: University of Chicago Press, 1985.

Gordon, Barry. *The Economic Problem in Biblical and Patristic Thought.* Leiden: Brill, 1989.

Gordon, Mary. *Reading Jesus: A Writer's Encounter with the Gospels.* New York: Pantheon Books, 2009.

Gowan, Donald E. "Wealth and Poverty in the Old Testament. The Case of the Widow, the Orphan, and the Sojourner." *Interpretation* 41, no. 4 (1987): 341-53.

Greene, Graham. *The Heart of the Matter.* New York: Penguin, 1971.

Greene-McCreight, Kathryn. "Feminist Theology and a Generous Orthodoxy." *Scottish Journal of Theology* 57 (2004): 95-108.

Grootaers, Jan. "The Collegiality of the Synod of Bishops: An Unresolved Problem." *Concilium* 4 (1990): 18-30.

Grese, William C. "'Unless One Is Born Again': The Use of a Heavenly Journey in John 3." *Journal of Biblical Literature* 107, no. 4 (1988): 677-93.

Gurevitch, Z. D. "The Power of Not Understanding: The Meeting of Conflicting Identities." *Journal of Applied Behavioral Science* 25, no. 2 (1989): 161-73.

Gutiérrez, Gustavo. *On Job: God-Talk and the Suffering of the Innocent.* 12th ed. Maryknoll. NY: Orbis Books, 1999.

Halfon, Mark. *Integrity: A Philosophical Inquiry.* Philadelphia: Temple University Press, 1989.

Hammarskjöld, Dag. *Markings.* Translated from the Swedish by Leif

Sjöberg and W. H. Auden. New preface by Jimmy Carter, 1964. Foreword by W. H. Auden. New York: Vintage, 2006.

Hamilton, Brian. "The Politics of Poverty: A Contribution to a Franciscan Political Theology." *Journal of the Society of Christian Ethics* 35, no. 1 (2015): 29-44.

Hart, Tobin, and Catalin Ailoae, "Spiritual Touchstones: Childhood Spiritual Experiences in the Development of Influential Historic and Contemporary Figures." *Imagination, Cognition and Personality* 26, no. 4 (2006–2007): 345-59.

Henderson, John. *The Construction of Orthodoxy and Heresy*. Albany: State University of New York Press, 1998.

Hicks, Jane E. "Moral Agency at the Borders: Rereading the Story of the Syrophoenician Woman." *Word and World* 23, no. 1 (2003): 76-84.

Holman, Susan. *The Hungry Are Dying: Beggars and Bishops in Roman Cappadocia*. Oxford: Oxford University Press, 2001.

———. "Rich City Burning: Social Welfare and Ecclesial Insecurity in Basil's Mission to Armenia." *Journal of Early Christian Studies* 12, no. 2 (2004): 195-215.

———. *God Knows There's Need: Christian Responses to Poverty*. Oxford: Oxford University Press, 2009.

Hoppe, Leslie. *There Shall Be No Poor among You: Poverty in the Bible*. Nashville: Abingdon Press, 2004.

Hosmer, Rachel. "Poverty and Human Growth." *American Journal of Psychoanalysis* 34 (1974): 263-69.

Ihssen, Brenda Llewellyn. "Basil and Gregory's Sermons on Usury: Credit Where Credit Is Due." *Journal of Early Christian Studies* 16, no. 3 (2008): 403-30.

Inauen, Emil, and Bruno S. Frey, *Benediktinerabteien aus ökonomischer Sicht. Über die ausserordentliche Stabilität einer besonderen Institution*. Working Paper No. 388. Institute for Empirical Research in Economics. Zurich: University of Zurich, 2008.

Jackson, Frank C. "Epiphenomenal Qualia." *Philosophical Quarterly* 32 (1982): 127-36.

———. "What Mary Didn't Know." *Journal of Philosophy* 83 (1986): 291-95.

Jackson, Timothy P. *Love Disconsoled: Meditations on Christian Charity*. Cambridge: Cambridge University Press, 1999.

Johannes Duns Scotus, *Über die Erkennbarkeit Gottes*. Texte zur Philosophie und Theologie. Lateinisch-deutsch. Edited and translated by Hans Kraml, Gerhard Leibold, and Vladimir Richter. Hamburg: Meiner, 2000.

Johnson, Luke Timothy. *The Literary Function of Possessions in Luke-Acts*. Missoula, MT: Scholars Press, 1977.

Jones, John D. "Poverty and Subsistence: St. Thomas and the Definition of Poverty." *Gregorianum* 75, no. 1 (1994): 135-49.

———. "Poverty as Malum Simpliciter: A Reading of Aquinas' *Summa contra gentiles* 3.11." *Philosophy and Theology* 13, no. 2 (1999): 213-39.

Jones, Rufus M. *The Church's Debt to Heretics*. New York: George H. Doran, 1924.

Kämpchen, Martin. *Leben ohne Armut: Wie Hilfe wirklich helfen kann—Meine Erfahrungen in Indien*. Freiburg/Breisgau: Herder, 2011.

Kardong, Terrence. "Poverty in the Rule of Benedict: Chapters 33 and 34." *Cistercian Studies* 20 (1985): 184-201.

Kaufmann, Ludwig. "Synods of Bishops: Neither *concilium* nor *synodus*." *Concilium* 4 (1990): 67-78.

Kearney, Thomas. *A Prophetic Cry: Stories of Spirituality and Healing Inspired by L'Arche*. Dublin: Veritas, 2000.

Keenan, John F. *The Works of Mercy: The Heart of Catholicism*. Lanham, MD: Rowman & Littlefield, 2008.

Knuth, Elizabeth. "The Gift of Tears in Teresa of Avila." *Mystics Quarterly* 20, no. 4 (1994): 131-42.

Kreeft, Peter. *The God Who Loves You*. San Francisco: Ignatius Press, 2004.

Ladik, Daniel, Francois Carrillat, and Mark Tadajewski, "Belk's (1988) 'Possessions and the Extended Self' Revisited." *Journal of Historical Research in Marketing* 7, no. 2 (2015): 184-207.

Langer, R., and U. Simon, "The Dynamics of Orthodoxy and Heterodoxy. Dealing with Divergence in Muslim Discourses and Islamic Studies." *Die Welt des Islams* N.S. 48, nos. 3-4 (2008): 273-88.

Levine, Robert. *The Cautionary Tale of Carolina Maria de Jesus.* Kellogg Working Paper 178. Notre Dame, IN: Kellogg Institute for International Studies, 1992.

Lewis, Clive S. *A Grief Observed.* London: Faber & Faber, 1966.

Linden, Ian. *Global Catholicism: Diversity and Change since Vatican II.* London: Hurst, 2009.

Lorance, Cody C. "Cultural Relevance and Doctrinal Soundness: The Mission of Roberto de Nobili." *Missiology* 33, no. 4 (2005): 415-24.

Louth, Andrew. *Maximus Confessor.* London: Routledge, 1996.

MacIntyre, Alasdair. *After Virtue.* 2nd ed. Notre Dame, IN: Notre Dame University Press, 1997.

Malherbe, Abraham J. *Moral Exhortation: A Greco-Roman Sourcebook.* Philadelphia: Westminster Press, 1986.

Malina, Bruce J. "Wealth and Poverty in the New Testament and Its World." *Interpretation* 41, no. 4 (1987): 354-67.

Margalit, Avishai. *The Decent Society.* Cambridge, MA: Harvard University Press, 1996.

———. "Human Dignity between Kitsch and Deification." In Christopher Cordner and Raimond Gaita, eds., *Philosophy, Ethics, and a Common Humanity: Essays in Honour of Raimond Gaita.* London: Routledge, 2011, 106-20.

Marins, Jose. "Base Communities, a Return to Inductive Methodology." In R. Pelton, ed., *Aparecida: Quo Vadis?* Scranton, PA: University of Scranton Press, 2008, 93-99.

Marshall, Bruce D. *Trinity and Truth.* Cambridge: Cambridge University Press, 2000.

Matthew, Suresh. "Evangelii gaudium: Pope Francis' Magna Charta for Church Reform." *SEDOS Bulletin online* 45, nos. 11-12 (2013).

Mben, Joseph Loic. "The Concept of 'Poor' in Evangelii gaudium." *Zeitschrift für Missionswissenschaft und Religionswissenschaft* 98, no. 1 (2014): 133-38.

McCabe, R. V. "The Meaning of 'Born of Water and the Spirit' in John 3:5." *Detroit Baptist Seminary Journal* 4 (1999): 85-107.

McFall, Lynne. "Integrity." *Ethics* 98 (1987): 5-20.

McSweeney, John. "Doctrinal Orthodoxy." *The Furrow* 61, no. 5 (2010): 306-8.

Menke, Christoph. *Die Gegenwart der Tragödie*. Frankfurt/Main: Suhrkamp, 2005.

Merton, Robert. "The Matthew Effect in Science." *Science* 159, no. 3810 (1968): 56-63.

———. "The Matthew Effect in Science, II: Cumulative Advantage and the Symbolism of Intellectual Property." *Isis* 79, no. 4 (1988): 606-23.

Merton, Thomas. *The Life of the Vows*. Initiation in the Monastic Tradition 6. Edited by Patrick F. O'Connell. Collegeville, MN: Liturgical Press, Cistercian Publications, 2012.

Miethke, Jürgen. *Ockhams Weg zur Sozialphilosophie*. Berlin: de Gruyter, 1969.

Miller, Daniel. *The Comfort of Things*. Cambridge: Polity, 2008.

Moreira, Alberto. "Orthodoxy for the Protection of the Poor?" In Johann-Baptist Metz and Edward Schillebeeckx, eds., *Orthodoxy and Heterodoxy*. Edinburgh: T&T Clark, 1987, 110-15.

Müller, Barbara. *Der Weg des Weinens. Die Tradition des Penthos in den Apophthegmata Patrum*. Forschungen zur Kirchen- und Dogmengeschichte 77. Göttingen: Vandenhoeck und Ruprecht, 2000.

———. "Das Gebet unter Tränen in der Benediktsregel und der Vita Benedicti Gregors des Grossen." *Erbe und Auftrag* 1 (2000): 47-59.

Myers, Bryant L. *Walking with the Poor*. Maryknoll, NY: Orbis Books, 2011.

Newman, John Henry. *An Essay in Aid of a Grammar of Assent*. Notre Dame, IN: Notre Dame University Press, 1979.

Noble, Tim. *The Poor in Liberation Theology. Pathway to God or Ideological Construct?* Sheffield: Equinox, 2013.

Nogosek, Robert J. *Nine Saints for Today: Different Spiritualities for Different Personalities*. Notre Dame, IN: Corby Books, 2015.

Nolan, Albert. *Jesus before Christianity*. Maryknoll, NY: Orbis Books, 1978.

Noll, Mark A. *Jesus Christ and the Life of the Mind*. Grand Rapids, MI: Eerdmans, 2011.

Noonan, Jr., John T. "Development in Moral Doctrine." *Theological Studies* 54 (1993): 662-77.

Notelle-Wildfeuer, Ursula. "Eine Frage der Authentizität. Arme Kirche—Kirche der Armen." *Stimmen der Zeit* 232 (2014): 579-90.

Nussbaum, Martha. *The Fragility of Goodness.* Cambridge: Cambridge University Press, 2001.

O'Grady, Desmond. *Eat from God's Hands: Paul Gauthier and the Church of the Poor.* London: Chapman, 1965.

O'Hanlon, Gerry. "The Pope's Interview: A Reflection." *Studies: An Irish Quarterly Review* 102, no. 407 (2013): 279-82.

O'Neill, Onora. *A Question of Trust.* Cambridge: Cambridge University Press, 2002.

Oord, Thomas Jay. *The Nature of Love: A Theology.* St. Louis: Chalice Press, 2010.

Oz, Amos. *The Story Begins: Essays on Literature.* Translated by Maggie Bar-Tura. New York: Harcourt Brace, 1999.

Paton, Alan. *Ah, but Your Land Is Beautiful.* New York: Scribner Paperback, 1996.

Phillips, L. E., and M. Garrett, *Why Don't They Just Get a Job?* Highlands, TX: aha! Process, 2010.

Pieris, Aloysius. "To Be Poor as Jesus Was Poor?" *The Way* 24 (1984): 186-97.

Pixley, George, and Clodovis Boff. *The Bible, the Church and the Poor.* Maryknoll, NY: Orbis Books, 1989.

Placker, William C. *Narratives of a Vulnerable God: Christ, Theology, and Scripture.* Louisville, KY: Westminster John Knox Press, 1994.

Planellas I Barnosell, Joan. *La iglesia de los pobres en el Concilio Vaticano II.* Barcelona: Herder Editorial, 2014.

Polanyi, Michael. *Personal Knowledge: A Post-Critical Philosophy.* Chicago: University of Chicago Press, 1962.

Pope, Stephen. "Poverty and Natural Law." In William A. Galston and Peter H. Hoffenberg, eds., *Poverty and Morality: Religious and Secular Perspectives.* Cambridge: Cambridge University Press, 2010, 265-84.

Potkay, Adam. "Spenser, Donne and the Theology of Joy." *SEL Studies in English Literature 1500–1900* 46, no. 1 (2006): 43-66.

Prostmeier, Ferdinand. "Christliche Paideia. Die Perspektive Theodorets von Kyrrhos." *Römische Quartalschrift* 100 (2005): 1-29.

Quash, Ben. *Abiding: The Archbishop of Canterbury's Lent Book, 2013.* London: Bloomsbury, 2013.

Quinn, Carol V. A. "On Integrity." *International Journal of Applied Philosophy* 23 (2010): 189-97.

Rahner, Karl. "Current Problems in Christology." In Karl Rahner, *Theological Investigations I.* Translated by Cornelius Ernst. London: Darton, Longman & Todd, 1961, 149-214.

———. "The Prospects for Dogmatic Theology." In Karl Rahner, *Theological Investigations I.* Translated by Cornelius Ernst. London: Darton, Longman & Todd, 1961, 1-18.

———. "The Resurrection of the Body." In Karl Rahner, *Theological Investigations II.* Translated by Karl Heinz Kruger. London: Darton, Longman & Todd, 1963, 203-16.

———. *On Heresy.* New York: Herder & Herder, 1964.

———. "What Is Heresy?" In Karl Rahner, *Theological Investigations V.* Translated by Karl Heinz Kruger. London: Darton, Longman & Todd, 1966, 468-512.

———. "Questions of Controversial Theology on Justification." In Karl Rahner, *Theological Investigations IV.* Translated by Kevin Smyth. London: Darton, Longman & Todd, 1966, 189-218.

———. "Reflections on the Experience of Grace." In Karl Rahner, *Theological Investigations III.* Translated by Karl Heinz and Boniface Kruger. London: Darton, Longman & Todd, 1967, 86-88.

———. "The Church as the Subject of the Sending of the Spirit." In Karl Rahner, *Theological Investigations VII.* Translated by David Bourke. London: Darton, Longman & Todd, 1971, 186-92.

———. "The Historicity of Theology." In Karl Rahner, *Theological Investigations IX.* Translated by Graham Harrison. London: Darton, Longman & Todd, 1972, 64-82.

———. "Experiences of a Catholic Theologian." In Declan Marmion and Mary E. Hines, eds., *The Cambridge Companion to Karl Rahner.* Cambridge: Cambridge University Press, 2007, 297-310.

Ras, J. M. Johan. "Jesus, Moral Recognition and Crime in the Gospel of John." *Inkanyiso. Journal for Humanities and Social Sciences* 2, no. 2 (2010): 115-21.

Ratzinger, Joseph (Pope Benedict XVI). *Milestones.* San Franciso: Ignatius, 1997.

———. *Introduction to Christianity.* San Francisco: Ignatius, 2004.

Rawls, John. *A Theory of Justice.* Rev. ed. Cambridge, MA: Harvard University Press, 1999.

Rhee, Helen. *Loving the Poor, Saving the Rich: Wealth, Poverty and Early Christian Formation.* Grand Rapids, MI: Baker Academic, 2012.

Richi Alberti, Gabriel. "Evangelii gaudium y la índole pastoral del magisterio." *Scripta theologica* 46 (2014): 611-34.

Richter, Vladimir. "Duns Scotus' Text zur Theologie als praktischer Wissenschaft." *Collectanea fransciscana* 60 (1990): 459-74.

Rippinger, Joel. "The Biblical and Monastic Roots of Poverty in the Rule of Benedict under the Aspect of Koinonia." *American Benedictine Review* 27, no. 3 (1976): 321-31.

Rhoads, David. "Jesus and the Syrophoenician Woman in Mark: A Narrative-Critical Study." *Journal of the American Academy of Religion* 62, no. 2 (1994): 343-75.

Ricoeur, Paul. *The Symbolism of Evil.* Translated by Emerson Buchanan. Boston: Beacon, 1969.

Rigney, Daniel. *The Matthew Effect: How Advantage Begets Further Advantage.* New York: Columbia University Press, 2010.

Roberts, Robert Campbell. *Spiritual Emotions: A Psychology of Christian Virtues.* Grand Rapids, MI: Erdmans, 2007.

Rost, Katja, Emil Inauen, and Margit Osterloh. "The Corporate Governance of Benedictine Abbeys. What Can Stock Corporations Learn from Monasteries?" *Journal of Management History* 16, no. 1 (2010): 90-115.

Roth, Philip. *Patrimony: A True Story.* New York: Simon & Schuster, 1991.

Sandel, Michael. *Liberalism and the Limits of Justice.* 8th ed. Cambridge: Cambridge University Press, 2008.

Scherkoske, Greg. *Integrity and the Virtues of Reason: Leading a Convincing Life.* Cambridge: Cambridge University Press, 2013.

Schlick, Moritz. "Über das Fundament der Erkenntnis." *Erkenntnis* 4 (1934): 79-99.

Schneider, John R. *The Good of Affluence. Seeking God in a Culture of Wealth.* Grand Rapids, MI: Eerdmans, 2002.

Sedláček, Tomas. *Economics of Good and Evil: The Quest for Economic Meaning from Gilgamesh to Wall Street.* Oxford: Oxford University Press, 2011.

Sedmak, Clemens. "Strukturen epistemischer Gerechtigkeit." *Salzburger Jahrbuch für Philosophie* 46/47 (2001/2002): 139-52.

————. *Katholisches Lehramt und Philosophie.* Freiburg/Breisgau: Herder, 2003.

————. "Utility and Identity: A Catholic Social Teaching Perspective on the Economics of Good and Evil." *Studies in Christian Ethics* 28, no. 4 (2015): 461-77.

Sen, Amartya. *Development as Freedom.* New York: Oxford University Press, 1999.

Senior, Donald. "Religious Poverty and the Ministry of Jesus." *American Benedictine Review* 26, no. 2 (1975): 169-79.

Shogimen, Takashi. "William of Ockham and Conceptions of Heresy, c. 1250–c. 1350." In Ian Hunter, John Christian Laursen, and Cary J. Nederman, eds., *Heresy in Tradition: Transforming Ideas of Heresy in Medieval and Early Modern Europe.* Hants, UK: Ashgate, 2005, 59-70.

Shrader-Frechette, Kristin. "Liberation Science and the Option for the Poor. Protecting Victims of Environmental Injustice." In Dan Groody, ed., *The Preferential Option for the Poor beyond Theology.* Notre Dame, IN: Notre Dame University Press, 2013, 120-48.

Signer, Michael A. "Social Justice in Judaism." In Daniel Groody, ed., *The Option for the Poor in Christian Theology.* Notre Dame, IN: University of Notre Dame Press, 2007, 290-301.

Silva, Sergio. "La exhortación apostólica del papa Francisco como desafío a los teólogos." *Teología y vida* 55, no. 3 (2014): 549-69.

Sobrino, Jon. *Jesus the Liberator: A Historical-Theological Reading of Jesus of Nazareth.* Maryknoll, NY: Orbis Books, 1993.

————. "La iglesia de los pobres desde el recuerdo de Monseñor Romero." *Revista lationoamericana de teología* 86 (2012): 135-55.

Söding, Thomas. *Die Verkündigung Jesu: Ereignis und Erinnerung.* 2nd ed. Freiburg/Breisgau: Herder, 2012.

Sosnoski, James J. *Token Professionals and Master Critics: A Critique of Orthodoxy in Literary Studies*. Albany: State University of New York Press, 1994.

Spadaro, Antonio. "The Heart of a Jesuit Pope: Interview with Pope Francis." *Studies: An Irish Quarterly Review* 102, no. 407 (2013): 255-78.

———. "Wake up the World!" Conversation with Pope Francis about the Religious Life, *La Civiltà Cattolica* 165 (2014/1), 4 (English translation by Fr. Donald Maldari, S.J.).

Stander, Hennie. "Chrysostom on Hunger and Famine." *HTS Teologiese Studies/Theological Studies* 67, no. 1 (2011), art. # 880.

Stanovich, Keith E. "Matthew Effects in Reading: Some Consequences of Individual Differences in the Acquisition of Literacy." *Reading Research Quarterly* 21, no. 4 (1986): 360-407.

Stark, Rodney. *The Rise of Christianity*. Princeton, NJ: Princeton University Press, 1996.

Steiner, George. *After Babel: Aspects of Language and Translation*. Oxford: Oxford University Press, 1998.

———. *Lessons of the Masters*. Cambridge, MA: Harvard University Press, 2003.

Stevens, R. Paul. "Living Theologically: Toward a Theology of Christian Practice." *Themelios* 20, no. 3 (1995): 4-8.

Stump, Eleonore. *Second-Person Accounts and the Problem of Evil*. Edited by K. E. Yandell. Faith and Narrative. Oxford: Oxford University Press, 2001, 86-103.

———. "Narrative and the Problem of Evil: Suffering and Redemption." In Stephen T. Davis, Daniel Kendall, S.J., and Gerald O'Collins, S.J., eds., *The Redemption*. Oxford: Oxford University Press, 2004, 207-34.

———. "The Problem of Evil: Analytic Philosophy and Narrative." In Oliver Crisp and Michael C. Rea, eds., *Analytic Theology: New Essays in the Philosophy of Theology*. New York: Oxford University Press, 2009, 251-64.

Tamez, Elsa. "Poverty, the Poor, and the Option for the Poor. A Biblical Perspective." In Daniel Groody, ed., *The Option for the Poor in Christian Theology*. Notre Dame, IN: University of Notre Dame Press, 2007, 41-54.

Taylor, Charles. *Varieties of Religion Today: Revisiting William James.* Cambridge, MA: Harvard University Press, 2002.

Ticciati, Susannah. *A New Apophaticism: Augustine and the Redemption of Signs.* Leiden: Brill, 2013.

Tirado, Linda. *Hand to Mouth: Living in Bootstrap America.* New York: Penguin, 2014.

Tracy, David. *Plurality and Ambiguity: Hermeneutics, Religion, Hope.* San Francisco: Peeters Press, 1987.

———. *Dialogue with the Other: The Inter-religious Dialogue.* Louvain: publisher, 1990.

Turner, Victor. *The Forest of Symbols.* Ithaca, NY: Cornell University Press, 1967.

Vacek, Edward Collins. "Orthodoxy Requires Orthopathy: Emotions in Theology." *Horizons* 40, no. 2 (2013): 218-41.

Vanier, Jean. *Drawn into the Mystery of Jesus through the Gospel of John.* Mahwah, NJ: Paulist Press, 2004.

Van den Eijnden, Jan G. J. *Poverty on the Way to God: Thomas Aquinas on Evangelical Poverty.* Leuven: Peeters, 1994.

van den Hoek, Annewies. "Widening the Eye of the Needle. Wealth and Poverty in the Works of Clement of Alexandria." In Susan R. Holman, ed., *Wealth and Poverty in Early Church and Society.* Grand Rapids, MI: Baker Academic, 2008, 67-75.

Vattimo, Gianni. "Dialectics, Difference, Weak Thought." In G. Vattimo et al., eds., *Weak Thought.* Albany: State University of New York Press, 2012, 39-52.

Vollman, William. *Poor People.* New York: Harper Perennial, 2007.

Ward, Benedicta, ed., *The Sayings of the Desert Fathers: The Alphabetical Collection.* Kalamazoo, MI: Cistercian Publications, 1984.

Wade, Robert H. "On the Causes of Increasing World Poverty and Inequality, or Why the Matthew Effect Prevails." *New Political Economy* 9, no. 2 (2004): 163-88.

Weaver, Rebecca H. "Wealth and Poverty in the Early Church." *Interpretation* 41, no. 4 (1987): 368-81.

Weil, Simone. *Notebooks.* 2 vols. Vol. II, translated by Arthur Wills. London: Routledge & Kegan Paul, 1956.

———. *Waiting on God.* New York: Fount, 1977.

———. "The Love of God and Affliction." In George A. Panichas, ed., *The Simone Weil Reader*. New York: David McKay, 1977, 439-43.

———. *Gravity and Grace*. London: ARK Paperbacks, 1987.

Wheeler, Sondra Ely. *Wealth as Peril and Obligation: The New Testament on Possessions*. Grand Rapids, MI: Eerdmans, 1995.

Whelan, Gerard. "*Evangelii gaudium* as 'Contextual Theology': Helping the Church 'Mount to the Level of Its Times.'" *Australian eJournal of Theology* 22, no. 1 (2015): 1-10.

Williams, Bernard. "Integrity." In J. J. C. Smart and Bernard Williams, *Utilitarianism: For and Against*. New York: Cambridge University Press, 1973, 108-17.

———. "Persons, Character, and Morality." In Bernard Williams, *Moral Luck*. Cambridge: Cambridge University Press, 1981, 1-19.

Williams, Rowan. *The Wound of Knowledge*. 2nd ed. London: Darton, Longman & Todd, 1990.

———. *On Christian Theology*. Oxford: Blackwell, 2000.

Wittgenstein, Ludwig. *Tractatus Logico-Philosophicus*. London: Kegan Paul, 1922.

———. *Philosophical Investigations*. Oxford: Blackwell, 1967.

———. *Culture and Value*. Edited by G. H. v. Wright in collaboration with H. Nyman. Text revised by Alois Pichler. Translated by P. Winch. Oxford: Blackwell, 1998.

Wolf, Susan. "'One Thought Too Many': Love, Morality, and the Ordering of Commitment." In Ulrike Heuer and Gerhard Lang, eds., *Luck, Value, and Commitment: Themes from the Ethics of Bernard Williams*. Oxford: Oxford University Press, 2012, 143-62.

Wright, Christopher J. H. *Old Testament Ethics for the People of God*. Downers Grove, IL: InterVarsity Press, 2004.

Wright, Scott. *Oscar Romero and the Communion of Saints*. Maryknoll, NY: Orbis Books, 2009.

Index